THE INTELLECTUAL CONQUEST OF PERU

THE INTELLECTUAL CONQUEST
OF PERU

The Jesuit College of San Pablo, 1568-1767

LUIS MARTIN

FORDHAM UNIVERSITY PRESS · 1968
NEW YORK

© Copyright 1968 by Fordham University Press
Library of Congress Catalog Card Number: 67-26159
Manufactured in the United States of America

To
PETER ARRUPE
whose friendship and generosity
made this book possible

" . . . se debe contentar quien lee historias de saber lo que desea en suma y verdadero, teniendo por cierto que particularizar las cosas es engañoso y aun muy odioso . . . . "

Francisco López de Gómara in the prologue
to his *Historia General de las Indias*

ABBREVIATIONS

AHN   Archivo Histórico Nacional, Madrid
ANP   Archivo Nacional del Perú, Lima
ARSJ   Archivum Romanum Societatis Jesu, Rome
AVP   Archivo de la Vice–Provincia del Perú (Jesuitas), Lima
     LC   Libro de Congregaciones MS
     LI   Libro de Instrucciones MS
     LO   Libro de Ordenaciones MS
CV   Colección Vargas (Private Collection of Rubén Vargas Ugarte, s.j., currently housed in Villa Kostka, Hacienda Huachipa), Lima
LCI   Library of the Colegio de la Inmaculada, Lima
MHSJ   Monumenta Historica Societatis Jesu, Madrid and Rome
     MP   Antonio de Egaña, s.j. (ed.), *Monumenta Peruana*, vols. 75, 82, 88 of MHSJ (Romae: Borgo S. Spirito, 1954–1961)
     SFB   *Sanctus Franciscus Borgia, quartus Gandiae Dux et Societatis Jesu Praepositus Generalis tertius*, 5 vols. of MHSJ (Matriti: typis Augustini Avrial, 1894–1903; typis Gabrielis Lopez del Horno, 1908–1911)

PREFACE

The rise and fall of the Jesuit Order in the new world has been retold several times. Spanish-, English-, and French-speaking historians have left us general accounts of the Jesuit march through the lands of the Americas, along the wind-swept trails of Canada, the scorched earth of northern Mexico, and the steaming rain-forests of the tropics. The revolving stage of history has moved many times, and has brought to us the epic of men who in the snows of New France tested the limits of human endurance; the efforts to build a bucolic Utopia in the forests of Paraguay; the romantic story of hundreds of *padres* who, on horseback, wove a web of paths and trails to eventually cover the entire South American continent. There are many outstanding Jesuits who played important roles against the backdrop of American history, and whose deeds have already been recorded by historians—men like Marquette, Brebeuf, Kino, Acosta and Vieira, to mention but a few.

The present book studies a Jesuit college and its role in colonial society. The school was the College of San Pablo in Lima, Peru, the first Jesuit foundation in Spanish America, and one which would last for two centuries (longer than any other Jesuit institution in the Spanish Empire) until the expulsion of the Order in 1767. San Pablo was the kernel from which all other Jesuit institutions in Spanish South America sprouted. It was, besides, the training ground for most of the Jesuits destined to work south of Panama, and the administrative center of the Order in the old Viceroyalty of Peru. Many of the pioneers who went forward to open the Jesuit schools and missions in Quito, Chile, Charcas, Nuevo Reino, and Paraguay were the products of San Pablo, which was for them a window kept open to the intellectual currents of Europe and a supply base for ideas, books, and all kinds of material goods. To understand the history of San Pablo is the key to the meaning of Jesuit activities in Spanish America.

Besides its role within Jesuit history, San Pablo, an early challenger of the intellectual monopoly of the University of San Marcos, must be studied in order to understand the ideological life of colonial Peru and the intellectual climate of the viceroyalty. In its school of humanities, San Pablo trained the best youth of Lima, and was instrumental in the foundation of other colleges, like the famous colleges of San Martín and El Cercado. The former was across the street from San Pablo and always remained its "intellectual colony," and the latter served in the outskirts of Lima as a special school for the Indian nobility. At times the faculty of San Pablo lent some of its best professors to the University of San Marcos, and graduated outstanding scholars who were to hold chairs in colleges and universities throughout the viceroyalty. San Pablo's tireless administrators built what was perhaps the best college library on the continent, besides founding a scientific laboratory to test the new knowledge received from Europe. The college pharmacy was a center of medical research. Its wide influence spread medical knowledge not only to America, but even throughout Europe. For all these reasons a knowledge of the history and educational structures of San Pablo is essential for a full comprehension of the intellectual life of the Spanish–American Empire.

The majority of the sources used in preparing this work are still preserved in manuscript form, and are described in the "Statement on Sources" which the reader will find on page 179. The printed material bearing on the history of San Pablo has certainly supported the contention of those scholars who believe that the intellectual history of the Spanish Empire in America is still partly hidden in the Latin volumes written by colonial authors. In addition to the topical arrangement of the data gathered in this research, a chronological sequence is followed within each chapter of the book. This sequence is obviously conditioned by the amount and nature of the sources available and, at times, by the need to preserve the topical pattern of the work.

PREFACE

Anyone familiar with modern scholarship knows that the type of research embodied in this book cannot be done without the help of many. The author wishes to express his gratitude, first, to his former professors and classmates in the Department of History of Columbia University, New York, where the work was conceived and planned. Many words of thanks are due to the officials of the National Library and the National Archives of Peru, whose cooperation matched the generosity of the proverbial *limeños*; to Fr. Enrique Bartra, a gentleman-scholar whose advice and encouragement provided the factor of perseverance during the arduous research; to Miss Maria Antonieta Regalado and Miss Macu Gil who slaved so many hours in transcribing documents, and patiently deciphered the author's handwriting in reading the first manuscript of the book. Finally, a sincerely grateful bow to the director and staff of Fordham University Press without whose interest and editorial care this book would not have come to its present state.

Ibero–American Institute   Luis Martín
Sophia University, Tokyo

ILLUSTRATIONS

CONTENTS

INTRODUCTION

On the 18th of January, 1535, Francisco Pizarro, the conqueror of Peru, signed the foundation act of the city of Lima with twelve of his followers. They planted the future capital of the Viceroyalty of Peru in a wide and fertile plain on the left bank of the river Rimac, seven-and-a-half miles from the sea and fifty from the barrier of the Andes. On the 30th of the same month, Pizarro held the first *cabildo* or town council, and Lima began playing its role as the Spanish administrative center of Peru. About seventy Spanish *vecinos*, or heads of households, moved into the new capital from the Andean valley of Jauja and began building simple houses of adobe by the Rimac. Allowing some five persons for each household, the initial population of Lima must have been between three and four hundred Spaniards, not counting the several hundred Indians who had been living on the banks of the Rimac before the foundation of the Spanish city.[1]

By the year 1539, the population of Lima had climbed to two hundred *vecinos*, which meant that about one thousand Spaniards lived in the city. The civil wars, which soon broke out among the conquerors, stifled the development of the capital, and the population remained unaltered for more than a decade.[2] When in 1543 Fray Jerónimo de Loaiza was received as the first bishop of Lima, the city was composed of only ten or twelve blocks of simple dwellings around the *Plaza Mayor*, and only a few hundred persons gathered in the streets to welcome Loaiza. Lima experienced a sort of boom after peace was finally established in the land through the efforts, first, of Pedro de la Gasca and, later, of the Marquis of Cañete. In the 1560s, a few years before the foundation of the College of San Pablo, the residents of Lima, the *limeños*, had

[1]

doubled and about 2,500 persons of Spanish ancestry dwelt in the city.[3]

In the thirty years between 1535 and 1565, and in spite of the bloody civil wars, Lima had become the head and center of a mighty viceroyalty. During those thirty years, five *Audiencias Reales*—Panama, Santa Fe, Quito, Charcas and Chile—had been created and had been placed under the central administration of Lima, which in 1544 had received its first viceroy in the person of Blasco Nuñez de Vela. Pope Paul III had also been persuaded to make Lima the center and head of the ecclesiastical organization. In 1546, Paul III severed the links which tied the bishopric of Lima to that of Seville and, at the same time, he elevated the colonial city to the rank of a metropolitan see with authority over the bishoprics of Cusco, Quito, Panama, León of Nicaragua and Popayán. Soon the famous provincial councils were held in the metropolitan see and the influence of Lima was felt throughout the entire ecclesiastical structure of Peru.[4]

After the end of the civil wars, civic and ecclesiastical life developed and throve in Lima. The economic acitivities of the city increased as a result of the exploitation of Huancavelica and Potosí. As early as the administration of the Marquis of Cañete, the merchants of Lima thought of forming the *Consulado* or college of merchants to solve, without the intervention of the regular courts, the problems and disputes arising among them. Currency was badly needed and royal approval was sought to mint coins in Peru, a privilege granted by the king in 1565. Legislation was passed to protect the Indians, and hospitals were founded to take care of both Spaniards and natives. Between 1561 and 1564, the Count of Nieva improved some of the public buildings and began constructing an aqueduct to bring fresh water to all sections of the city.[5] The great religious orders (Franciscans, Dominicans, Augustinians and Mercedarians) opened convents in Lima, which soon became comfortable residences of hundreds of men who lived by the generous gifts of the *limeños*. Their numbers increased to such an extent that years later Don Francisco de Toledo, the fifth viceroy of Peru, would be appalled to see almost three thousand priests, monks and religious living in a city that had only six thousand *vecinos*. As a result of this situation, he realized that great numbers of Indians throughout the viceroyalty were left without pastoral care.[6]

The first three decades after the foundation of Lima were not the best years in which to foster and develop a strong cultural and intellectual life. Peace and leisure are essential to cultivate the intellect, a Peruvian historian has remarked, and up to the second half of the sixteenth century Peru only offered a "clash of swords and war cries" to stimulate the minds of men.[7] It is a tribute to the pioneer settlers of Lima that, in spite of adverse conditions, they did not neglect the instruction and education of their children. The intellectual life of the colony would grow years later into a powerful tree, but the seeds had already been planted before 1568.

The absence of proper institutions of learning in the new city made parents turn at first to private tutors for the education of their children. Legal contracts were drawn up in the presence of a notary public and the teacher took charge of instructing the children of the family, which in turn paid the agreed-upon salary. One of the first men to make a living as a teacher in Peru was Gonzalo de Segovia whose profession was recorded in an official document as "maestro de mostrar a leer." His professional qualifications must not have been great: he did not go beyond teaching small children how to read. Toward 1543 he became restless and joined the faction of Gonzalo Pizarro. Years later, because of his participation in the revolts, Gonzalo de Segovia was condemned to perpetual exile in Chile and to the confiscation of his property, and Lima lost one of its first teachers.[8]

Another private teacher, better qualified than Gonzalo de Segovia, was Florestán de Lasarte who had been living in Lima at least since 1551. Lasarte was a protégé of some of the leading families, wrote plays inspired by the dramas of Terence, Plautus and Seneca, and was highly regarded as the private tutor of the best youth of Lima. Lasarte not only taught reading and writing, but also gave instruction in arithmetic and Latin, of which he had perfect command. The contracts signed by Lasarte in 1552 and 1554 are still preserved, and are proof that the play-

[3]

wright Lasarte taught not only reading but also writing with "letra caligráfica," besides mathematics and Latin grammar.[9]

Florestán de Lasarte was not the only qualified teacher in a city whose population at the time did not surpass the five hundred *vecinos*. Lasarte died before 1561, but another famous teacher was already carrying on his tradition among the best families of Lima. His name was Enrique Garcés and he was perhaps a better humanist than Lasarte. Garcés knew not only Latin, but also Italian and Portuguese, and had done valuable work translating Camoëns and Petrarch into Spanish. Garcés' teaching career in Lima seems to have been limited to the higher levels of lecturing on Latin and Spanish grammar, leaving the basic courses in reading and writing to less-qualified teachers.[10]

The families established in Lima before 1568 relied a great deal upon private instructors like Segovia, Lasarte and Garcés for the education of their children. But before 1568 one could already detect efforts to institutionalize the instruction of youth in the colonial city. Those efforts were made mainly by the secular clergy and religious orders, while the attention of the civil authorities was absorbed by the more demanding needs of preserving peace and building a city. The Augustinians, for instance, made plans in 1551 to open schools in which the Indian children could learn reading and writing in Spanish, in addition to religion, arithmetic and a skilled trade. By 1550, the Dominicans had sixty such schools in different parts of Peru. The Franciscans also gave instruction in their *doctrinas*, or Indian parishes, although, as late as 1571, they did not have a school in Lima and could not even train their own members properly.[11]

The bishop of Lima, Jerónimo de Loaiza, was also concerned about education during the first years of his residence in the colonial city. In 1549, when he was planning the establishment of a hospital for the Indians, he ordered the establishment of a school for Indian children where they could learn religion, reading and writing. Following the European tradition, the bishop of Lima opened a school for Spanish children in the shadow of his cathedral. Gonzalo de Trejo was put in charge in 1561 and he taught grammar and music for a salary of twenty-five *pesos* each semester. By 1564, the bishop's example had been followed by others, and Loaiza wrote the king that grammar was taught "in three or four other places of the city, and other disciplines [were taught] in some monasteries."[12]

Loaiza's last remark referred, among others, to the Dominicans who were undoubtedly the best intellectuals in the colony. In 1548 they had decided to create a full-fledged college in their convent of Lima, and by 1549 Fray Domingo de Santo Tomás was already lecturing on theology. On the 23rd of January of the following year, the *Cabildo* of Lima, obviously impressed by the accomplishments of the Dominicans, petitioned the emperor to make the Dominican college a university with the rights and privileges of Salamanca. The intellectual efforts of the Dominicans and the formal petition of the *cabildo* were the roots of the future university of San Marcos, whose cradle was the Dominican convent of Lima. The courses taught by Fray Domingo de Santo Tomás and his brethren were the only courses in philosophy and theology available in Lima in 1550.[13]

In the educational spectrum of Lima before 1568, one could detect still another important element. Not only the disciplines traditionally taught in Europe were in vogue in the colonial city, but a new one had been established: the language and culture of the conquered race. The cleric Alonso Martínez had taught *Quechua* since 1561 in a chair founded by the bishop in the cathedral. Martínez followed in the steps of the great Fray Domingo de Santo Tomás, the first linguist of Peru, who for years had studied and taught the language of the Indians, and who had published the first *Quechua* grammar in Valladolid in 1560.[14]

Lima of the 1560s, a city of about 2,500 Spaniards still struggling to recover from the wounds of an era of civil unrest, was already in the early stages of an intellectual life. The Dominicans ran a university in their convent with the privileges of Salamanca. Private tutors were hired by the wealthy families to teach their children, and classes on grammar and music were offered in the cathedral and in several other places. The religious orders were trying to instruct the Indians while themselves learning their native languages and customs at the same

[5]

time. From these humble beginnings would grow, in a few decades, the great Lima colleges of the seventeenth century—the colleges of San Ildefonso, San Martín, San Felipe y San Marcos, El Cercado, San Antonio, Our Lady of Mount Carmel and Santo Toribio—the crown and glory of the University of San Marcos. We now turn to the study of one of those colleges, the College of San Pablo. After witnessing its establishment and early developments, we shall enter its imposing cloisters to follow from within the intellectual life of the institution.

I

TWO VICEROYS AND A VISITOR

In February of 1556, Don Fernando Álvarez de Toledo, fourth Count of Oropesa, left the city of Plasencia in the Spanish province of Cáceres and headed for his own town of Oropesa in the province of Toledo. His small entourage was soon crossing the plain, bordered on the north by the river Tietar and the Sierra de Gredos, and enclosed on the south by the Tajo and the mountains of Toledo. The shepherds and peasants working in the fields recognized the banner and shield of Oropesa, and whispered the name of Don Fernando as the count passed by on his horse. But nobody suspected that two great Spanish viceroys accompanied the count on that cold February day along the Castilian plain. One of them, wearing the humble robe of a Jesuit, was Francis Borgia, an old friend of the Emperor Charles, the Duke of Gandía, and former Viceroy of Catalonia. The other was the count's younger brother, Don Francisco de Toledo, who was destined to become years later the supreme organizer of the Viceroyalty of Peru.[1]

Borgia and Toledo had been drawn to each other since the day they first met. Both were members of noble families, trained in an unbreakable fidelity to the crown, and in a deep Christian faith. Francisco de Toledo had taken his religious vows as a member of the Military Order of Alcántara, and Francis Borgia, renouncing his titles after the death of his wife, had joined the new Jesuit Order, founded by a soldier-saint. Both Toledo and Borgia lived in a world of absolute values, represented

[7]

by the Church and the crown. Before the year 1556 was over, these two men met again at Yuste, the monastery where the Emperor Charles was preparing to fight his final battle. Toledo was one of the few attending the ailing emperor, and Borgia was summoned to Yuste, as priest and friend, to deal with problems troubling the imperial conscience.[2] Borgia and Toledo watched, with religious emotion, the man who had made Europe tremble, trembling himself at the sight of his Maker.

The respect and friendship between Borgia and Toledo grew with the years. In May of 1559, the Jesuit Borgia, still very much the aristocratic statesman in spite of his priesthood and his religious vows, wrote a long report to young King Philip, proposing names for the most important posts of Castile. Francisco de Toledo was recommended as the man to fill the position of President of the Military Orders, as a "man of great Christianity and prudence, endowed with great talent. . . ." Borgia knew, he assured the king, that the younger brother of the Count of Oropesa had all the qualifications necessary for the delicate position, and that his counsels would be excellent both in war and in peace.[3]

Toledo, on the other hand, took more and more interest in the Jesuits, and soon began thinking of founding a Jesuit college in Oropesa, within the shadow of the family castle. By 1565, the same year his friend Borgia was elected third General of the Jesuit Order, Francisco de Toledo had two Jesuits laying the foundation of the College of Oropesa, and was dreaming of vying with the already famous Jesuit colleges of Coimbra, Paris, Gandía and Rome.[4] But the College of Oropesa would languish, while Don Francisco de Toledo and Borgia were destined to play a vital role in the foundation of another Jesuit college, not in an obscure Castilian town, but in the capital city of Peru, one of the mightiest viceroyalties of Spain.

The idea of founding a Jesuit college in Lima was an old one. Twice, in 1555 and in 1559, Borgia, then Jesuit Superior in Spain, had laid the ground-work for the foundation, but twice he failed to see his idea come to fruition. The Jesuits appointed by Borgia to accompany the

Viceroy Andrés Hurtado de Mendoza and the Count of Nieva to Peru never sailed from Seville. But the project of sending Jesuits to Lima was never forgotten, and it was fully revived in 1566 by a letter from King Philip to Borgia, who was by then Jesuit General in Rome. The king asked his father's former counselor to appoint twenty-four Jesuits to be sent to the Indies of the Ocean Sea, wherever the Royal Council should decide. Francis Borgia was happy to see the door open to the realization of his old dream, but he knew that the number requested by the king was too high for the limited strength of the Order, and he appointed only eight.[5]

The First Jesuit Trip to Peru

By May of 1567, the chosen superior of the first Jesuit expedition to Peru, Father Gerónimo Ruiz de Portillo, was in Seville busying himself with the endless details of the long trip to the Indies, and waiting for his companions, who, from different parts of Spain, were slowly converging on the Andalusian capital. They moved slowly indeed. The Armada of 1567 sailed down the Guadalquivir before the Jesuits arrived, and Fr. Portillo, still waiting for those whom he was supposed to take to Peru, was forced to watch its sails sink below the horizon.[6]

The delay obliged the small group of Jesuits to live through the scorching Sevillian summer. Well provided by the royal officials with the essential elements for the voyage, they set out to gather a few more items, visiting friends and benefactors of the Order. The Jesuits, waiting at Seville in the summer of 1567, were different from other religious groups sent before them to the Indies. They had been founded with a clear teaching vocation, and they were going to Lima to open not a monastery but a college. Their superior, Portillo, was fully aware of that, and he knew that to fulfill their mission books were paramount. From the minute he was appointed, Portillo was concerned about the books to be taken to Peru; and now he crisscrossed the narrow streets of Seville, dropping by the best bookdealers of the city, and began gathering a small library. Portillo spent more than two hundred *ducados* on books, a larger sum than the one invested in religious articles and sacred vestments. The teacher was already overshadowing the missionary.[7]

Weeks went by. To break the long, monotonous hours of waiting in the unbearable heat and humidity of Seville, the Jesuits, led and encouraged by Portillo, turned to the study of the language and culture of Peru. Even before they set foot in the new world, that group of men was making a serious effort to study and to comprehend the new human environment of America.[8]

By the end of September, 1567, Portillo led his men from Seville to Sanlúcar; finally, on the 2nd of November, in a small, solitary ship, they began the crossing of the Atlantic. It was a lonely crossing without the friendly sails of the Armada dotting the seas. The books, packed in Seville, began passing from hand to hand, and reading was widely used to soothe the tensions and harshness of the journey. Soon the Jesuits were dividing the passengers and sailors into groups of three or four, according to their taste and capacity, to listen to the reading of "useful histories and pious books." In each group, a Jesuit did the reading and made comments on the things read. On certain days at given hours, when the winds and currents had subsided and they were almost nailed to the sea, the ship was like a floating school.[9]

A New Peruvian Viceroy

While the Jesuits were inching their way ahead at the mercy of the winds, rumors circulated in Madrid about impending changes in the colonial administration. By February of 1568, a month before Portillo and his companions moored at Callao, the seaport of Lima, Don Francisco de Toledo was summoned to the court and offered the position of Viceroy of Peru. When the news reached Rome, Francis Borgia, the Jesuit General and former Viceroy of Catalonia himself, was genuinely delighted. His long years of friendship with the House of Oropesa, and particularly with Don Francisco, were indeed solid grounds on which to build great hopes for the future of the Order in Lima. The man who had worked for years to begin a Jesuit college in Oropesa would certainly help to found and develop the more important college of Lima.[10]

Francisco de Toledo arrived in Madrid on the 13th of March of that year to spend several months of studies and consultations before taking up his official duties in Lima. Assisted by members of the Royal Council and some theologians, Toledo tried to familiarize himself with conditions in Peru. Because religion was for him a matter of principle and of conscience, Don Francisco plunged with zest into the study of the *patronato* and committed himself to being its champion in America. For him, to serve the Church was to serve the king, and the boundaries between altar and throne became dangerously blurred in his mind.[11]

On the 5th of July, 1568, Toledo wrote a confidential letter to Francis Borgia in Rome which shows his profound commitment to the faith and to the crown. The chosen viceroy was already aware of the eight Jesuits gone to Peru, but he insisted on his friend Borgia's appointing four or six more to be "his consolation and companions" on his own journey. On the 4th of September, somewhat dejected and tired after six months of long meetings, discussions, and consultations, Toledo wrote again to the Jesuit General. This time he requested that one of the Jesuits should be named his confessor; and, after reminding Borgia of some business of the Jesuit college in Oropesa, Toledo confided to the Father General his intention of opening more colleges of that nature in Peru under the care of the Jesuits. The man who directed those letters to Borgia considered himself not only the viceroy but also the vice-patron; and he was going to sail for Peru both to take care of the civil administration of the viceroyalty and to spread the faith by working for the well-being of the Church at the same time. Within that ideological frame of mind, it was only natural that Toledo thought of opening Jesuit colleges in Peru wherever and whenever he, the viceroy, might judge convenient.[12]

In that autumn of 1568, rereading Toledo's letters, the keen eye of Borgia must have seen suddenly that the Jesuits and the new Viceroy of Peru were on a collision course. Borgia knew too well that independence from outside pressure was an essential condition for the efficiency of the

Jesuit Order, and postulated by its *Constitutions*. But he knew also that, in Toledo's world, the Jesuits were by virtue of the *real patronato* an instrument in the hands of the crown like other religious groups. Francis Borgia, as former Viceroy of Catalonia, was too familiar with the political administration of the Spanish Crown and with the imperious character of Francisco de Toledo not to have sensed the dangers ahead on the road to building and developing a Jesuit college in Lima.

On the 9th of December, with the soft but steady hand of a diplomat, Borgia tried in a letter to Toledo to steer away from this dangerous path. He informed the new viceroy that the worth of the Jesuits resided in the perfect observance of their *Constitutions*. If that basic legal instrument, written by the Order's founder himself, were neglected, then the Jesuits would be able to serve neither God nor king. Borgia did not say anything more, but he hoped that Toledo would remember that the Jesuit *Constitutions* imposed a special vow of obedience to the pope, who should always enjoy the direction and control of the Order from Rome.[13]

In spite of his deep misgivings, Francis Borgia granted Toledo the Jesuits he had requested, and by the beginning of the year 1569 the second Jesuit expedition to Peru was standing by, ready to sail with the new viceroy.

The Beginnings of San Pablo

Meanwhile, the first Jesuit group had arrived in Lima, led by Portillo, on the 1st of April, 1568. The city, only thirty-three years old, deeply impressed the Jesuits. They admired the checkered pattern of the streets, the beautiful public square in front of the viceregal palace, the monasteries of the religious communities, and the buildings of civil and ecclesiastical administrators. Father Diego de Bracamonte paid a handsome compliment to Lima when he wrote home saying that the city was "another Seville."[14]

One of the first acts of the newly arrived Jesuits was to visit Lope García de Castro, President of the *Audiencia* and Acting Governor of Peru. They presented him the royal *cédula*, in which the king explained the coming of the Jesuits and ordered Castro to provide them with a suitable place for their foundation. Before going to Castro, the Jesuits had studied the city, the location of other religious communities, the density of population in the different quarters, and they had set their eyes on a particular square of the chess-board that was Lima. They requested the president of the *Audiencia* to grant them that particular location. It was only three blocks to the east of the public square, and three blocks from the Franciscans, in a rather thickly populated section of the city.[15]

Lope García de Castro, after reading the king's *cédula* and listening to the Jesuits, named the *Oidor* Gregório González Cuenca to handle the case. A public hearing was scheduled for the 12th of April, less than two weeks after the arrival of the Jesuits, and seven witnesses took the stand. All of them declared under oath that the place proposed and requested by the Jesuits was suitable for the new foundation, being in an excellent location, healthy, and surrounded by already populated areas. Three of the witnesses specified that the location was the best for a college, and very convenient to the student body. García de Castro, seeing the success of the hearings, signed a decree on the 17th of April expropriating the property, and granting it to the Jesuits, who had to pay more than twelve thousand pesos to the former owners.[16]

Castro's decree was for Father Portillo the beginning of the headaches so well known to all school administrators. The Royal Exchequer gave him two hundred pesos, but Portillo had to begin knocking on doors to collect the rest of the money to buy the property. Once the property was in his hands, Portillo began with feverish activity to make the place suitable for its new purpose. He knocked down walls, set up classrooms, a chapel, private rooms, and even built a small library to house the books brought from Europe. Portillo named Diego de Bracamonte the first rector of the incipient community, and the College of San Pablo was a reality.[17]

The Jesuits began their pedagogical activities in Lima by teaching the humanities, and two classes of twenty students each were soon under way. The new teachers were interested in training the whole man, and

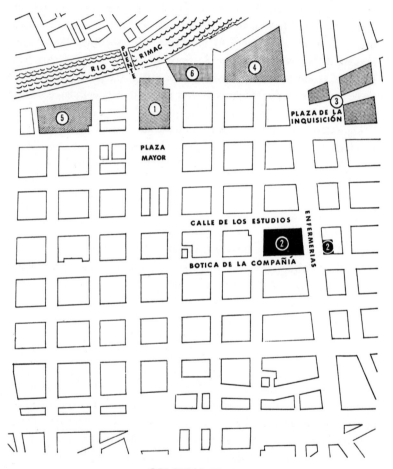

COLONIAL LIMA

1. Viceroy's Palace.
2. College of San Pablo,
3. San Marcos University.
4. Franciscan Convent.
5. Dominican Convent.
6. Desamparados.

they considered forty students to be the number adequate to attain that purpose, given the limited strength of the school in its first year.[18]

Besides teaching the humanities, the Jesuits displayed an amazing variety of activities from the day the college opened its doors, activities that would become characteristic of San Pablo during the two hundred years of its existence. Father Portillo gave a weekly lecture on canon law for the clergy of the city, preached several times a week, and was soon *the* speaker at the great solemnities. He attracted a group of fervent Spanish laymen and led them into the hospitals to do charity work. Father Rector Bracamonte visited the grammar schools of the city almost every day to teach religion, and began apostolic work among the Indian population of Lima. Father Luis López, years later condemned by the Inquisition for moral turpitude, was the first Jesuit to penetrate the world of the Negroes. On Sundays he gathered more than two thousand slaves in San Pablo for their weekly religion class, and was soon accepted as peacemaker and counselor in the slaves' quarters. All the ordained members of the community were available as confessors and consultants on problems of conscience.[19]

The Jesuits startled Lima, accustomed to the traditional and more contemplative religious orders, with the new style of teacher-priests who engaged freely in all sorts of social activities. The impact created by the Jesuits of San Pablo in the viceregal capital was profound, as can be gathered from the economic support given the college and the number and quality of those who requested admission to the Order. The Rector informed Rome on the 21st of January, 1569, that by his calculations the college had received well over thirty thousand ducats in the first six months, and was supported at the time of the report by the free donations of the citizens. This generosity of the *limeños* continued for several years until San Pablo acquired, also through the generous donations of some benefactors, its own sources of revenue.[20]

The new, flexible structure of the Jesuits had attracted a great number of candidates to the Order since its foundation in 1540, but in the Lima of 1568 the number of vocations to the Jesuits went far beyond anybody's expectations. Of the many who requested admission to San Pablo

[15]

to become Jesuits, twenty-three were accepted. They had come to knock at the doors of the college from every walk of life: old men, like Juan Toscano who had been dean of the Cathedral of Lima and joined the Jesuits at sixty-four; mature men, like Pedro Mexia who was *Fiscal* of the *Audiencia* of Lima and a master of laws; youngsters, like Martín Pizarro and José de Ribera, related to the oldest families of the city; the first *mestizo*, Blas Varela; and even a foreigner, the Portuguese Alonso Pérez, who was the pioneer of the many non-Spanish Jesuits later to go through the cloisters of San Pablo.[21]

The Clash of Two Old Friends

When Don Francisco de Toledo sailed from Sanlúcar on the 19th of March, 1569, he was unaware of the great increase of Jesuits in the infant college at Lima. For months he had written letters begging, cajoling, persuading the Jesuit General, his friend Borgia, and royal officials that the eight Jesuits sent in the first expedition were a number utterly insufficient for the needs of his viceroyalty. Now that his ships were weighing anchor at the mouth of the Guadalquivir, Don Francisco had twelve new Jesuits on board as a result of his own efforts, and the vice-patron of the Church was already making plans on how to use them for the service of God and king.[22]

On the last day of November, 1569, stern and solitary, weary from the long trip and deeply concerned for the problems awaiting him, without the soothing company of a wife or children, Don Francisco de Toledo, fifth Viceroy of Peru, entered his capital city of Lima for the first time. Hardly had he settled in the viceregal palace, when on the 8th of December he began his first direct contact with the religious orders. On the morning of that day, he walked the two blocks separating his palace from the Franciscans, and in the afternoon he visited the Jesuit College of San Pablo. A community of forty-four Jesuits, twice the number expected by Toledo, assembled in the cloister, richly decorated for the occasion and filled with students, who entertained the viceroy with a play, poems and excellent music.[23]

Three weeks later, on the 1st of January, 1570, Toledo paid his

second visit to San Pablo. With his deep Christian faith, he joined the
Jesuits in the religious services of the morning and suddenly decided to
stay for dinner with the community. As did his master, Philip II, the
Solitary of the Escorial, Toledo sincerely enjoyed the company of monks
and priests, and the silence and discipline of the cloisters. On that 1st
of January, the viceroy seemed to be in an excellent mood. He gave
the college 15,500 silver pesos, and spent the day chatting amicably
with the fathers. But in the course of the conversation, Don Francisco
showed the iron hand of the vice-patron ready to grasp the helm of the
Church in Peru. As a matter of fact, without the slightest suspicion that
his ideas could meet with anything but approval and gratitude from the
Jesuits, Toledo informed them of his desire and determination to use
the manpower concentrated in San Pablo to open many new colleges
through the viceroyalty, and to man the *doctrina* of El Cercado, an
Indian village begun in the neighborhood of Lima by his predecessor
Lope García de Castro. [24]

By February of 1570, Toledo had every reason to be satisfied with
the Jesuits. While the Archbishop, Loaiza, had begun resisting his
rights as vice-patron, the Jesuit Provincial, Portillo, was submitting to
Toledo's plans to overhaul and mend the structures of the ecclesiastical
administration. Toledo's report to His Most Catholic Majesty of the
8th of February, 1570, was all praise for the Jesuits. They had accepted
the spiritual care of the Indian village of El Cercado, and had sent eight
missionaries southeast of Lima to Huarochiri, a *doctrina* abandoned by
the Dominicans in the heart of the Andes. The viceroy was so satisfied
that he began thinking of attaching to the College of San Pablo a new
institution, a special college for the children of the Indian nobility. [25]

While Toledo wrote to the king and developed his ecclesiastical
policies in his palace on the *Plaza Mayor*, three blocks away, in the
College of San Pablo, several Jesuits sat down in their cells to write to
Francis Borgia in Rome. Reading these reports on the latest developments in Lima, the wrinkled face of the old aristocrat become
Jesuit General became somber. The clash with Toledo that he sensed
two years before was now unavoidable. If the college at Lima was to be

what the *Constitutions* of the Order demanded, controlled only by Jesuit superiors, Toledo's interference had to be checked with promptness and determination. On the 14th of November, 1570, Borgia locked himself in his cell in the Jesuit headquarters in Rome to consider the Peruvian problems. He wrote two letters, one to the Provincial Portillo, the other to the viceroy himself.

In his letter to Toledo, Borgia was all diplomat and politician handling an explosive issue with kid gloves. His tone was mild and respectful, though firm. The Jesuit General thanked the viceroy for his great interest in the Order and its development in Peru, and humbly requested that, in every undertaking in which the viceroy might want to use the Jesuits, care should be taken to observe the *Constitutions* and basic legislation of the Order at all times. In his letter to Portillo, Francis Borgia was the General who gives clear-cut commands and expects to be obeyed without delay. Borgia blocked step by step, by his orders to Portillo, everything that Toledo was planning to do with the Jesuits of Peru. Besides San Pablo, no more colleges should be opened in the viceroyalty, with the exception of one in Cusco. The Jesuits should not even discuss the possibility of opening other colleges, even if the viceroy claimed that he had orders from His Majesty to do so. Borgia was also cold to the idea of a college for Indian nobles. The Indians, like anybody else, could attend classes in San Pablo, but the Peruvian Jesuits were forbidden to administer and take charge of the new institution envisioned by Toledo. The *doctrinas*, if they required the ordinary pastoral care of a parish priest, were against the Jesuit *Constitutions* and should not be accepted. The Jesuits could work among the Indians with temporary missions, but their superiors should always be able to recall or remove them without interference from viceroy or bishop.[26]

When Francis Borgia sealed those two letters on the 14th of November, he must have known that they were an open challenge to the *real patronato*, the "most precious jewel in His Majesty's crown." He must have known that his clash with Toledo was going to occur, not in the arena of mutable policies, but in the bedrock of principles, and

[18]

that the clash was going to rock the still-tender foundations of San Pablo. Borgia and the viceroy had opposite views on the function of the Jesuits in Peru. By character and training they were incapable of compromise, and they could not help clashing like the unyielding steel of two swords of Toledo.

The viceroy was in Cusco, in the middle of his famous *visita*, when he became aware of the new Jesuit attitude imposed by Rome. He was a practical man, born for action and command, who could not suffer contradictions. As soon as he sensed the Jesuit opposition, Toledo made up his mind to fight back. By the 12th of February, 1572, he had chosen Father Bracamonte, former rector of San Pablo, and over the head of the Jesuit provincial sent him to Madrid and Rome. Bracamonte was to explain to Borgia the viceroy's point of view, and to win the Father General's approval for Toledo's ideas. The viceroy felt truly conscience-bound to send priests among the Indians, and the only place he could find them was in the religious houses of Lima, filled like San Pablo with large communities. As for the temporary missions suggested by Borgia, they were utterly insufficient for the conversion and religious education of the natives.[27]

When Father Bracamonte, Toledo's envoy, reached the shores of Spain, Francis Borgia had been dead for three months, and Juan de Polanco, private secretary to the first three Jesuit Generals, was temporary superior of the Order with the title of Vicar General. Even before he met Bracamonte, Juan de Polanco had already written to the college at Lima, renewing Borgia's orders. With the same inflexibility of the old General, but lacking his diplomacy, Polanco commanded the Jesuits of San Pablo to abandon immediately the two *doctrinas* of Huarochiri and El Cercado, a measure never taken by Borgia, which would antagonize still more the already alienated viceroy.[28]

The Visitor and the Scholar

On the 23rd of April, 1573, Everard Mercurian, a native of the Low Countries, was elected fourth General of the Jesuits, and inherited the Peruvian crisis. On the 27th of June he wrote his first letter to Toledo.

After a few details on Borgia's death and his own election as General, Mercurian announced to the viceroy the appointment of a Jesuit Visitor who would go to Peru with all the powers of the General, and would try to solve all the difficulties developing in Lima.[29]

The man chosen in Rome as the first Jesuit Visitor to Peru was Doctor Juan de la Plaza, a stern, scrupulous person, who had long years of experience in the government of the Order. He was given instructions to iron out the differences between the Jesuits of Lima and the viceroy, to whom he should always show affection and respect. On the issue of the *doctrinas*, Plaza was told to maintain an open mind, trying to find new ways for a solution. But new colleges should not be accepted for the time being, and the Visitor was given the charge to reinforce and develop the still shaky foundations of San Pablo, the heart and center of the Order in Peru. The new Flemish General of the Jesuits had certainly that development of San Pablo in mind when he chose the men who would accompany Plaza to Peru. Among them were Doctor Juan de Montoya, who had taught philosophy in the Roman college; Baltasar Piñas, twice rector of Spanish colleges and a master of arts; Antonio López, a good humanist; the Italian Bernardo Bitti, a painter; and Melchor Cano, who was an expert in music. Always thinking of making San Pablo a sister institution equal to the great Jesuit colleges of Europe, Mercurian ordered Plaza to select from among the Spanish Jesuits two or three more men who could become professors of theology and scripture in the college at Lima.[30]

The elected Visitor, Juan de la Plaza, had to wait in Spain for more than a year before being able to sail for Peru. His long and frequent correspondence of that year shows a man crushed under the weight of an office bigger than himself. Like Toledo before him, Plaza plunged into the study of Peruvian conditions, listened to everybody, read and reflected; but lacking the stubborn personality of Toledo, he was haunted by fears, scruples and doubts. Forgetting the limited scope of his *visita*, Plaza even tortured himself with burning doubts about the rights of the Spanish Crown to be in Peru. The conscience-stricken Plaza, plagued by thorny questions, soon began distorting an issue which he should have kept in constant sharp focus: the future development of San Pablo.[31]

By December of 1573, Doctor Plaza was in Seville, and, influenced perhaps by the exaggerated mystical tendencies of some Andalusian Jesuits, seriously doubted the advisability of opening colleges of the Order in the new world. A college always meant the need of solid economic foundations, and its administrators were soon burdened with the ever-growing pressures of material needs. Many days, in his cell in the college at Seville, or in his walks through the city, Plaza asked himself whether the Jesuits would not do better in Peru by opening simple houses, living in poverty, and being content with preaching the Gospel and administering the sacraments to the Indians. In spite of his doctorate, Plaza felt uncomfortable when confronted with the idea of a big college and the life of a professional teacher.[32]

Rent by these doubts, Plaza could not but react negatively to a proposal sent to Spain by the rector of San Pablo. Father Miguel de Fuentes, then rector of the college at Lima, had written to Madrid, asking that the Order's papal-granted privileges of conferring degrees be cleared through the *Consejo de Indias*, the Council of the Indies. In that way, the rector hoped, San Pablo would be fully recognized by both Church and state, and able to confer degrees in its own right, without leaning on the university. Plaza's alarm before such a reasonable proposal is reflected in a letter written to the General on the 15th of March, 1574. For Plaza, the aim of the Order is to save Indian souls, and he does not seem to understand how the conferring of degrees fits into the picture. At most it is something "very accidental," and Plaza would prefer to bury Fuente's request altogether, unless the Father General should think otherwise.

Before the beautiful Andalusian spring began filling the narrow streets of Seville with sun and light, the Visitor of the Peruvian Jesuits had conceived a plan that represented more danger for the future expansion of San Pablo than his scruples and doubts and all the interference of Toledo. Plaza began seriously thinking of founding a theological seminary in Spain to train all the men destined to work in the

Indies. This seminary, he hoped, would make unnecessary the major faculties of philosophy and theology in the College of San Pablo, which would remain at most a school of humanities for young children. The idea was discussed at Seville and proposed to Rome, but the Father General prudently ordered Plaza to wait and take up the subject with the Jesuits of Lima.[33]

While Plaza was toying with the new idea of a missionary college in Spain to supplant the college in Lima, news arrived from the viceregal capital bringing glowing reports of the progress of San Pablo. The courses in philosophy had been established, and young Father Martínez was giving the lectures. There were also some occasional lectures on theology. Passing on this information to the Father General in Rome, Doctor Plaza sounded truly downcast. Things were moving too far and too fast for the Father Visitor, who feared that before his arrival in Lima San Pablo would be a full-fledged college with all faculties.[34]

Father General Mercurian in Rome must have understood, reading Plaza's letters, the interior crisis of his Visitor who could not square his conscience with the Spanish conquest and exploitation of the new world, and who appeared more and more irresolute in every letter. Mercurian tried several times to ease the qualms of conscience suffered by Plaza, and in one of his letters he advised Plaza to discuss all his doubts with José de Acosta, the "brain" of San Pablo, as soon as they could meet in Lima. Writing to Lima the same month, April of 1574, the Father General asked Acosta to meet the Visitor and to discuss with him all important issues concerning the Peruvian Jesuits.[35]

The Jesuit General had written two letters from his office in Rome and had placed two entirely different men face to face, hoping they would complement each other. If Plaza was irresolute and wavering, scrupulous and biased against the intellectual pursuits of the Order, José de Acosta was a self-assured, born intellectual who had gone to the Indies in 1572 with a clear and determined teaching vocation, convinced that the training of new missionaries had to be done in America, not in the colleges of Spain.[36]

On the 31st of May, 1575, the Visitor finally arrived in Lima, met

[22]

José de Acosta in the cloisters of San Pablo, and the first Jesuit visitation of Peru was under way. Not too many days had gone by before those two men, Plaza and Acosta, were facing each other across a desk in the main office of the college. Following Rome's suggestions, they exchanged ideas, and Plaza began falling under the spell of one of the greatest talents that the Jesuits ever had in Peru. His old idea of a theological seminary in Spain was punctured like a balloon, and the Visitor was led by Acosta to the conclusion that the budding San Pablo was the place which had to be built into the training ground for all the Jesuits destined to work south of Panama.[37]

Three months had passed since the Visitor's arrival in Lima, when on the 1st of September he named José de Acosta rector of San Pablo, only to promote him to the office of provincial of all the Jesuits of Peru on the 1st of January of 1576, a day on which Viceroy Toledo honored the Jesuits with his presence for dinner. The new provincial, Acosta, decided to analyze and find a reasonable solution, once and for all, to all the problems that the Jesuits had found since they had arrived in Peru eight years previously—especially to those problems which had poisoned their relations with the viceroy. With characteristic determination, and only a fortnight after his appointment as provincial, Acosta called a meeting in San Pablo of the most influential Jesuits of Peru and invited Plaza to attend as an observer.[38]

On the third day of the convention, Father Acosta came to one of the crucial points, clearly stating that the main purpose of the Jesuits' coming to Peru was to work for and to help the Indians, and that the methods of carrying out that purpose were now called into question. The Viceroy Toledo had proposed two items, the *doctrinas* and a school for Indian nobles, and both had been rejected in Rome. The traditional thinking of the Order was to send Jesuits among the Indians in temporary missions like those used in Europe, and perhaps to open small houses in Indian territory as headquarters of those missions.

The results of the discussion proved a clear victory for Toledo's thinking. The fathers assembled in San Pablo had the honesty to affirm that the temporary missions, although useful, were greatly insufficient,

[23]

and that all the difficulties raised against the acceptance of *doctrinas* by the Order could be solved. If the Jesuit legal code forbade their taking the regular pastoral care of the *doctrinas*, the solution was not to refuse the *doctrinas*, leaving the Indians without competent spiritual assistance, but to seek a dispensation from the Jesuit legislation on this point. The suggested school for the sons of the Indian nobility, an idea received in Rome with caution and reserve, was hailed by the assembly with warm enthusiasm; and a resolution was passed to request, in the name of all the Jesuits of Peru, the General's consent to open such a school.[39]

With the intellectual Acosta at the helm of the convention, and the Visitor Plaza reduced to the condition of an observer without a vote, it is not surprising that the attention of the fathers turned also to the problems in the field of education. The same halls of San Pablo, in which they had convened, were mute reminders not to neglect this important aspect of Jesuit activities in Peru. The members of the convention were concerned, for instance, with the Indian languages. *Quechua* and *Aimara*, already taught and practised at San Pablo, were given a boost when the assembled fathers decreed that two grammars and two dictionaries should be written, and two catechisms prepared that could satisfy theologians and linguists alike. Another setback for Plaza's ideas occurred when the convention took notice of the fact that the Spanish population of the viceroyalty could be helped better by teaching and training the youth of the city than by any other priestly work. The fathers consequently thought of giving San Pablo the solid economic foundation that it was still lacking, asking the viceroy and the king for some financial support similar to that given to the university.[40]

When the Jesuit assembly was suspended for a time on the 27th of January, 1576, Acosta had every reason to be satisfied with the results. The College of San Pablo, whose development could have been stifled by the animosity of the viceroy and the odd mentality of the Visitor, was now free to proceed and take its place as an equal among the flourishing Jesuit colleges of Europe. The future of the college at Lima appeared bright indeed in January of 1576. From his office, Acosta could hear the rattling and voices of two hundred and fifty youngsters reading aloud

[24]

Cicero and Homer, or playing in the patio of the school of humanities. Fifty more mature students were enrolled in the courses in philosophy and almost the same number was regularly attending Acosta's own lectures on theology. The weekly round-table on practical moral problems, a forum where Jesuits and lay friends tried to study the issues of the day in the light of Christian principles, drew an attendance of two hundred persons. The chairs of Indian languages were the pride of San Pablo, and all the Jesuits, some fifty of them, were following the courses together with the great majority of the secular clergy of Lima.[41]

José de Acosta left behind that thriving college, and on mule back he followed twisted Indian trails up the Andes to arrive at Cusco on the 3rd of October. There he reconvened the Jesuit assembly begun in Lima. The Jesuits who gathered in Cusco confirmed the resolutions made at the earlier Lima meeting, took charge of a new *doctrina*, discussed the future of the College of San Pablo, and elected a representative to be sent to Madrid and Rome to explain to the metropolitan authorities the new course they were about to take. The representative to Madrid and Rome was Baltasar Piñas, who had arrived in Peru with the Father Visitor in 1575, and who took over the rectorship of San Pablo when Acosta was named provincial.[42]

The Jesuit College and the State University

Piñas was summoned to Cusco to receive a report signed by Acosta and the Visitor, which was to be taken to Rome. A long paragraph of that report dealt with the College of San Pablo and its relations to the state university, a creation of Toledo, which had been holding classes since April of 1575 in San Juan de la Penitenciaría just a few blocks away from San Pablo. Acosta, with his sharp insight, sensed that the activities of the two institutions should be coordinated to avoid academic clashes in the future, and he informed the Jesuit General that this was also Toledo's opinion. The viceroy, taking into account the present accomplishments of San Pablo and having the acquiescence of the university faculty, had proposed that the Jesuit college handle the

[25]

teaching of the humanities and be officially considered *escuelas menores*, a sort of undergraduate division of the university.

Toledo's proposal sounded reasonable and promising, but the Jesuits feared that San Pablo would be harnessed to a state-controlled institution where the last word would always be had by the viceroy. Acosta, therefore, laid down his own conditions before accepting the idea proposed by Toledo, and once again we witness a revival of Borgia's unshakable principle of absolute freedom from state interference in the activities of the Order. Acosta was ready to accept association with, but never subjection to, the university. He would permit the students of San Pablo to register in the university at the beginning of the school year and to receive their degrees from the academic authorities of the university; but classes should be held in San Pablo, taught by Jesuits, and run according to the pedagogic theories of the Order. No authority should be exercised by the university within the walls of San Pablo, and the students should only be subject, both on academic and disciplinary levels, to the Jesuit rector, not the university's. If the university should try to interfere, then the Jesuit students would be given a choice: either to register at the university and stop coming to San Pablo, or to come to San Pablo and give up their official registration at the university.[43]

While Father Piñas journeyed with these proposals toward Madrid and Rome, and Acosta tried to gain friends for his views in Lima, academic life in the viceregal capital went on peacefully as before. The Jesuit students who finished their courses in philosophy in 1576 took their final exams and received their degrees at the university. Acosta, who knew Spanish academic circles well, assured the General that the Order's students in the college at Lima could have won honors either in Alcalá or Salamanca. The new school year, 1576–77, began and ended, it seems, without any major friction between the university and San Pablo. The Jesuits enrolled forty-four lay students plus six members of the Order in their course in philosophy. The school of humanities drew to its classes all the youngsters following those studies in Lima; and it had to open, for the first time, a student dormitory to house eighteen boys sent by their parents from Chile and Tierra Firme to study with the Jesuits of San Pablo. Languages also continued to be taught with the viceroy's approval.[44]

By the first half of 1578, the first serious tensions had developed between the Jesuits and the state university, confirming Acosta's fears. When the students of San Pablo walked the two blocks separating the college from the university to take their final exams in philosophy and receive their degrees, they met an unusual rigor and severity on the part of the university professors. In April of that year, enrollment for the new school year opened and all the lay students ready to begin the courses in philosophy, thirty of them in the whole city, went over to San Pablo, while the lectures at the university were deserted. A good number of theologians also preferred to attend the lectures of Acosta and Esteban de Ávila in San Pablo rather than to attend regular classes at the state institution.[45]

By May, Doctor López Guarnido, for the second time rector of the university, surveyed his empty classrooms and came to the conclusion that, in a still developing city with a limited number of students, San Pablo was a real threat to the university. As rector, he could not tolerate that situation. He called a faculty meeting and the decision was taken to appeal to the viceroy, patron and father of the university.

In their letter to Toledo, the university doctors described well the academic situation of Lima in the winter of 1578. The university, an institution "so important for the service of His Majesty," was empty, deserted by the students and without any authority. The reason for this lamentable situation was not a lack of interest in studies on the part of the city's youth; it was rather the fact that they all went regularly to the colleges run by the religious orders. The students were persuaded to do so under false pretences or compelled through family pressures. So far, its doctors complained, all the peaceful means taken by the university to correct this state of affairs had failed. The faculty of the university asked the viceroy to take this problem into his own hands, and they made a request which would have honored the narrower mentality of the Holy Tribunal of the Inquisition. They asked the viceroy to forbid the

[27]

attendance of lay students at the private colleges, and to forbid it with all the authority and power of the state under the severe penalties of exile from the kingdom and perpetual ineligibility to hold any public office within the boundaries of the viceroyalty. If any religious order would dare to oppose the viceregal command, it should be immediately deprived of all its properties.[46]

While reading the university's report, Don Francisco de Toledo was filled with mounting anger. Since his arrival in Lima he had dreamed of a new Salamanca on the Rimac. He had taken the university away from the Dominicans, moved it to a new and better location, and had assigned financial support to maintain its chairs. Now the Jesuits, with their College of San Pablo, were again blocking his way. San Pablo refused to become an integral part of his university and, based on papal-granted privileges, was sailing an independent course which was both the ruin of the university and a new challenge to the *real patronato*. Besides, the Jesuits could exercise and had begun exercising more influence on the viceregal society than was suited to His Majesty's interests.

By the first week of October, 1578, His Excellency, heeding the university's request, had signed a decree to confirm the state university as the only unchallenged source of ideas in the viceroyalty, destroying all freedom in the field of education. On Saturday, the 11th of October, a body of trumpeters formed in front of Toledo's palace, and soon the sound of trumpets filled the plaza, reverberating far out into the city. A multitude of the curious gathered at the plaza, but there was complete silence when the town crier ascended the platform and began reading Toledo's decree in a clear and loud voice. The viceroy, following step by step the suggestions of the university, forbade under threat of grave punishment the attendance of lay students at any private colleges and imposed the obligation of attending classes at the university. A social death of civil ineligibility and exile was decreed for those who would not obey the new law, and the same punishment was also applicable to the parents and tutors of the guilty students.[47]

After the decree was read to the multitude, royal officials went to the Dominican convent, a block away from the viceregal palace, to repeat the decree to the Dominican Fathers. The superior accepted the law, expressed his agreement with its content, and promised obedience to His Excellency's orders. Sunday the 12th of October, 1578, was a day of waiting and tension at San Pablo. The Jesuits knew that Toledo's decree was meant for them, and that to accept it without a challenge was the end of San Pablo. Throughout the day, the fathers studied and discussed the situation, listened to the warning and advice of friends, gathered the rumors wildly spreading throughout the city, and offered special prayers in the college chapel. Before the day was over, José de Acosta, as Jesuit provincial, had made the decision: with respect but firmness, the viceroy's decree had to be resisted.

On Monday, the viceroy's officials knocked at the doors of San Pablo and summoned the rector. When he came to the front door, a great number of Jesuit students was already surrounding Juan Delgado, royal notary and secretary of the university, who was in charge of reading Toledo's decree to the Jesuits. Silence was imposed and Delgado slowly read, word by word, the long, despotic decree. The Jesuit rector reacted with coldness, asking for an official copy of the document and requesting a suspension of the law until that legal requirement was fulfilled. When, a few days later, a notarial copy of the document was handed to José de Acosta, the doors of San Pablo had to be closed and the students dispersed.[48]

The year 1578 ended in sadness for the Jesuits. The classrooms and cloisters of their college, alive a few months before with the best youth of Lima, were now emptied and silenced by the imperious will of a man embodying in himself absolute monarchy. Ten years before, the Jesuits had come to Lima dreaming of building a college in the European tradition of the Order. Only a decade had elapsed and the old dream was coming true, when it abruptly ended in a complete failure.

With the coming of 1579, the Jesuits closed ranks in the empty college around their Provincial Acosta, ready to fight Toledo's decree with the only weapon available in their type of society: a strong appeal to Madrid and Rome. With great secrecy, fearful of Toledo's violent reprisals, the Jesuits made contacts with friends and benefactors, asking them to write to the king and the council in favor of San Pablo. Acosta himself sat down at his desk and wrote a long report instructing Father Piñas, who was in Spain representing the Peruvian Jesuits, on how to fight Toledo's drastic measures against San Pablo in Madrid. His ideas in 1579 were similar to the ones he expressed in the report signed with the Visitor in Cusco in December, 1576, and which had been taken to Spain by Piñas. Acosta demanded for San Pablo the freedom to teach, and, for the students, freedom to learn and attend classes wherever they might choose, without being restricted or compelled by the viceroy or the university.[49]

The news and reports of the closing of San Pablo arrived at Seville in August of 1579. Father Piñas, as former rector of the college at Lima, was heartbroken and indignant. In a letter to the Father General, written from Seville before rushing to Madrid to oppose the viceroy's orders, Piñas almost called Toledo a tyrant who had treated the Jesuits in a manner unheard of even among the Lutherans and heretics of Central Europe. Piñas arrived in Madrid to join forces with Father Francisco Porres, the able Jesuit procurator in the royal court, and both tried by all the means at their disposal to win a reversal of Toledo's decree. The king, always irresolute and fearful of making the wrong decision, took his time reading the documents which had arrived from Peru and listening to his counselors. Finally, on the 22nd of February, 1580, he signed a *cédula* in which he tried for a compromise between the Jesuits of San Pablo and his Peruvian viceroy.

The *cédula* of 1580 ordered Toledo to reopen San Pablo and empowered the Jesuits to teach the humanities and languages, Indian or European, to anybody and at any time the Jesuits might choose. The major faculties of philosophy and theology could also be taught at San Pablo, but not at the same time that the university offered its regular lectures on those subjects. A greater restriction for San Pablo and a greater victory for Toledo's idea was the absolute prohibition contained in the *cédula* of granting any degrees in San Pablo. The students could attend the Jesuit college freely and get a Jesuit education, but if they wanted an official degree, they had to register in and to attend courses at the university.[50]

The dream of Toledo had been realized. The state university would always be the only institution in Lima capable of creating doctors, masters and bachelors, and the main currents of the intellectual life in Peru would run through state-built and state-controlled channels. The Jesuits, with their dangerous ideas on freedom and their resistance to the king's *patronato*, would be restricted to teaching children. If any adults chose to attend their classes in philosophy and theology, they would never be able to exercise any strong influence in society, having no recognized degrees to give them social stature.

II

ATHENAEUM ON THE RIMAC

The king's *cédula* of 1580 did not end the feud between San Pablo and the university, and the legal battle for academic freedom and supremacy continued well into the seventeenth century. It was a frustrating legal battle with all the subtleties, endless rebuttals and appeals so characteristic of the Spanish courts of the era, and made even more frustrating by the clash of different jurisdictions, by the overlapping of executive and judicial powers, and by the lamentable confusion between the Church's and the state's spheres of action.[1] Caught and almost strangled in the legal maze, San Pablo would never be able to develop its full potential in the major faculties of philosophy and theology. The school of humanities and languages of the Jesuit college, less hampered by the university, was soon free to grow and become the training ground where the youth of Lima received that humanistic culture which had made famous the Jesuit schools in Europe.

The Viceroy Toledo had left for Spain, and to his successor, the gentle Martín Enríquez, fell the task of establishing and maintaining, following the king's wishes, the difficult equlibrium between San Pablo and the university. In February of the year 1581, the new viceroy informed the king that the Jesuits were now ready to take care of all the teaching of the humanities in Lima, as an integral part of the university.[2] The rector of San Pablo at the time, Juan de Atienza, was a former rector of the Jesuit college at Valladolid, where he had run the Jesuit institution as the *escuelas menores* of the university. The arrangement had worked in Spain since 1576, and now, five years later, Atienza and the viceroy were determined to make it work in Lima. On the 24th of July, Martín Enríquez finally proclaimed the royal *cédula* of 1580, and the Jesuits could reopen the school of humanities at San Pablo without any restriction.[3]

By the end of the sixteenth century, San Pablo's department of humanities was the official preparatory school for the University of San Marcos, and the Jesuits had the exclusive right to teach the classics in Lima. The academic authorities of San Marcos were satisfied. The Jesuits were teaching Latin and Greek in San Pablo without salaries and without tuition; and the endowment furnished to maintain the chairs of humanities in the university could be diverted to increase the number of chairs in the major faculties. The Jesuits were also satisfied to a certain extent. In the closing years of the century, the Marquis of Cañete had given them the exclusive right to teach the humanities, making their college the normal door for entrance to the university.[4]

On the 10th of September, 1621, the king had put the royal seal of approval to this situation by making it compulsory for any student who sought admission to the university to have a certificate signed by the Jesuits of San Pablo, stating that he had completed the courses in the humanities at the Jesuit institution.[5] For two hundred years, the professors of San Pablo would mount guard at the entrance of San Marcos, zealously screening the candidates and giving them the knowledge of Latin and Greek and the humanistic background which were considered at the time to be the indispensable prerequisites to following fruitfully the courses in the major faculties.

The Schedule of Classes

Being an integral part of the university, San Pablo's school of humanities followed, during the entire colonial period, the academic rhythm of San Marcos. The school year opened on the first Monday after Easter Week with a gathering of the faculty and the student body to listen to a solemn academic lecture by one of the professors. Given the widespread religious spirit of the times, the principal holidays coincided with the religious festivities, and classes were interrupted from the 24th of December, eve of the Nativity of Christ, to the 7th of January; then during the two weeks preceeding Lent, and during Holy Week and Easter Week.

The doors of San Pablo opened daily at seven-thirty in the morning and classes began fifteen minutes later. For two full hours, the younger students wrestled with the intricacies of Latin grammar, while the senior students read the classical authors of antiquity, trying to imitate their written and spoken styles, and to comprehend and assimilate their literary beauty. At ten the bell rang, and the students gathered in the chapel for half an hour of religious services. The rest of the morning was free for games, school plays, and other extra-curricular activities. In the afternoon, the first class began at two-thirty to last for a full hour, followed by thirty minutes of recreation on the large patio of the school. The final class was taught from four to five, and the students were dismissed after a few minutes of evening prayers in the school chapel.[6]

This daily routine was frequently broken by literary and scholastic academies, a characteristic feature of Jesuit education. On Saturday, for instance, some of the regular classes were suspended, and a general review was held to go over the main points studied during the week. On occasions, to give a greater solemnity to these reviews, outsiders were invited to be present and to fire all sorts of questions at the students. Several times each semester, literary competitions were organized to foster emulation and sharpen the creative qualities of the students. On very special occasions, the entire school presented to the general public a classical performance, re-enacting a passage of ancient history, delivering Cicero's speeches or reciting selections from Homer and Virgil.[7]

The Student Body

The study of the humanities, so popular in the post-Renaissance period, plus the fact that San Pablo was the only regular way to eventual attendance at the university, attracted more students to the Jesuit

[34]

school each year. The two classes, begun in 1568 with only forty students, had one hundred pupils by 1571. Five years later that number had doubled, and in 1578, the year Toledo closed the school, three hundred students were regularly attending the humanity courses at San Pablo.[8]

After the deadlock imposed by Toledo's decree was broken, the school began its painful recovery, and by January of 1583 the first three classes of the curriculum were once again functioning normally. There were also plans under way to begin a fourth class in the humanities soon, and to begin the final year with courses in rhetoric. Two years later, in 1585, more than two hundred students again enlivened the cloisters of San Pablo, while the faculty engaged in a renewed effort to improve the standards of the college. The chair of rhetoric was offered to José de Arriaga, a young Jesuit recently arrived from Spain, who was already an accomplished humanist; and with this chair the curriculum of humanities was completed, having now the five classes demanded by the *Ratio Studiorum*, the Jesuit code of education.[9]

During the first decades of the seventeenth century, while the scholarly alumnus and subsequent professor of San Pablo, Bernabé Cobo, was writing his famous *Fundación de Lima*, the number of students climbed to five hundred, and by the year 1648 six hundred students crowded into the old classrooms. When freshman classes of almost two hundred and fifty pupils began entering San Pablo, the Jesuits determined upon remodeling the old building and increasing the number of professors. The work was undertaken and, for the second half of the seventeenth century, San Pablo had a new, "sumptuous" building to house the one-thousand-odd students who became the standard number in attendance during the last one hundred years of the school.[10]

Not far away from San Pablo, to the rear of the viceregal palace, the Jesuits conducted an elementary school which they founded in 1666, and three hundred and thirty-six younger children were prepared there for the humanities, learning reading, writing and simple arithmetic. The number of pupils in that school also grew with the years. Before the end of the seventeenth century five hundred young boys tested the patience of their Jesuit masters, and during the recess periods played bullfighters, *conquistadores* and Indians, making a racket easily heard in the viceroy's office.[11]

To select the students to be accepted into their colleges, the Jesuits had in their code of education a simple, clear-cut principle. No one should ever be excluded or rejected because of birth or the socio-economic status of his family. But the practical implementation of this principle was quite different for the humanists who had written the *Ratio Studiorum* in post-Renaissance Italy, and for the men building a school at the edge of an ever-expanding empire. In colonial Lima, the color boundaries were sharp, and the Indians and Negroes vastly out-numbered the white, Spanish citizens, who styled themselves the *gente decente*, the decent people. San Pablo stood in the midst of a society in which decency was related to the color of the skin, not to moral behavior.

The Jesuits had tried from the very beginning of their college to avoid any segregation on economic grounds, making the teaching of the humanities tuition-free, and forbidding the imposition on the students of any expense by reason of extra-curricular activities. They even tried to ignore the racial boundaries, and the *Carta Anua* sent from Lima to Rome on the 1st of January, 1570, speaks of several Indian boys, "students of our college," who had taken part in a school play to the great admiration of the *limeños*, who had never before seen anything like it.[12] But when, in 1618, the Viceroy the Prince of Esquilache, a direct descendant of Francis Borgia, put into effect Toledo's old idea of a special school for Indian nobles under the care of the Jesuits, San Pablo's school of humanities was definitely closed to the aboriginal races.

Up to the first decade of the seventeenth century, the Jesuit college had been a microcosm of that colonial society, a melting pot of Indians, Negroes and Caucasians. White boys from the best families of Lima, tracing their ancestors back to the founders of the city, freely mixed in studies and play, under the eyes of the Jesuits, with all shades of mestizos, and with youngsters whose flat noses, protruding lips, and kinky hair were the unmistakable seal of the Negro. But soon the administrators of San Pablo were under serious social pressures to turn the school into an exclusive institution for those of pure Spanish ancestry.

"Decent" people, who naturally did not see any major objection to occasionally bedding down with an attractive slave-girl, began to object to the Jesuit policies of freely accepting mestizos and mulattos in San Pablo. They presented to the Jesuit rectors their arguments in favor of a segregated San Pablo, and even appealed to the Jesuit authorities in Peru. These must have been difficult years of soul-searching for the men teaching in the Jesuit college. Those men formed a compact group under military discipline, and they knew that policy-setting decisions had to come from above, that only the superiors could exclude mulattos and mestizos from the college; but they knew also, that when the decision was finally made, their duty was to carry it out with true religious obedience.

The men who held the higher Jesuit offices in Peru had the last word on the issue of segregating the school; they alone could change the course of the institution. The Jesuit superiors in Lima believed that all men were equal, and knew that a constitutional principle of all Jesuit schools forbade discrimination on the basis of birth or economic status. However, those men, unable to resist the social pressures in seventeenth-century Lima, fell victims of the prevailing ideological climate of the viceroyalty and gave orders to segregate San Pablo.

In 1648, Father Lupercio Zurbano, then Jesuit Provincial of Peru, gave a warning to the rector of San Pablo, reminding him that no mulattos or those clearly mestizo should be accepted into the school. And the provincial sounded almost apologetic, when he wrapped his orders in the soft excuse that "grave persons" of the city had requested that the Jesuit college follow this policy of excluding those not pure Spanish.[13]

A few years later, Andrés de Rada in Rome was named Visitor of the Peruvian Jesuits and had, therefore, an authority higher than that of the provincial himself. He not only maintained Zurbano's discriminatory orders, he made them even stronger. Rada wanted mulattos and all mestizos excluded from the school, and, besides, all those to whom the "decent people" of Lima should seriously object. Father Visitor thought that those "decent people" of Lima were justified in pressing for an exclusive school where the racially lower classes would not mix with the Spanish boys, and accordingly he gave orders to the rector to acquiesce in the wishes of the colonial elite. That was indeed a low point in the history of San Pablo.[14]

During the second half of the seventeenth century, the Jesuit college tended to be a segregated school, not as a *de facto* situation, but as a state of affairs created by deliberate orders of those superiors who ruled the Jesuits in Peru. Yet, not all the members of the Order could accept this new, unchristian policy imposed by the Visitor, and some of them must have written to Rome, opposing Rada's orders and appealing to the Jesuit General. By the closing years of the century, Thyrsus González, a former professor of the University of Salamanca and then General of the Jesuits in Rome, was fully aware of the situation prevailing at San Pablo. In 1692, he sent to Peru his own supreme orders, which showed that he knew well the existing segregation in the college at Lima and did not like it at all. González tried, too hesitantly perhaps to be really effective, to revert to the basic Jesuit principle of non-discrimination. He ordered the college to accept mestizos in San Pablo again, if social pressures could be overcome, but he said nothing of the mulattos, who seemed to have entirely faded from the cloisters of San Pablo, as the Indians did many years before.[15]

Laws and orders have never been able to change overnight culturally rooted prejudices, and Father González' weak orders from faraway Rome could do very little to affect the mentality of men caught in the web of a city that not only in its layout but also in its social patterns was a checker-board of alternating colors.

This color-consciousness seems to have endured among some Spanish and Peruvian Jesuits well into the eighteenth century. In 1715, Provincial Antonio Garriga visited the Jesuit primary school behind the viceregal palace and saw that it was open to all the children of the

THE COLLEGE
OF
SAN PABLO

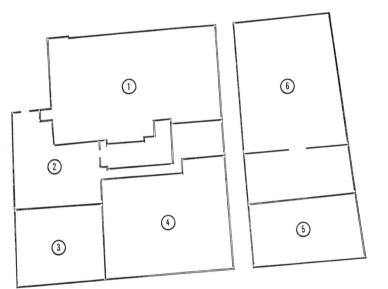

1. Church.   2. Jesuit Residence.   3. Offices, storerooms and pharmacy.
4. Classrooms, library, private rooms.   5. Infirmaries.   6. School of
Humanities.

neighborhood, including mestizos and mulattos. Although the Jesuits had adopted a freer racial policy there than in the school of humanities, still the provincial objected to an indiscriminate mixing of races, and imposed an "equal but separate" sort of principle to handle the problem. The classrooms were built with ascending steps to enable the teacher to easily watch the restless swarm of younger children. Garriga ordered the Spanish children and those of noble birth to sit on the higher steps, reserving the lower ones for the young mulattos and mestizos. He reasoned that this measure was necessary to meet the objections of those good families who abhorred seeing those "who [were] separated by nature" united in the school.[16]

Textbooks, Poetry and Theater

The students accepted in San Pablo were exposed to the same authors and were taught by the same methods used in the Jesuit schools in Europe. Faithfully following the *Ratio Studiorum*, the youth of Lima read, studied, and on occasion memorized Cicero, Sallust, Caesar and Livy, three of the great historians of antiquity, and the poets Virgil and Horace. For the Greek lectures, the Jesuits favored the use of Plato and Plutarch, John Chrysostom and Gregory Nazianzen, among others.[17]

Since 1579 San Pablo had had as an official textbook the famous *De Institutione Grammaticae Libri Tres*, which had been published as recently as 1572 by the Portuguese Jesuit Manuel Álvarez. For many decades, Álvarez' work, so quickly adopted in San Pablo, was a genuine bestseller in Europe. It became the required textbook in the schools of humanities all over the world, and was translated into many modern languages, including Polish, Hungarian, Croatian and Chinese. The youth of Lima were led into the magnificent world of the classics by the same mentor who was, for more than three centuries, to initiate thousands of students of all nationalities in the beauties of the Latin language. Other famous European textbooks adopted very early in the courses at San Pablo were the *De Arte Rhetorica Libri Tres*, written in

1560 by the Spanish Jesuit Cipriano Suárez, and Bartolomé Bravo's *Thesaurus Verborum*, published in 1597.[18]

But the Jesuit college at Lima was not going to rely forever on European authors. In the first years of the seventeenth century, the brilliant José de Arriaga wrote in Lima, as a textbook for San Pablo, his *Rhetoris Christiani Partes Septem*. The manuscript was sent to Europe, where it was examined and approved by several Jesuit humanists, and it was finally printed in Lyons, France in 1619. Arriaga's purpose was to teach the advanced students of humanities at San Pablo the rules and methods of becoming effective public speakers. Inspired by the classical orators of Greece and Rome, Arriaga taught his Lima students how to select proper subjects for each occasion, how to compose speeches, and how to deliver them in a pleasant and persuasive manner. Elocution was stressed, and voice, pronunciation, gestures, and bodily position and control were fully explained in Arriaga's textbook.[19]

Toward 1672, an anonymous professor of San Pablo wrote (although it was never published) his own Latin grammar adapted to the peculiar needs of the colonial students, and it contained a collection of Latin proverbs for the moral and ethical training of the younger children.[20]

One of those young students, who, in his school days at San Pablo, had used the grammar of 1672 and Arriaga's book, was a bright youngster by the name of José Rodríguez. Rodríguez joined the Jesuit Order in 1680, and years later became one of the best humanists on the faculty of San Pablo. In the first decades of the eighteenth century, he was teaching in his alma mater and writing a textbook, which became a small classic, for his class. His *Gramática Ilustrada*, modeled after Nebrija's great work, was printed in Madrid in 1734, went through several editions in Lima before the end of the century, and was reprinted again in 1839, in already independent Peru, seventy-two years after the Jesuits were banished from the Spanish dominions and San Pablo had ceased to be.[21]

In the humanistic climate created in the Jesuit college at Lima, the writing of poetry and drama grew through the years with baroque luxuriance. The Jesuits had always fostered the writing of poems as a means of mastering the language and to improve literary style; and men like Lope de Vega, Calderón, John of the Cross, and later in France Descartes and Voltaire, wrote their first compositions in Jesuit schools and under Jesuit masters. In colonial Lima, the professors of San Pablo would maintain for two centuries the tradition of the Jesuit schools in Europe.

Poems were written in San Pablo by the thousands, not only by the students but by the Jesuits themselves, to solemnize the entrance of new viceroys or the installation of new bishops, to mourn the death of a royal person, to compete in the literary contests organized in the city, or as ordinary school exercises. Language did not create any barriers, and the Jesuits of Lima produced poetry in the classical languages, in Hebrew, in the modern European and in the Indian languages. Perhaps the outstanding example of this poetic babel occurred in 1761, when the college mourned the death of Queen Amalia and the students and faculty members wrote poems in Latin, Spanish, Basque, Italian, German, Portuguese, Hungarian, English, French, Catalan, Quechua, Aymara, and the language of the Moxo Indians. At times a combination of languages was used as in the octosyllabic macaronic *romance*, Quechua-Spanish, which begins:

> Sonecollay imanasuguim
> Que tan perdido te veo,
> Iscai rumip nitiscatam
> Te contempla el universo
> . . . .[22]

Other poems were written, in which the authors, employing a high degree of ingenuity, though with dubious taste, tried to weld Spanish and Latin, using only words and syntactical constructions common to both languages, to produce a work which could be read either as Latin or Spanish. In the second half of the seventeenth century, Rodrigo de Valdés, professor of theology and the busy dean of studies at San Pablo, found the time to write the outstanding work in this macaronic vein—his *Poema Heroyco Hispano-Latino*, which sings and extols the great-

ness of the "very noble and loyal city of Lima." The poem was considered good enough to be printed in Madrid in 1687, a few years after
the death of Valdés. But Rodrigo de Valdés was the exception, and many
of those Spanish-Latin compositions, void of all literary value, were soon
forgotten, although some of them could have been important landmarks
for philological studies.[23]

If the poetic production of San Pablo was written in an amazing
variety of languages, it also shows a wide knowledge of all the metrical
patterns used at the time in the best literary circles of Spain. The
Jesuits of Lima and their students wrote hexameters in the style of
Virgil; Pindaric, pseudo-Pindaric, and Horatian odes; *liras*, *sonetos*,
décimas, *endechas reales*; and *romances*, the pattern of eight syllables so
popular in Spanish literature and polished to perfection by Lope de
Vega. They also wrote solemn *endecasílabos* in the Italian style, a pattern
newly introduced by Garcilaso de la Vega from Italian into Spanish
poetry, and one can even find samples of the "modern" twisted and
conceptual poetry that, under the spell of Góngora's genius, was
growing out of hand, like a rain-forest, in the Spanish literature of the
seventeenth century. Góngora's poetry, incidentally, was to have in San
Pablo the same devastating effects it had in Spain—a great deal of the
Jesuit prose written in the college was infected with *culteranismo*, the
literary cancer eating away at the marrow of the best Spanish literature.[24]

If poetry filled so many hours in the curriculum of San Pablo and was
constantly used as a mind-training tool, drama also occupied a prominent place in the college as an essential device to impart the humanistic
outlook on life, the aim of all Jesuit education. Since 1568, the year
San Pablo opened its doors to the youth of Lima, theatrical performances were a well-known feature in the Jesuit institution. But theater
was never a mere social entertainment to break the monotony for the
Peruvian Jesuits, or to brighten the tempo of slow-moving colonial life.
The historian Jacinto Barrasa, for years teacher and writer at San
Pablo, goes out of his way to make it clear that drama had high academic
value in the college. It was an anvil on which the Jesuits tried to shape
into perfect forms the future lawyers, preachers and public officials of

Peru, who found on the stage at San Pablo the best living arena in which to practice all the precepts and rules learned in the classes on rhetoric.[25]

The academic value of these theatrical performances was further increased by the fact that they were conceived, written and produced by the Jesuits and their students primarily as a practical exercise in literary expression. The school library had some of the best plays written in Europe, both by Jesuits and professional playwrights, but San Pablo's professors preferred, obviously for academic reasons, to write their own plays in collaboration with their students. From the very first years of the school, we see men of the intellectual stature of José de Acosta writing and producing these plays.[26]

As in the case of poetry, so the diverse styles of plays written and presented in San Pablo show a remarkable familiarity with the theatrical currents then in vogue in Spain. One of the forms most frequently used in the Jesuit college at Lima was the *colóquio*, a simple performance, usually in one act, almost devoid of any plot, which served as a mere frame within which to deliver a famous speech, to recite poems, or to stress some ethical or religious principle. The Viceroy Toledo was the guest of honor in 1576 at one of these *colóquios* in which, due to the solemnity of the occasion, the Jesuits combined prose with verse in the dialogue and Spanish with the two classical languages. Also on the stage, in true baroque spirit, the Jesuits loved to display the languages known in the college.[27]

The *auto sacramental*, which had become a jewel of Spanish literature at the hands of Lope de Vega and Calderón, was highly favored by the Jesuit professors because of the religious content of this type of drama. Virtues, ideas and abstract principles were personified and thrown onto the stage to reveal in graphic fashion their hidden works in society and in the mind of man. In 1569, the students of San Pablo presented, also before the Viceroy Toledo, the "Challenge and Duel Between Work and Laziness"—a subject closely related to the social conditions of colonial Lima, where the higher classes tended to live in leisure and leave hard labor to the Indians and Negroes. The following year, the viceroy was again treated to a solemn *auto*, the "Victory of Wisdom over Folly," in which the importance of the intellectual life was stressed. The Jesuits once again combined Latin with Spanish and prose with verse in the dialogue.[28]

This tradition was continued throughout the seventeenth century and well into the eighteenth. In 1661, for instance, when the Count of Santisteban was received for the first time at San Pablo and the walls of the school were practically covered with poems in Latin and Spanish exalting the virtues of the new viceroy, an *auto sacramental*, this time with a farcical twist, was presented by the students. Mars, the war-god of the Romans who symbolized the military qualities of the count, and Minerva, their goddess of wisdom, competed for supremacy over the viceroy's heart. After the conflict had been joined and the outcome appeared uncertain, a nymph representing the Jesuit Order appeared who settled the dispute and reconciled Mars and Minerva in the heart of Santisteban.[29]

In 1723, Salvador de Vega, professor of philosophy at San Pablo, wrote and produced a highly theological play, which depicted on stage the different spiritual effects caused in the Christian soul by the reception of Holy Communion. It was a short masterpiece of only three scenes, written in light Spanish verse of different patterns, with a background of music and songs. The author's aim was clearly religious, to exhort his young audience to proper preparation for the reception of the Sacrament of the Last Supper, but he succeeded in attaining that aim in a pleasant, entertaining manner. De Vega introduced in the plot, as one of the main figures, the foolish steward or *gracioso*, epitomized in Spanish literature by the eternal Sancho Panza, and through him he managed to keep the play from becoming a dry theological lecture.[30]

Besides the Jesuit professors' original works, San Pablo also occasionally produced plays written by professional playwrights. Lope de Vega, with Calderón, the king of Spanish dramatic authors, was read at San Pablo at least after the first years of the seventeenth century, and some of his comedies, retouched here and there, found their way onto the school stage. The pleasant, easy reading of Lope's great comedies

[45]

became a serious danger to the hardier studies of the Latin and Greek authors, and the Jesuit superiors in Peru had to forbid the reading and presentation of Lope's work several times. Yet, the Spanish genius left his imprint on San Pablo, and the Jesuits wrote comedies in the style popularized by Lope, interwoven with popular music and dances, and in the rhythmic stanzas of the Spanish *romance*.[31]

Mindful of the young actors and the pedagogical purpose of their theater, the Jesuits regularly chose biblical and historical themes for the plots of the school comedies. The clash between Mary, Queen of Scots, and Elizabeth of England was the subject of a play presented in honor of the Viceroy the Marquis of Cañete. The secular and political life of Francis Borgia provided the plot for another play offered to the Count of Salvatierra. The life of Saint Paulinus, Bishop of Nola, so closely related to the ever-present problem of slavery, was also brought to the stage of San Pablo, and the bishop's role was played on that occasion by the young student Gerónimo de Montesinos, who years later became the best public speaker in the viceroyalty, and was known as the "Demóstenes Indiano."[32]

The dynamic, anarchistic spirit of the baroque was making artistic masterpieces of the Jesuit churches in Peru in those years: twisting columns created an exuberant anarchy of colors and shapes and made walls, pilasters, and domes burst into a luxuriant, ever-growing, ivy-like ornamentation. The same baroque spirit also took hold of the dramatic art produced at San Pablo, and as in Europe, the Jesuit theater in Lima became a baroque theater. As the seventeenth century advanced, many a drama became a mere excuse to display a wealth of robes, silver and gold ornaments, fireworks, music and dances. The action could no longer be limited to the regular stage and overflowed into the plaza at the entrance of the college, there to be prolonged at times for two and even three days. "The History of Joseph, the Ancient Patriarch," a veritable forerunner of the modern Hollywood Biblical extravaganza, was produced at San Pablo to honor the arrival of the Viceroy Montes-claros; the stage was the entire plaza, and the action lasted for two days. When the news of the canonization of Ignatius Loyola, the founder, and Francis Xavier, the most illustrious son, of the Order, arrived in Lima in 1622, the Jesuits surpassed all expectations in their efforts to honor the occasion. Besides elaborate religious festivities, they prepared a dramatic presentation extolling the glories of the new saints. The action overflowed again into the plaza, and for three seemingly endless days the *limeños* were treated to one of the most extraordinary outbursts of the baroque spirit known to colonial Lima.[33]

The plots of the plays no longer mattered and they disappeared behind the dazzling glare of the baroque scenography, just as the superb neo-classic lines of the school church, still standing in the heart of old Lima, had all but disappeared under superimposed baroque decoration. The school stage was furnished with wings and flies to give depth and perspective and to create the illusion of several levels of action, something the *Carta Anua* of January, 1675, claimed the Jesuits had helped to introduce into Lima. Music had been used in the school plays from the beginnings of San Pablo, but in that second half of the seventeenth century the dialogue itself melted into lyrics, and the Jesuit students produced the first musical comedies ever to be heard in Lima. The exotic, indigenous elements which had delightfully crept into the Jesuit churches, giving American Baroque its unique beauty, were also present in the scenic art of San Pablo. Negro musicians, trained at the college, frequently took part in public performances, and aboriginal Indian costumes and songs also found their way onto the stage of the school.

This flair for scenography and elaborate scenic display sometimes led the Jesuits of San Pablo to extremes of realism bordering on bad taste. Bernabé Cobo, professor at the college, recorded in his *Historia del Nuevo Mundo* a play produced in San Pablo, presenting in a grandiose manner the mystery of the Last Judgment. Indian mummies and skeletons were brought to the college from the *huacas* or burial mounds in the valley of Lima, and when the angel's trumpet sounded in the play, the mummies and skeletons appeared from every corner, answering the call to their final judgment, terrifying the gasping audience.[34]

Languages

If poetry and drama were well-known characteristics of the Jesuit college at Lima during the colonial period, the study of languages was even more so. The Jesuits, founded in an age of discoveries and travels, had been good linguists since the first years of the Order. Many of them had learned to handle with ease, besides classical languages, the modern European tongues. The men who lived for two hundred years at San Pablo kept alive this tradition of the Order and made it even richer by the study of some of the aboriginal languages of America.

Several European languages could be heard at any given time in the classrooms and patios of the college. Even before the end of the sixteenth century, the Jesuits tried to break the Castilian monopoly of sending men to the Indies, and they succeeded in bringing to San Pablo many non-Spanish-speaking Jesuits who made the college a fine sample of the internationality of the Jesuit Order. Italian Jesuits, already requested in 1576 by the far-seeing Acosta because of their facility in learning new languages,[35] had been going steadily to Peru since the last decades of the sixteenth century; in 1605, of the fifty-odd Jesuits who left Europe for Peru, about twenty were Italians. German-speaking Jesuits had been on the Peruvian route since 1616, and in 1647 seventy-five of them waited in Seville for royal approval to go to different parts of America. Basque, Catalan, Portuguese and French Jesuits also went to work in Peru at certain periods.[36]

Most of those men stayed only briefly at the college on their way to the missions, but some of them remained longer to complete their studies or to serve as teachers, administrators, and even rectors. They gave San Pablo a certain international and multilingual flavor, as in the case of the famous poetic competitions, and they greatly increased the manpower of the college, which reached at times the number of one-hundred-sixty Jesuits, engaged in the academic and the apostolic ministries of the Order.

All of these men, regardless of their nationality or language, had crossed the seas to expand the frontiers of Christendom by preaching the Gospel to the Indians, and it was only natural that they turned with zeal to the study of the Indian languages. Toward the end of November of 1568, only a few months after the arrival of the first Jesuits in Lima, the mestizo Blas Valera, "a good language" (sic), as he was described in a document sent to Rome, was received in San Pablo and began teaching Quechua to all the members of the college. In a few months they had prepared their first translations, and by 1569 the courses in Quechua, compulsory for all the Jesuits in San Pablo, were formally established with two weekly classes.[37]

That same year, in the group of Jesuits brought to Peru by the Viceroy Don Francisco de Toledo, the Andalusian Alonso de Barzana arrived at San Pablo. If José de Acosta was the thinker and the theologian of the college, and José de Arriaga the humanist, then Alonso de Barzana became the outstanding linguist. With an unquenchable thirst for knowledge he had taken up the study of Quechua even before his arrival in Peru, and once in Lima he was soon considered one of the "best languages" in the college. On the 25th of June, 1570, when the Jesuits of San Pablo took over the nearby *doctrina* of El Cercado, Barzana delivered a flawless sermon in Quechua in the presence of the viceroy and the *Audiencia*, and a few months later he was *the* teacher of Indian languages at San Pablo. Before his death at Cusco in 1598, he had mastered half a dozen aboriginal languages, writing grammars and dictionaries of several of them.[38]

Barzana had set the tone, and the study of Indian languages in San Pablo became not only a needed apostolic tool but a serious scientific endeavor. The Jesuits not only studied those languages; they tried moreover to reduce them to rules, to rearrange logically the unwritten Indian languages, and to produce the dictionaries required for systematic study. The Archbishop of Lima, Jerónimo de Loaiza, recognized the significance of this linguistic effort, as the historian Antonio de Herrera would recognize it years later, and ordered all the clergy of the city to enroll in the courses given at San Pablo. When the famous Third Provincial Council of Lima convened in 1583, and the council fathers approved the motion of writing a new catechism for the instruction of the Indians, several Jesuits were among the linguistic experts in charge of the work. San Pablo made history on that occasion by housing the first Peruvian printing press, brought from the Jesuit college in Mexico City by Antonio Ricardo, and by printing in its cloisters the bilingual catechism of 1584, the first book ever printed in the Viceroyalty of Peru.[39]

The Indian languages became such a serious matter with the Jesuits of San Pablo that orders were given for all the newly arrived in Lima, regardless of age, nationality or previous studies, to spend six months taking intensive courses in Quechua. The young Jesuits still in training at the college were obligated to speak the Indian languages among themselves, and to prepare Quechua sermons to be delivered before the community. It was an amazing sight, perhaps the unique product of the intermingling of Christian, humanistic and baroque spirits, to see that large group of highly-educated Europeans, who had absorbed the esthetic values of ancient cultures and were conversant with the latest literary development of the Romance languages, trying to channel their thoughts and feelings into the novel guidelines of the Indian languages. They were committed to reaching the soul of the Indian to graft him into the universal world-view of Christianity; to master the aboriginal languages became for them not only a scientific curiosity, but, above all, a truly religious duty.[40]

With the passing of the years, the Jesuit linguistic center was shifted from San Pablo to the *doctrinas* of El Cercado and Juli, where Quechua and Aymara could be taught and learned in a more living environment. But in the college, the linguistic activity never died and the young Jesuits continued to study and practice the languages learned in the *doctrina* while they completed their studies in philosophy and theology. In 1596, Father General Aquaviva signed into law a proposal received from Peru that no Jesuit should be promoted to the priesthood in San Pablo unless he had first a good command of the Indian language, and that the newly ordained priests should spend three full years working among the Indians perfecting their knowledge of the aboriginal language. In the same spirit, General Thyrsus González made these rules even stricter. In August of 1692 he ordered that no Peruvian Jesuit should ever abandon his long course of studies to do apostolic work until he had a good knowledge of the aboriginal language.[41]

The Jesuits who studied, taught and worked at San Pablo during the colonial age were also in close contact with another linguistic group, that of the Negro slaves. Luis López, a member of the first Jesuit expedition, had worked among them, and from that time there had always been Jesuits at San Pablo appointed to minister to the slaves. The need to communicate with the Negroes, together with the humanistic climate of the college, soon led some of the Jesuits to turn their attention to the "language of Angola," and a serious proposal was referred to Rome asking whether it would be advisable to establish formal courses in that language to be followed by the members of the Order in Lima. At the same time, an inquiry was made about the advisability of printing some linguistic works in the language of the slaves, already prepared at San Pablo: namely, a simple dictionary, a grammar and a guide for confessors.[42]

Rome's answer must have been positive, at least to a certain extent, because in 1629 San Pablo was using and distributing, even to the furthest ends of the viceroyalty, prayer leaflets, catechisms and instructions printed in Lima in the language of the slaves. In 1630, fourteen hundred and forty copies of a simple grammar came off the press, and the Jesuits of San Pablo were furnished with the essential tools to begin the systematic study of the "language of Angola." For these linguistic publications in the African language, the Jesuits of San Pablo did not produce an original work as in the case of Quechua, but rather used a work edited in Portugal by Mateo Cardoso, a Jesuit theologian born in Lisbon, adapting it to the needs of America.[43]

These publications circulated among the Jesuits during the same years that Alonso de Sandoval's famous book *De Instauranda Aetiopum Salute* was fresh from the printing shops of Seville. This book was inspired even to its title by Acosta's great work on the Indians and was widely read at San Pablo. While Sandoval, a former student of the College of San Pablo, where he learned humanities, philosophy, and his boundless love for the Negro, was toiling among the slaves in

Cartagena de Indias (where one of his students was St. Peter Claver), his brethren in Lima studied his great book, learning the nature, customs, political and religious organization of the Negroes and the ways to bring them to the Christian vision of the world. As in the case of the linguistic publications in the ''language of Angola,'' San Pablo became a distributing center for Sandoval's book, and between 1628 and 1631 many copies of that great work were sent from the college at Lima to the four corners of the viceroyalty.[44]

Over the span of two centuries, the Jesuit college at Lima was an intellectual bridge uniting two different worlds—the Christianized, Greco-Roman world of the European, and the somber, exotic world of the Indian and Negro. In the cloisters of San Pablo, two currents of humanity intermingled their cultural mainstreams, and many men, like a Barzana and a Sandoval, emerged from that encounter mestizos and mulattos of the soul and of the heart.

III

THE SILENT BATTLE

The Jesuits, who from the beginning had admired the "City of the Kings" and had sent to Europe glowing reports comparing Lima with Seville and Toledo, soon began feeling the coarse texture of life in the colonial city. In an era and culture in which conscience was still queen, the drive for gold and power had become white-hot, while moral sense and moral values grew dimmer.

A white minority had subdued Indians and Negroes and was trying to use them as mere pawns in the financial games played daily on the huge chess-board that was the viceregal capital. An elite of landholders, civil servants, retired soldiers, priests and merchants lived off the fruits of the labors of the conquered race, and fell victims of that secret erosion which slowly eats away the interior worth of those who live in leisure. Silver from Potosí and silk from China had combined to give Lima a glow of luxury unknown in the stern, almost monastic cities of Castile. Violence erupted and swords easily crossed to win power or to avenge honor. It was a new world in the making, with new perspectives and new patterns, where men could at times acquire the stature of heroes or saints, but where they could also sink below the human, Christian level.[1]

The eyes of the priest-scholars who taught at San Pablo, in the midst of that boiling society in search of its identity, were accustomed to look beneath the surface of things, and soon became aware of those moral reefs, hidden menaces to the Christian course of colonial life. In the confessional the Jesuits tried to cure minds and souls wrecked by greed or lust; but the confessional, because of its personal nature, could not have an influence wide enough to check the unchristian ideas and practices creeping around and lurking in the city. The professors of San Pablo decided to establish in the college a seminar course on practical moral problems to charter the routes to be followed by the Christian conscience in the adventure of colonizing a virgin world.

The seminar, according to Jesuit legislation, was not a regular lecture on moral theology, but a weekly meeting conducted under the chairmanship of one of the professors in the informal way of a roundtable discussion. Abstract moral principles were not at issue, but rather their practical implications in the concrete setup of a given human situation. Local and temporal circumstances were described, and the question was raised on how the Christian conscience should act in that situation, and why. The participants could offer suggestions, object, propose possible solutions, agree or take exception. The chairman usually summed up and, *salvo meliore judicio*, offered his own reasoned solution.[2]

Until 1577, the gifted José de Acosta held the chairmanship of the bi-weekly seminar, and attracted to the discussions almost two hundred persons, both Jesuit and secular clerics. In 1608, the provincial of Peru, Esteban Páez, insisted that the seminar be held twice a week, and ordered that practical issues, which should be carefully studied beforehand by the chairman and the participants, be taken up. In 1637, the same order was renewed by Antonio Vázquez, then provincial, who, recognizing the great utility of the meetings, ordered all the Jesuits to be present, unless excused by the rector himself. If for any unforeseen reason the seminar could not be held at the appointed day or time, Vázquez ruled that it was to be postponed, but never cancelled. In the last decade of the seventeenth century, Father General Thyrsus González approved this established procedure at San Pablo, and again urged that all Jesuits always be present at the meetings, unless bedridden.[3]

Justice for the Indians

The relations between conquerors and conquered were one of the issues most frequently discussed at San Pablo. It was a common practice of the times to impress Indians for public works, especially in the mines, and even allot them to work in shifts for private owners within the city limits. The Jesuits of San Pablo raised some questions about this practice. Was it right for good Christians to force free men into hard labor? Considering the extreme lack of a labor force in the kingdom, could public officials do so? Could they assuage their consciences by saying that it was the king's will?

In the spirit of the seminar on practical moral problems, those questions could not be answered in the abstract, but only by studying the concrete nature of forced labor in Peru. In 1576, José de Acosta decided not to rely on reports any longer, but to see for himself the labor conditions in the Peruvian mines. He made a detour on his way to Cusco, and, following twisted trails up the Andes, he arrived at Villa Rica de Oropesa, better known as Huancavelica. Huancavelica had become not only a magic key to unlock the wealth of Potosí, but also a burning thorn in the conscience of many Spaniards, for whom the quicksilver mines were a symbol of all the greed of the conquerors, and of all the injustices heaped on the crushed Indian race.

Acosta made the rough trip to Huancavelica to be able, as he wrote to the Jesuit General in February of 1577, ". . . to understand the affairs of those mines, which seemed to me important in dealing with the consciences of many persons in this kingdom. . . ." With his characteristic intellectual curiosity, Acosta looked into every aspect of the mines, their history, the layout of the *socavones* or mining-pits, labor conditions, housing, dangers for the miners, the monetary reward they received, and the climatological conditions of the region. The Jesuit knew well that, from the viceroy on down, many Spaniards were deeply involved in the affairs of the mines, and he needed to know every possible detail to be able to judge correctly if a Christian could in good conscience cooperate in the exploitation of Huancavelica.

His greatest objections were two: the complete spiritual and human

[55]

forlornness of the Indians, and the low salaries paid to them. Both things, Acosta thought, would cause serious, well-founded concern to any Christian conscience. But, comparing the reality of labor conditions with the alarming rumors widespread in Lima, he found the latter grossly exaggerated. Of everything he saw, good and bad, Acosta did not hesitate to write to the Viceroy, Francisco de Toledo, who was dreaming of a wondrous wedding between Huancavelica and Potosí to beget the wealth and the power of Spain.[4]

Toward the *mita*, or forced-labor draft, Acosta had a realistic view. He thought that without some sort of forced labor it was impossible to establish a viable society in Peru, but he campaigned for a human approach to this thorny problem.[5] Much more than the *mita*, the tributes levied by Toledo on the Indians were considered an outrage, and he even dared to write to the king himself, trying to prick the royal conscience into revoking Toledo's unjust taxes.[6]

By the end of the sixteenth century, the authority of San Pablo's professors on practical moral problems was well established, and their seminar well attended. Persons from every walk of life knocked at the door of the college seeking advice and guidance to face as Christians the social and economic realities of a new society. The human experience of life in America did not have a parallel in Europe, and many persons of good will were lost in their efforts to inject a Christian spirit into the modes of existence formed in the new world. It was only natural that they turned to the priest-scholars of San Pablo.

Among those who came to the college in those closing years of the century was Don Luis de Velasco. The viceroy could not entirely square his conscience with the system of forced Indian labor. He had studied the issue, reviewed the existing legislation and practice, consulted his advisors, and through it all he had spent more than one restless night. In January of 1599, Don Luis came to San Pablo with a hard question: regardless of what had already been done by his predecessors, might he force additional Indians to work in mines newly discovered?

Some of the best Jesuit minds then at San Pablo, among them Esteban Ávila and Juan Pérez de Menacho, the two Jesuit theologians who also taught at San Marcos,[7] got together in the spirit of the seminar on moral problems to discuss the issue and to find an answer. They shrewdly remarked that they were not going to say anything about forced labor in general ". . . because we were not asked that question. . . ." But the answer to the specific question raised by the viceroy was clearly negative. The viceroy might not force additional Indians to work in mines newly discovered.

The Jesuits backed their answer with the authority of known authors, and pointed out that it would not be right for a Christian to force men to do what the pagans had already abhorred as the worst kind of slavery. They went on to explain that forcing Indians to the mines, aside from the ethical issue, was bad policy and bad administration. So, at a time when more hands were needed in agriculture, the few ones available were taken away to work the mines. This was a work profitable perhaps to the Kingdom of Spain, but certainly not to the Kingdom of Peru.[8]

Years went by with the roundtable discussion being held regularly at the college twice a week, when in 1624 Pedro de Oñate, an extraordinary intellectual personality, came to San Pablo to take over the seminar on moral problems. Oñate had obtained the best education available in Europe at that time. An alumnus of Salamanca and Alcalá, he studied in the latter university under that intellectual giant, Francis Suarez. Since 1615, he had been entrusted with one of the most important positions the Jesuits had in America, that of provincial of Paraguay, where the famous Reductions demanded only the best administrators. From that Indian world lost in a tangle of rivers and dark forests, Pedro de Oñate came to the glitter of Lima "to solve problems of conscience," and to feel the economic pulse of the viceroyalty.[9] For years, in his quiet cell at the College of San Pablo, Oñate worked within the boundaries of economics and moral theology, and produced his three volumes *De Contractibus*, one of the best and least-known works written in colonial days. Oñate, the first to attempt such a work in the colonies, tried to systematize the "infinite chaos" of laws and regulations governing the contractual life of the empire. The first volume of his work deals with contracts in general; the second concerns itself with all the lucrative contracts then in vogue throughout the viceroyalty; the third volume is a thorough study of the onerous contracts which impose a legal burden on the contracting parties. The Jesuit professor described the legal and economic aspects of all those contracts and discussed their ethical and moral implications. Pedro de Oñate was persuaded that, by guiding the conscience of lawyers, judges and merchants, he was making a serious contribution to the effort of building a Christian society in America.[10]

In 1629, Oñate had to face the problem of forced Indian labor in the mines of Huancavelica. It was in August of that year that the Viceroy the Count of Chinchón asked the Jesuits of San Pablo for advice on a personal moral question. The province of Huancavelica was depleted, and the labor force in the mines had become utterly insufficient. The viceroy wished to know if he might, in good conscience, force Indians from new provinces, not obligated to the *mita* of Huancavelica, to go to the mines. Moreover, the count asked if he could be absolved by his confessor in case he took that measure, and if he had any moral obligation to inform the king about the present situation in the mines.[11]

As in the case proposed by Don Luis de Velasco in 1599, Chinchón's moral problems were discussed at the college, and all the arguments, pro and con, were carefully examined. It fell to Oñate, as the expert on moral problems, to put in writing the answer to the viceroy's doubts. He rose to the occasion and produced a document which places him among the great fighters for justice in America. Oñate lacked the fire of a Las Casas or a Vieira, his brother in religion, but the punch of his iron logic made his cry for justice more scholarly, articulate and, therefore, more effective. In the document he wrote for Chinchón, Oñate pruned every oratorical excrescence, but by compressing his thoughts he made irony and cutting scorn ooze from every line.

With a greater courage than the professors who answered Luis de Velasco in 1599, Oñate dismissed the viceroy's specific questions and cut right to the bare bone of the issue. Was it morally right for the viceroy to compel any Indians to mine in Huancavelica, given the deaths and desolation following upon the present mining system? Was

[58]

forced labor of that nature permissible in a Christian society? The Jesuit blocked every possible way to an affirmative answer, and clearly maintained that to compel Indians, any Indians, to work in Huancavelica was illicit and unjust and could be shown with "grandissimas evidencias." He then heaped argument upon argument until the reader's mind is crushed under the weight.

Oñate's scholarly detachment was momentarily lost and replaced by a burning scorn which inflamed every word when he examined the arguments of certain devout persons who had tried to justify the horrors of Huancavelica on religious grounds. Spain was the strong arm of Holy Mother Church, they said, the defender of the faith and the wrecker of heresies in Europe. To give blood and muscle to that arm, and to assure it a mortal punch, the silver of Potosí was vitally needed. But without Huancavelica, there was no Potosí; without forced Indian labor, there was no Huancavelica. The conclusion was obvious: the quicksilver of Huancavelica, dug out by the sweat and blood of the Indians, was the rampart of the faith and the bulwark of the Church.

This argument was mocked and torn to pieces by Oñate, whose pen became piercing with irony when he suggested that the Spaniards themselves work the mines to exalt and defend their Church and their faith. And the professor of San Pablo went far ahead of many men of his generation when he made a clear distinction between the temporal realm of the crown and the spiritual realm of the Church. The king had no right, Oñate wrote, to force men to work or to pay taxes for the defense of the faith and the Church in Germany and in the Low Countries. And if he imposed those types of tribute, then they were unjust and no one had an obligation to pay them.

The Jesuit professor, familiar with the political organization of the empire, also expanded a line of thought timidly hinted at in the answer to Don Luis de Velasco in 1599. Peru, he said, was a true kingdom united to the Kingdom of Spain only in their mutual subordination to the same crown. The crown was the only political link between those kingdoms, and it was illegal for the king to tax or compel the citizens of Peru for the benefit of Spain. If nobody would dare to say that it was licit to tax the peninsular Spaniards for the benefit of the Indians, or the Indians of Paraguay for the benefit of those of Peru, how could they justify forced work and taxes laid on the shoulders of the Peruvian Indians for the benefit of Spain and its European entanglements?[12]

If the viceroy knew how to read between the lines, he must have been startled by some of Oñate's ideas and the Jesuit's courage and freedom in defending them. The viceroy had asked a specific question in trying to ease his moral scruples on a local issue, and he got a full lecture on justice and political theory in which the absolute power of the crown was cogently challenged on the basis of the peculiar nature of the Spanish Empire and of the different fields of action of Church and state.

Human exploitation, of course, was not halted in Peru by the efforts of men like Oñate. However, they freely sowed the ideas which, like the roots of a powerful tree slowly cracking the pavement, would eventually break the established system. Walking through the cloisters of the college, feeling under foot the hard, stony floor, one could sense the seedlings of a new, vigorous ideology springing up through the cracks. Onate was not a solitary figure in the faculty of San Pablo: his predecessors and successors were men with the same ideas.

Diego de Avendaño was one of these men. He had perhaps even a greater intellectual stature than Pedro de Oñate. With great versatility, he had taught the humanities, philosophy and theology at San Pablo; had twice become rector of the college, in 1659 and in 1666; and had also twice held the position of provincial of Peru. All along he had been one of the most active members of the roundtable discussions on problems of conscience. In the last decades of the seventeenth century, already an old man with almost fifty years spent in Peru, he wrote and published the six large volumes of his *Thesaurus Indicus*, undoubtedly the most extraordinary work produced in the College of San Pablo. Into the *Thesaurus*, a veritable treasure written in superb Latin, Avendaño packed all his ideas of half a century of fighting for the freedom of man and of trying to implant a Christian way of life in America.[13]

Like Acosta, Ávila, Menacho and Oñate, all professors of San Pablo, Avendaño was not a fiery preacher or a revolutionary social reformer, but a gentle scholar working with ideas. Yet he soared to heights of true classical eloquence when he opposed the slavery of so many men thrown every year into the mines. Avendaño had no fewer than forty-two accusations against the mining system and its controllers in Peru, and, as he had proclaimed them in his lectures at San Pablo, so he listed them in the first volume of his *Thesaurus* for all in Europe and America to read.[14] He was an old man and feared nothing but the concealment of the truth and the approaching judgment of God.

Speaking and writing about the *mita* of Huancavelica, Avendaño's hard line became even harder. As provincial, he visited the Jesuits throughout Peru and must have gone to Huancavelica where the Jesuits had had a small residence since 1644. He certainly had received reports from the Jesuits living there on the situation in the quicksilver mines. His judgment on the *mita* as practiced in Huancavelica toward the end of the seventeenth century is unmistakable. Avendaño thought that it was against all justice, and that labor conditions had deteriorated to the point of being utterly inhuman. He has left us a masterful literary description of the horror-stricken Indians, who sacrificed to the mountains surrounding the village as to wrathful gods, to placate them so that the natives might not be swallowed up by the dreadful *socavones*.[15]

During the seventeenth century, the faculty of San Pablo fought a silent battle, trying to establish the principle that the Indians were free human beings, and should be treated as such. The Jesuit professors lectured and wrote on the subject and discussed it freely in their weekly seminar on Peruvian moral conditions, without fear of viceroy or king, whose absolute demands were at times checked at the college.

In this battle, the Jesuits found a more sympathetic ear in their friend the saintly Count of Lemos, whose heart is the most precious relic kept even today by the Jesuits of Lima. Lemos epitomized the best in the Christian conscience of Spain, and could not peacefully accept forced Indian labor. The viceroy had consulted with his advisors about the *mita* of Potosí, and had come to the conclusion, as he wrote to the king, that it was not silver but Indian sweat and blood that Potosí was sending to Spain.[16] In 1670, he turned to the faculty of San Pablo, asking the

Jesuit professors' opinion on the *mita* of Potosí. The usual meetings were held at the college in order to sift all the data available on labor conditions in the silver mines. On the 26th of June, a report was sent to Lemos with the results of the discussions. The Jesuits thought that the *mita* of Potosí should be discontinued, and they offered this opinion as a serious moral obligation binding in conscience, not as a mere counsel of greater perfection. About a week later, on the 4th of July, Lemos wrote his well-known letter to the king proposing to abolish, altogether and for good, forced labor in the mines of Potosí.[17] This new, more humane way of dealing with the thorny problem of labor in the silver mines did not, unfortunately, last long. After Lemos' death, men without his unbreakable commitment to Christian principles reverted again to the practice of forcing Indians to work in the mines.

Moral Counselors to the Viceroyalty

The fame of the Jesuit professors of Lima as moral counselors traveled far and wide, and moral and legal problems were referred to San Pablo for consultation from places as far away as Tucumán, Chile, and Paraguay. The cases submitted dealt not only with Indian affairs, but also with the sensitive issue of the *patronato*, the authority of royal officials, taxes and tributes, selling and buying of public offices, and ecclesiastical matters relating to the morality of the clergy. Through the opinions rendered at San Pablo, the college's influence reached to the far ends of the viceroyalty, and Lima became the central head-quarters, as it already was in the economic and political sphere, so now of the efforts to build a Christian society in America.

In 1641, Fray Bernardino de Cárdenas had been appointed bishop of Paraguay by royal designation, and was in a hurry to be consecrated. The Jesuits of Córdoba were asked if the bishop-designate could receive episcopal consecration based only on the royal appointment, without waiting for the pope's confirmation. It was a delicate question. The need for a bishop in Paraguay was urgent, and the authority of the king in ecclesiastical affairs was great in virtue of the *patronato*. Many persons thought that the consecration could take place without Rome's knowledge, but the Jesuits, bound to the pope by a special vow of fidelity, upheld his authority against the demands of the crown's officials. The Jesuit professors of Córdoba resolved that Fray Bernardino had to wait for the approval of the Holy See. Only the pope had the authority to make him a bishop, and the crown's right in the matter was only one of presentation.

Considering conditions in Paraguay, doubts were cast on the soundness of this opinion by the defenders of the crown's power in ecclesiastical affairs, and the case was referred to Lima and came to the attention of the Jesuits of San Pablo. They sided with their brethren in Córdoba, and maintained that the consecration without Rome's approval was illicit. When this opinion was ignored and Fray Bernardino received the episcopal consecration only in virtue of his royal designation, the Jesuits of Lima decided that they could not remain silent. In 1647, Francisco de Contreras, Rector of San Pablo, published a short treatise on the subject, showing that such a consecration was clearly illicit. Contreras tried to remain on the level of principles, as a canon lawyer arguing his case, but he produced a work which was basically anti-*patronato*, and a fearless protest against royal interference in the ecclesiastical realm.[18] For the Jesuits of San Pablo, the king and the viceroy could not interfere at will in the affairs of the Church. As in the case of Fray Bernardino, the Jesuit professors defended this theory in their lectures and writings, and they faithfully maintained throughout the colonial period that attitude of independence, already stubbornly taken in the days of Viceroy Toledo.

But the Jesuits did not always oppose royal authority. At times they were its strong defenders. In the first decades of the seventeenth century, Tucumán was torn by a dispute in which moral theology, practical economics, and politics had become hopelessly entangled. The royal Visitor, Francisco de Alfaro, had overruled the provincial governor by strictly forbidding the *servicio personal*, and by abolishing certain taxes imposed by the governor on the Indians. The professors of San Pablo were called, once again, to pass judgment on the involved situation in faraway Tucumán. The colonizers of the region thought that the *servicio personal* could not be abolished without serious harm to the economy and without tearing to shreds established social patterns. The governor had recognized and legalized that unchangeable fact, and the Visitor should not modify the existing situation.

The meeting held in San Pablo to discuss the case reached a unanimous verdict on the last day of August, 1631. The letter written that day to Tucumán was presented as the "Opinion of the Fathers of the Society of Jesus in Lima. . . ." No individual, but rather all the Jesuits of San Pablo stood behind the opinion. The Jesuits thought that the Visitor, Alfaro, had all the legal powers to overrule the governor, and that his orders abolishing the *servicio personal* were binding in conscience. No one could ignore those orders without being guilty of mortal sin; one could not, therefore, be absolved in the confessional unless ready to abide by the Visitor's regulations, by doing justice to the Indians.[19]

The case of Tucumán was not unusual, for the faculty of San Pablo always opposed the *servicio personal* and maintained that it was a serious sin before God to extort such services from the Indians. Not even the *corregidores*—the chief magistrates—might break that principle, and if they did, they were bound to make restitution like anybody else.[20]

General problems of public administration also were treated at the college. The sale of public offices, for instance, had become such a widespread custom in the Spanish Indies under the Hapsburgs that the practice could not pass unnoticed by the watchdogs of justice and morality who met every week in San Pablo to listen to the heartbeat of the viceroyalty. Was it right for men in a Christian society to buy their advancement into the hierarchy of government? Could the crown be justified in selling positions of power within the structure of government? These questions were asked at times in the roundtable discussions and in the lectures held at the college.

The outspoken Pedro de Oñate had faced the problem with the same zeal and courage with which he had faced the *mita* of Huancavelica, and his ideas on the subject had been taught at San Pablo since the middle of the seventeenth century. Oñate thought that the practice of selling public offices could be permissible only if several conditions were strictly observed; otherwise it was immoral.

The first condition set by Oñate in his lectures at San Pablo was that the crown should determine beforehand a just and moderate price, not letting the selling degenerate into a public auction with the office going to the highest bidder. The second condition was that only those persons proved worthy and capable should be considered as potential buyers. A third provision urged by Oñate was that the monetary reward attached to the office should be strictly determined by the crown, without the office-holder's being allowed to increase it at the expense of the common citizen. Finally, the professor of San Pablo requested that the financial reward fixed by the crown should be high enough to maintain the office-holder decently, so that he would not be tempted to use his position of power to improve his economic status.[21]

Avendaño was even more concerned than Oñate with problems of public administration. He did not hesitate to review the entire hierarchy of offices in the empire, from the king down to petty officials, to criticize errors and point out new ways found by sound reason and Christian ethics. When he did not like the official policies determined by the crown, the old professor opposed them, always giving pungent reasons for his opposition. He attacked, for instance, the tendency to name military men to the position of civil governors, warning against the dangers of entrusting civil administration to hands which had been trained to hold weapons. He also opposed the policy of excluding foreigners from the spiritual conquest of America, and argued the need of accepting Italians, Germans, and men of other nationalities for the great adventure of civilizing the new world.

Diego de Avendaño was also fearless in pointing out to the viceroys that, within a Christian society, their position was one not of power and honor, but of great responsibilities toward God and man. The viceroys might not, the Jesuit proclaimed, engage in personal commercial dealings within the boundaries of their viceroyalties without being guilty of mortal sin. In order to preserve an administrative continuity, they should not change at will laws and regulations established

[65]

by their predecessors. But more than anything else, the viceroys had to respect the free elections of ordinary judges and of the members of the *cabildo*. Avendaño would lose his temper at the mere thought of the viceroy's tampering with those elections; in 1658, when the viceroy did interfere in the judicial elections, Avendaño protested and declared the elections of that year to be the laughing stock of all prudent persons. Electors who would succumb to such outside pressures were also guilty of mortal sin, in Avendaño's mind. San Pablo's old warrior also did not hesitate to call his students' attention to the shameful smuggling in oriental goods, brought to Acapulco by the Manila Galleon and smuggled down to Peru with the connivance of royal officials.[22]

Jesuits and Negroes

In the post-Reformation period, the problem of human freedom became an obsession with philosophers and theologians. The Reformers had dealt a deadly blow to Renaissance man's self-confidence, and even the freedom of the human will was called into question. Within the Catholic Church, Jesuits and Dominicans fought bitterly to support opposed theories on man's freedom. Public debates were held to discuss the merits of the two schools, and public imagination was caught up in the issue. From the heights of philosophy and theology, the dispute on human liberty was channeled down into popular songs, folk-tales, and even the theater, until it became public domain and even bullfights and dances were organized to celebrate the victories of one or the other theory.[23]

The waves of these disputes also broke on the shores of America. The Jesuits of San Pablo eagerly read Molina and Suarez, the two champions of the Order in its intellectual encounter with the Dominicans. The philosophical and theological questions related to the human will were freely discussed in lectures and in private meetings. Human freedom was presented in the lectures on moral theology as the root and condition of all true morality, and the men teaching and studying at San Pablo fully realized that one could not even talk about a Christian ethic unless human liberty was first presupposed.[24]

[66]

This intellectual concern with the problems of man's liberty, plus the overwhelming presence in America of Negro slaves, made the Jesuits of Lima turn inevitably to the study and discussion of slavery and legal freedom. In the intellectual effort to build a framework for a new Christian society, could one find any room for slavery? More than once the issue was raised at San Pablo. The fathers also asked how a true Christian should face the all-pervading world of the slaves.[25]

The subject was complicated. It could not be solved from a religious point of view alone, for history and economics were deeply entangled in the social reality of slavery. The complicated issue became, besides, an extremely delicate one to be discussed in the cloisters of San Pablo, for the college was one of the largest slave-holders of the entire vice-royalty, and the institutions survived and could operate only thanks to slave labor. Negro slaves helped to build the first residence of the Jesuits in Lima, and were soon serving in the house. As early as October of 1578, the Jesuit General, Everard Mecurian, had to instruct the Jesuits of Lima to dismiss all the Negro women from the service of the college and to reduce as much as possible the numbers of Negro men.[26] But like so many commands coming from Europe, Mercurian's precept was easier to give in faraway Rome than to be obeyed in the unique socioeconomic setting of Peru. In spite of Mercurian's wishes, the Jesuits of San Pablo continued to have and to augment their Negro slaves.

In 1581, Diego de Porres Sagredo and Juan Martínez Reginfo placed San Pablo economically on its own feet, donating a vineyard, a sugar cane *ingenio*, and some valuable land. With the land came more Negro slaves to work it: eight were attached to the Martínez Reginfo property, and about fifteen to the land given by Porres Sagredo.[27] All through the seventeenth century, San Pablo received new land grants. The Jesuits, convinced that land without expert hands to cultivate it was useless in itself, had to increase the number of their Negro slaves, the only efficient labor force available in Peru for agricultural purposes. The administrators of the college bought slaves all through the colonial period, always replacing immediately those who died or were incapable of doing the hard work in the *haciendas*.[28] By the year 1764, San Pablo owned 1,550 slaves, and three years later, when royal officials confiscated the Jesuit properties, the college had a small army of Negro slaves working its extensive landholdings. The final count, ordered by the Viceroy Amat, rendered 1,848 slaves as property of the Jesuit college.[29]

In this situation it was difficult for the Jesuit professors to attack and condemn the system of slave labor, and it was a testimony to their intellectual honesty that they faced the problem at all, both in their lectures and in the weekly seminar on practical moral problems. The great Avendaño wrestled with the thorny issue, and was torn between the commonly accepted practice of slavery in the viceroyalty, including the college, and his objective understanding of the problem on the speculative level of principles. In itself, Avendaño thought, slavery was illicit and utterly unjust, and should be condemned. The Portuguese and everybody else on the slave route were doing something very "dangerous to a Christian conscience," and they must not buy and sell men as if they were cattle. Consequently, slaves could not be bought from the slave-traders without being guilty of serious sin. And the reason was that justice had been damaged, and the entire negotiation was poisoned at the very root. Avendaño would not hesitate to impose on the traders and the slave buyers the duty of restitution.[30]

This was his speculative understanding of the problem, but when Avendaño came down to the practical implications in Peru, his position softened a great deal. As a Jesuit, he was a staunch defender of the moral theory of probabilism, which allows an opinion favoring liberty of action to be followed even though another opinion is more probable, if the more liberal opinion commends itself to judicious minds.[31] Avendaño could not accept slavery, and thought that it was unjust and to be condemned, yet he knew that many serious theologians justified the practice in America, and that God-fearing Christians, priests, religious orders, and even bishops owned and bought their own slaves "without any scruple of conscience." He was impaled on the horns of a painful dilemma. His own conscience condemned slavery, but his belief in the theory of probabilism obligated him to allow people to follow the softer opinion of those who justified the practice in Peru.[32]

Pedro de Oñate, who had fearlessly defended the Indians from his chair in San Pablo, also came out in the middle of the seventeenth century to condemn slavery. It was clear to him that no man could have perfect dominion over the life and actions of another, and that servitude was against natural law, having been introduced by the positive law of nations. Oñate could recognize only three just ways for a free man to become a slave: when a given individual sold himself into perpetual servitude; when prisoners of war justly condemned to capital punishment were forced to labor instead under permanent bondage; and finally, when offspring were born to those who were justly held in servitude. Outside of that, to reduce a free man to slavery by force was the "greatest capital crime and could not be justified . . .," and Oñate quoted to this effect the classic proverb: *Non bene pro toto libertas venditur auro*, not even for all the gold in the world can freedom be sold justly.[33]

The thought of men like Oñate and Avendaño was not a revolutionary manifesto against the social system of slavery, but the deep roots from which true freedom would eventually grow. During the seventeenth century, thanks to the thinking and writing of the Jesuit professors, the dawn of a new concept of the slave slowly broke in the college of San Pablo. The slave was no longer a mere piece of property to be used at the owner's absolute will, but a person who, through insurmountable odds, had been placed in a situation which was against the laws of nature. He had certain inalienable rights, among them life, health, bodily integrity, and at least a minimum of human development. And the slave owner was justly obligated to respect those rights.

In line with this thinking, and influenced by the professors of moral theology, the Jesuit administrators made a constant effort to improve the human condition of the slaves who were the property of the college. The harsh punishment of the era—jails, stocks and lashes—common even among free men, were tempered and the provincial superiors constantly reminded the rectors of San Pablo to treat the slaves with

[69]

humanity and Christian charity. Delinquents should not be kept in jail and stocks more than a week, nor punished with more than fifty lashes, even if the fault was grave, nor should they ever be hurt or harmed in their limbs. If a slave was guilty of serious crimes, he should be sold or given away, but never condemned to capital punishment while under the ownership of the college.[34]

On the 6th of May, 1661, the Provincial Andrés de Rada wrote a letter to the rector of San Pablo, determining certain policies that should be followed at the college. Regarding the slaves, Rada insisted that physical punishment should be avoided, and that everybody should talk to the slaves with consideration and respect. He ordered that working conditions be reviewed and made more humane, that slaves be well fed, and that they be abundantly provided with the clothing proper to each season. He stated also that the college had a real obligation to give the slaves a religious and human education. Under directives like Rada's, some of the slaves of San Pablo became accomplished musicians, bakers, vintners, and even pharmacists.[35]

The same sense of obligation towards the slaves made the Jesuits of San Pablo take special care of the old and of the sick. Early in the seventeenth century the college established, and maintained until the expulsion of the Jesuits, a small hospital and rest home for the slaves. Each hacienda had a tiny infirmary to take care of emergencies and mild cases, but the more serious ones were brought to Lima to be treated at the hospital, run by the Jesuits in a house across the street from the college.[36]

In the hospital the Negro slaves received the same basic treatment accorded the Jesuits themselves when ill. Comfortable beds with clean sheets were provided, and food was carefully cooked according to the needs of the patients. A Jesuit brother was assigned as a nurse to wait on them, and one or two fathers were charged to visit and comfort them. In 1648, about the same time as Oñate was championing justice in San Pablo, the Provincial Francisco de Zurbano visited the college, and took time to inspect the slaves' infirmary to make sure that everything was in order. He was satisfied with the care given the slaves, but also ordered the Jesuit in charge to always have a "good doctor" available, and to have all the medicines needed to treat the Negro patients, regardless of the expenses involved. Zurbano explained that this measure was not only demanded by justice and charity, but also by good economic administration.[37]

This medical care was not restricted to the Negroes in the college's infirmary, for those working in the haciendas were not forgotten, and regular shipments of medicine were sent to treat the milder cases. Pregnant Negro women could always have a competent midwife to assist them in childbirth, and many Jesuit administrators were godfathers of those Negro children born in the haciendas, thus becoming *compadres* of their own slaves.[38]

By the year 1767, when the Jesuits were abruptly expelled from Peru, the relationship between them and their eighteen-hundred-odd slaves had moved a great deal ahead towards the Christian ideals of brotherhood, justice and love. It had not been an easy, smooth road. The administrators of the college and its landholdings had depended on the slaves to make the institution economically viable, had bought and sold Negroes without any scruples of conscience, and had not always avoided cruelties in the process. But the professors of moral theology had never fully recognized the system, had kept hammering at the principles of justice in their lectures and writings, and slowly and painfully the system of slavery at San Pablo began to change from within. By 1767, it was not yet midday, but a luminous dawn was beginning to light the patios of San Pablo.

The Redress of Justice

Thousands of moral and legal cases had been studied, discussed, and solved in the weekly seminars held at the college in the two hundred years of its existence, and a great number of them had dealt with the redress of justice. In the relationships between conquerors and conquered, masters and slaves, governors and governed, clergy and bishops, the Jesuits had found that justice had many times been ignored or violated, and so it had to be restored before God and man. Several treatises were written in San Pablo on the problem of restitution, *De Restitutione*, as an intellectual effort to determine the rules by which justice had to be restored.[39]

It was a universally accepted principle that restitution became a grave moral obligation for anyone who had seriously injured another's spiritual or material goods. But to determine when a given injury was serious, thereby imposing the duty of restitution under grave, moral obligation, was a matter of prudence as related to local, historically concrete situations. The theologians of San Pablo fully realized this point when they put aside the great European authors, whose works filled many shelves in the library of the college, and began writing their own treatises. They felt that America presented a unique human situation, that the social, economic and cultural environment of the new world had never been encountered before by the *homo Christianus*, and that one could not simply accept in Lima the concrete application of unchangeable principles made by theologians in Salamanca, Paris or Rome.

This conviction had driven Diego de Avendaño, already an old, broken man, to begin the towering work of his *Thesaurus Indicus* as a moral guide for the Christian conscience "in those things which belong to the Indies." It had impelled Pedro de Oñate to study the commercial life of the viceroyalty, so different from that of Spain, and to write his three volumes *De Contractibus*. The same spirit moved Martín de Jaúregui. who had been professor in San Pablo for years and its rector in 1681, to write his *Tractatus de Restitutione*. Both Jaúregui and the anonymous author of the *Tractatus de Restitutione Fortunarum*[40] show that as early as the second half of the seventeenth century there was a strong *esprit de corps* among the moral theologians of San Pablo. Time and again they quoted the former Jesuit professors of Lima: José de Acosta, Esteban Ávila, Juan Pérez Menacho, Diego Álvarez de Paz, Juan Zapata, and others who were identified as "our theologians," and whose opinions were frequently accepted over those of the Europeans. Jaúregui went so far as to openly reject the solutions on economic matters given by the European masters, and to add that their solutions might hold true in Spain, but not "in this kingdom of Peru," where things were different.

[72]

He even dared to list Juan Pérez Menacho, glory of San Pablo, among some of the greatest theologians of Europe—Tomas Sánchez, Molina, Vázquez and Suarez—and to call him *sapientissimus*, the wisest of them all.[41]

The principles of economic restitution, pruned of their European outgrowth in the lectures and seminars of San Pablo, were applied to specific penitents by the confessors and retreat masters of the college. A continuous stream of men and women went through San Pablo in the two hundred years of its existence, to purify their souls in the confessional or to spend several days among the Jesuits, making the retreat conceived and written by Ignatius Loyola. A great number of those persons had sinned against justice, and were bound to make restitution to repair injuries caused to others. Many of their fortunes had been built on shaky moral grounds, and the Jesuit confessors had to impose on them the duty of restitution so as to guide them to redress justice by this process.[42]

During the two centuries the Jesuits were in Lima, the struggle for justice was never interrupted in the classrooms of San Pablo. For two hundred years, the weekly seminar on moral problems had slowly shaped the mind of men who became not only confessors and retreat masters, but also teachers, counselors, preachers, administrators, and missionaries throughout the viceroyalty. San Pablo was the training ground of an army of Jesuits who went forth to fight for justice and Christian love in America, and it was also the central headquarters where the strategy was conceived, and from which the battle was always directed.

The public seminar on moral issues begun by José de Acosta in the sixteenth century, was still in session, and still fearlessly airing the unchristian thoughts and deeds of colonial society, when in 1767 the liberal King Charles III, for reasons still hidden in his royal breast, put an end to the College of San Pablo. The Jesuit army was dissolved. Hundreds of veterans from the coastal plains, the highlands of the Andes, and the Amazon rain forest, now considered enemies of the state, had to sail from Peru on the long journey into oblivion and exile.

IV

JESUITS AND BOOKS

In March of the year 1522, a short, limping man in his thirties changed his fine clothes of a Spanish nobleman for the tatters and rags of a beggar, in the Catalonian town of Manresa. Ignatius Loyola, future founder of the Jesuits, shaken by deep religious emotions had abandoned his military career, and dreamt of reviving the ascetic life of the ancient Christian hermits. For a year he lived in a cave on the outskirts of Manresa, not far from the thriving port of Barcelona, spending his days and part of his nights in prayer and penance. Christianity was in a crisis, and the man of Manresa soon felt in his solitude a call to go among his fellow men as a server of God and a preacher of the Gospel. His intellectual baggage was scanty, and Ignatius understood the need for study before turning to an apostolic life among men. He began a long intellectual pilgrimage, painful because of his years, through the schools of Barcelona, the Universities of Alcalá and Salamanca, to arrive finally at the University of Paris. The Jesuit Order was born there, in the cloisters of the greatest European university and in the midst of its busy academic life.[1]

The decade from 1547 to 1557 was spent by the former hermit of Manresa in Rome writing the *Constitutions* of the Jesuits, a revolutionary document in the history of Christian clericality. In the *Constitutions* Ignatius described a new type of religious life, in which the reformed priest and the scholar were welded together to be placed at the uncon-

ditional service of Christian ideals. In the fourth part of his great document Ignatius mapped the course to be followed in the intellectual
training of the Jesuits, and left a blueprint for the future schools,
colleges and universities of the Order. As one of the most important
means to foster the intellectual life, the founder of the Jesuits mentioned
the existence of a good, accessible library, and he ordered that a good
one be established in every Jesuit college. Besides the general library of
the college, Ignatius wanted every Jesuit to have all the books needed
for private studies. [2]

The heirs of Ignatius who sailed for Peru in 1568, under the leader-
ship of Gerónimo Ruiz de Portillo, knew that they were going to Lima
to open a Jesuit college, and carried with them the *Constitutions*. It was
not a mere coincidence that, in their months of waiting at Seville, they
had spent more than two hundred ducats to buy books. After a long trip
in which the Jesuits introduced sailors and fellow travelers to the
pleasures of good reading, they arrived in Lima with their books on the
first day of April, 1568. As soon as they bought the property for their
college, they began building classrooms, a chapel, dining room and
kitchen, private rooms and a library. The lack of money and the hurry
to open the college obliged the Jesuits to attend first to the most
essential things, and a library was one of them.

Before the year 1568 ended, and only nine months after their arrival
in Peru, the Jesuits of Lima had put the finishing touches on the first
library at San Pablo. They chose a quiet corner of the garden, next to
some of the bedrooms, and built a tiny library, twenty-seven feet
four inches by twenty-three feet eight inches. It was very small, but it
was well lighted by a window looking onto the garden. It was quiet
and sufficiently housed the books brought from Spain with the first
Jesuit expedition. During the year 1569, building activities continued
in the inchoative San Pablo, and the library was improved to the point
of making it "very convenient" for the purposes of the new foundation. [3]

Right from the start, every Jesuit group that crossed the Atlantic
brought along a new shipment of books. The Visitor Doctor Plaza, for
instance, followed this tradition in 1574, when he secured from the king

[75]

an endowment of five hundred ducats to be spent on books to increase the holdings of San Pablo's library. By the first days of January, 1574, he had the books safely stored in the hold of a ship, which on the 17th weighed anchor at the mouth of the Guadalquivir. Twenty-four hours later and not too far away from shore, the rudder broke and the ship had to be abandoned. The Jesuits were rescued by some of the escorting galleons, but their books, securely packed under the lower deck, went to the bottom of the sea with the rest of the cargo. Back in Spain the Visitor Plaza negotiated a new grant of another five hundred ducats to replace the lost books, and he sailed again with this new library on the 19th of October, 1574.[4]

The following year—taking into consideration the fast development of the Order in Mexico and Peru—the Jesuit General Mercurian confirmed the appointment of a procurator in Seville to take permanent care of the affairs related to the Jesuits working in the new world. The General sent him private instructions on how to discharge properly his obligations. In those instructions Mercurian, filled with the spirit of the Jesuit founder and knowing that books were paramount to attain the aims of the Order in the Indies, commanded his man in Seville to take special care of collecting and buying books for the Jesuit colleges on the other side of the sea. He should not wait to be asked for specific books, but buy and send all the books he could gather. Moreover, the Jesuit procurator should not be satisfied with the books offered by the book dealers of Seville. The Father General ordered him to keep himself informed of the new books printed each year and to go beyond the Spanish frontiers to acquire them, which could be easily done, Father Mercurian thought, through the many merchants converging each year upon Seville from every corner of Europe.[5]

While the Jesuit procurator was trying to carry out the General's orders from his headquarters in Seville, in faraway Lima the Visitor, Doctor Plaza, had taken time to inspect the fledgling library at San Pablo. Many pressing problems—the clash with Toledo, the tense relations with the university, the interior organization of the Order— were absorbing Plaza's time, but he did not fail to examine carefully the

[76]

Jesuit library of Lima, and to send his findings to the General on the 12th of December, 1576. In spite of the improvement of 1569, the library was placed in a very humid location, the Visitor thought, and some books had been badly damaged. In addition, the administration of the library had been negligent. The old catalogue had been destroyed and never replaced. There were no signs on the shelves to indicate the location of the different classes of books, many of which had become misplaced in the library. Worse yet, many of the books brought to the college from Europe had been lost by the end of 1576. They had been either borrowed by outsiders without notifying the librarian, or simply taken by unscrupulous readers. Seeing these conditions in the library, Plaza took care to have the books moved to a better, drier place, and gave orders to correct the shortcomings he had noticed in the administration of the library.[6]

Ten years had passed since Plaza wrote his remarks on San Pablo's library, when in 1586 the first edition of the Jesuit *Ratio Studiorum* was published in Europe, and arrived in Lima shortly thereafter. In that fundamental code of Jesuit education, the instructions given by the Jesuit General in 1575 concerning the buying of books for Peru became universal law for all the Jesuit colleges. The rectors and deans were ordered in the *Ratio Studiorum* to keep in touch with the book dealers and provide abundance of books for the common libraries and for the individual students. A budget for library expenses should be approved every year in each school, and the rector should not allow those funds to be diverted to any other purpose. This new legislation had its impact in the College of San Pablo, where there was already a remarkable interest in building a good library. Since those closing years of the sixteenth century, the Jesuit college at Lima never lacked funds to buy books, and in due time the college library had its own sources of income. Three brothers, John, Francis and Gabriel Perlín, joined the Jesuits in Lima between 1586 and 1604, and they donated a house, owned by them in Madrid, to the library of San Pablo with instructions to spend its entire rent on books for the college in Lima.[7]

In 1602, the holdings of the Jesuit library were greatly increased by a generous gift. Francisco de Coello, a former professor of the University of Salamanca, *Alcalde de Corte* or syndic of the *Audiencia* since 1592, counselor of two viceroys, and an expert on civil and ecclesiastical law, joined the Jesuit Order in Lima, and donated his private library to the College of San Pablo. Coello had, since the days of his professorship at Salamanca, a very "large" collection of legal books, and some works on mathematics and geometry, two disciplines he had always cultivated. All his books went to rest on the shelves of the library at San Pablo, but the scholar Coello did not lose access to them. For years he was stationed at the college, and in 1614 he became rector of San Pablo.[8]

José de Acosta, José de Arriaga, Alonso de Barzana, Esteban de Ávila and Juan Pérez de Menacho had already used that library as an essential tool in their extensive researches, when in the first decades of the seventeenth century the scholarly Bernabé Cobo locked himself for hours at a stretch in that same library to read and collect material for his own works. The wealth of direct quotations from the most diverse authors which is found in the books written by those Jesuit professors is only an indirect witness to the richness of San Pablo's library. Cobo in his *Fundación de Lima* has fortunately described it as it was in the 1610s. It was ample and roomy, and furnished with taste. It had up to four thousand volumes without counting duplicates, and it was valued at more than ten thousand pesos. As a former student of San Pablo and, later on, a member of its faculty, Cobo knew the library well and he commented that not only theological works, but all kinds of books were among the library holdings—a very valuable remark coming from a man who was not a theologian, and who had used the library as a source for his historical, scientific and socio-anthropological studies. He was perhaps a bit over-enthusiastic when he said that the book not found in the Jesuit library of Lima must have been a rather rare print.[9]

Distributing Center of Books

Since the first decades of the seventeenth century a continuous stream of the most diverse types of publications arrived steadily at San Pablo, not only from Seville, but also from Madrid, Lisbon, Lyons, Paris,

Antwerp, Venice and Rome. The General's directive of 1575, sanctioned later by the *Ratio Studiorum*, became established policy, and in those first years of the new century the College of San Pablo was in contact with the best publishing centers of Europe through the Jesuit procurator in Seville. The administrators of San Pablo were not satisfied with ordering single copies of each work for the college library: they bought an abundant supply of the great books of the day, to the point of making San Pablo a distributing center of the printed word for the entire Viceroyalty of Peru. The college in Lima was the heart of Jesuit intellectual activity in Peru, and all through the colonial period it beat with a steady rhythm, sending continuous waves of books and ideas through the entire viceroyalty.

New shipments of books, consigned to the College of San Pablo, arrived every year at Callao in the South Sea Fleet, which shuttled between Panama and Peru. The amount of books varied, from a few volumes lost in the personal baggage of individual Jesuits to the thirty-three hundredweight chests filled with books which arrived in 1629, or to the one hundred trunks of books which came in 1665. The shipments were unpacked in San Pablo's *Patio de los Procuradores*, an ample cloister in the southwest corner of the college, single copies of all the new publications were immediately placed in the library, and the rest of the books were set aside to be sent to other Jesuit colleges throughout the viceroyalty.[10]

At regular intervals, mule trains were formed at San Pablo and the books which had arrived from Europe, together with many other goods, began their long trip to the four corners of the viceroyalty. During the seventeenth century thousands of books left San Pablo and went north, to the college of Trujillo and the missions of Mainas, south to the colleges of Arequipa, Pisco and the Jesuit haciendas of Ica and La Nazca, and east to cross the formidable barrier of the Andes to begin and later to enrich new Jesuit libraries. San Pablo sent books to the Jesuit libraries in Huamanga, in Huancavelica, in the imperial Cusco, in Juli, at the shores of Lake Titicaca, in La Paz, in Oruro, in Chuquisaca (which received more than one hundred volumes from San Pablo in 1627 alone),

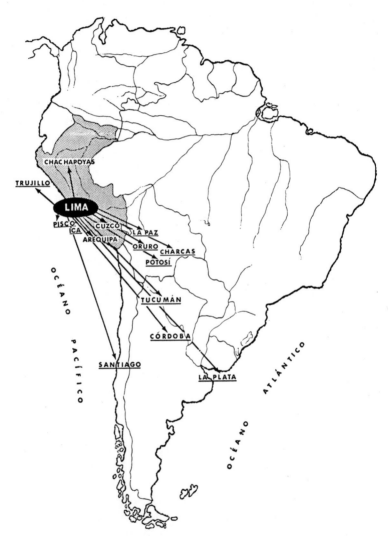

San Pablo's Sphere of Influence in South America

in Cochabamba, and in the thriving silver city of Potosí. The intellectual sowers of the college of San Pablo scattered the seeds so far and wide that the stream of books originating in their college overflowed the soaring peaks of the Andes to reach the college of Tucumán and the University of Córdoba, and even to the cities of La Plata and Santiago de Chile.[11]

The Jesuits of San Pablo not only increased the holdings of the common library of the college every year but helped create new ones from Chile to the frontiers of Quito, and from the Pacific seacoast to the mouth of the Paraná river. They also formed additional libraries within the walls of San Pablo itself, which developed and acquired a certain importance during the seventeenth century. The students' library was one of these and it already existed as a separate library before the year 1620. It was always open to the students, and it contained a few hundred volumes, mostly of Greek and Latin authors, theological and philosophical works, and a small selection of modern Spanish books.[12]

The Private Libraries

Encouraged perhaps by the advice of the Jesuit *Constitutions* that every individual Jesuit should always have all the books needed for his private studies, and encouraged also by the abundance of books available at San Pablo, the professors and writers of the college began early in the seventeenth century to form their own private, personal libraries. One of those booklovers was the bright Italian Nicolás Durán who had arrived at San Pablo from Rome in 1592, and was rector of the college in 1623. From the shipment of books which arrived at the college in 1630, Durán took for his own library more than fifty volumes, valued at four hundred and forty-four pesos. The following year he secured up to twenty-six new works from the new acquisitions of the college. Besides philosophy and theology, Durán was interested in the history of his own people, and in his library one could find Antonio Balerini's *De Re Militari Veterum Romanorum* and a general history of the Romans. Characteristic of an Italian of the sixteenth century and of a man who was a Jesuit superior most of his life, Durán was also interested in diplomacy

[81]

and politics, and in 1631 he selected for his personal library two works entitled *Thesaurus Politicus* and *Politicus Christianus*, together with the numismatic work of Hubert Goltzi and a treatise on the thought and ideas of the Egyptians.[13]

Durán's case was not the exception but the rule, and every time a new shipment of books arrived at the college from faraway Europe, many Jesuits rushed to the storeroom in the *Patio de los Procuradores* to browse and make their own selections. Before the second half of the seventeenth century, the private libraries of San Pablo had begun posing serious administrative problems in the college. In the 1630s, the Jesuit Provincial Antonio Vásquez, in a letter to the rector of San Pablo, complained that some of the Jesuits had too many personal books, disposed of them with absolute liberty, lent them to and borrowed them from lay friends, and went so far as to take their own libraries with them when they were assigned to another college. The Provincial Vásquez knew that this practice was against religious discipline and common enough to require the direct intervention of the college's rector.[14]

This type of warning had been issued several times, when in 1659 Andrés de Rada came to San Pablo as official Visitor from Rome. The situation had not changed, and Rada found too many personal libraries in San Pablo, and made a renewed effort to control and reduce them. He gave orders forbidding the Jesuits to lend or sell personal books to outsiders, and his words implied that the practice was quite common in San Pablo. The Visitor also objected to the books being taken from San Pablo when the owner was sent to another Jesuit house. To avoid this misuse of so many precious books, the Visitor ordered every volume existing within the walls of the college to be stamped with the name of San Pablo and the mark of the common library. If anybody alleged that his books were borrowed from lay friends and did not belong to the Jesuits, he was commanded to give them back to their rightful owners within the term of six days. Also within the term of six days every one in the college was to give a complete list of all his books to the librarian. If someone had too many books and said that he could not complete the list within a week, the rector would supply extra help to finish the work within the alloted time.

The Visitor Rada was a reasonable man and he explained the reasons for his orders. He wanted the catalogues of all the personal libraries carefully made, to enable the college's librarian to make a general, master catalogue of all the books in the college. This master catalogue, Rada thought, was indispensable for the professors and the students to know how many and what kinds of books were available in the college, and Rada quoted to this effect the fifth rule of Jesuit librarians, which implied that an uncatalogued book was like a non-existent book.[15]

Rada's efforts of 1659 to control the use and ownership of books by the Jesuits of San Pablo were not successful, a *démarche* undertaken by many a Jesuit rector with equal success since that time. On the 27th of October, 1660, he had to write a very serious letter to the rector of the college, then the great scholar Diego de Avendaño. Among other things, Rada complained in his letter that the liberty taken by many in the use of books was causing serious harm to the college's holdings, and it was scandalizing even the laity, who wondered how the Jesuits, bound by a vow of poverty, could use such liberties in disposing of so many expensive books. Rada ordered Rector Avendaño not to allow the Jesuits leaving San Pablo to take with them anything more than the works of Ignatius Loyola, the Roman Breviary, the Bible, a compendium on moral theology, and Thomas à Kempis' famous ascetic work, the *Imitation of Christ*. All the other books should be left behind in the college's library.[16]

Rada's letter to Avendaño did not have the desired effect either, and the Jesuits of San Pablo went on building and keeping their own libraries. Eleven years after Rada's visit, when the new Provincial Luis Jacinto de Contreras came to San Pablo, he found that the situation had not changed greatly in spite of the Visitor's firm directives. Individual Jesuits still kept their own libraries, and even bought and sold books without the control of the college's administrators. On the 31st of October, 1671, Contreras felt obliged to forbid this practice with a very strict command. Like his predecessors, the new provincial did not object to the wide reading of the Jesuits, but to the lack of proper discipline and to the faults against the vow of poverty, broken by those buying and selling books without the rector's permission.

Two years later, in 1673, a new Roman Visitor, Hernando Cavero, arrived at San Pablo to again find the same problem. He wrote in the *Memoriale* of his visitation that some faculty members still had libraries of "great value," used them with complete liberty, and took them away from San Pablo when they were appointed to another college. He let the community know that the Jesuit General in Rome seriously disapproved of this conduct, and had ordered him, the Visitor, to take those libraries from the individual Jesuits and place them in the common library of the college.[17]

The seventeenth century came to an end without a solution having been found to regulate the use of books and the ownership of private libraries in the College of San Pablo. On the 30th of August, 1692, the Jesuit General Thyrsus González had to intervene directly from Rome. He sent orders to San Pablo not to lend books to lay persons outside the college without proper permission, and always with the assurance that the books would be returned. He also reminded the Peruvian Jesuits that nobody, Jesuits or lay friends, should ever take books from the library without writing the borrower's name, title of the book, and the date when the book was borrowed. The provincials of Peru endorsed the General's directives, and among them Antonio Garriga made a very remarkable effort to organize the Jesuit libraries in Peru during his two terms in office, from 1714 to 1716, and from 1717 to 1724. Garriga insisted on having a good master catalogue and a proper classification of the books in the library to facilitate their location when needed. He also urged the strict observance of the library rules, always listing the name of the borrower, title of the book and the date. Like Plaza in 1576, Antonio Garriga was also deeply concerned in 1715 with the great humidity of Lima which was so harmful to books, and with the damage caused in the library by insects. He gave orders to clean the library and dust the books at least twice every week.[18]

In spite of the efforts of so many superiors during this long period of time, the private Jesuit libraries were a reality in San Pablo up to the very day the college was closed. When the royal officials came in 1767 to confiscate the Jesuit college, they took a careful inventory of some of those private libraries. In the office of José Rocha, General Procurator of San Pablo, royal officials found 4,101 volumes. One hundred and fifty books belonged to Rocha's personal library, and the rest were books recently arrived from Europe, destined to be sold to outsiders or to be sent to other Jesuit institutions throughout the viceroyalty. The Dean of Studies, Alejandro Cazeda, owned two hundred and ninety volumes. Among the professors, Mateos de los Santos had one hundred and eleven books, Ramón del Arco one hundred and ninety-seven, Antonio Bacas one hundred and thirty-two, Casimiro Bohórquez one hundred and eighty-eight, Martín del Castillo ninety-eight, Juan Antonio Rivera seventy-three, and several others had libraries of more than fifty personal volumes. Even a Jesuit lay brother, the German Henry Deker, had his own private library consisting mostly of scientific works, fifty-two of them in German. The royal officials did not take the inventory of those fifty-two volumes because they were ''en lengua tudesca,'' and none of the officials could understand that language.[19]

The Common Library

The private libraries of San Pablo, important as they were to indicate the intellectual climate of the college and the amount of books available, represented only a very small fraction of the books owned by the Jesuit college at Lima. The heart of San Pablo was the common library, and the superiors, administrators and professors worked together constantly to make that library the best in Lima. By the end of the seventeenth century they had totally succeeded, and San Pablo had the best library existing within the boundaries of the old Viceroyalty of Peru, a library which could also easily compete with the best libraries in similar European institutions. The four thousand volumes mentioned by Bernabé Cobo in the first decade of the seventeenth century had climbed steadily, and in the 1760s San Pablo's common library housed more than twenty-five thousand volumes, housed mainly in two ample rooms covered with shelves from floor to ceiling. Eleven large windows provided plenty of natural light, and in the open spaces along the walls hung twenty-one portraits of the best Jesuit writers, men like the Spaniard Suarez, the Italian Bellarmine, and the German Canisius. The center of the library was occupied by wide, solid wooden tables, and on them rested several globes, maps and compasses.[20]

The men who organized San Pablo's library went about it with the touch of the professional. They were not satisfied with acquiring all kinds of books in the European publishing centers, but were also concerned with classifying them properly and making them available. The librarians of San Pablo owned several treatises, at least one of them in French, on how to build, organize, and care for a library. They also had a book explaining the system and organization of the French library of the Jesuit Collège de Clermont in Paris, and large bibliographies and catalogues of famous European libraries. Among them San Pablo boasted a fifteen-volume work described as *Catálogo de Varias Bibliotecas en Todas Lenguas*, and twenty-one volumes of Juan Tomás de Rocaberti's *Index Operum Omnium Bibliotecae Maximae Pontificiae*, which listed all the works in the main papal library in Rome, and which was published in the Holy City in 1699.[21]

The fact that San Pablo was a great linguistic and humanistic center was fully reflected in the library, which was a true Babel of books printed in Greek, Latin, Hebrew, Arabic, Spanish, Portuguese, Italian, Catalan, French, German, and in the most important aboriginal languages of the new world. The Jesuits had grammars and dictionaries of all these languages, and even a Coptic grammar. The dictionaries in San Pablo's library showed all kinds of language combinations, and among them one could find a multi-volume Latin-Portuguese dictionary, Manuel Larramendi's *Diccionario Trilingüe del Castellano, Bascuence y Latín* published in 1745, another dictionary of four languages, and Ambrosio Calepino's well-known dictionary of eight languages.

Dictionaries and grammars were only the key to unlock the literary beauties of each language, and San Pablo was well provided with the best literature then available. All the literary figures of the Golden Century were present with a swarm of lesser personalities. Among the great Spanish writers one could find the Jesuit Baltasar Gracián, perhaps the sharpest mind in seventeenth-century Spain and second only to Quevedo in literary creativity. Gracián's great works were all in San Pablo's library, and they were read by the Jesuits of Lima during the same years that Europeans of all latitudes were reading them in the Latin, French, Italian, English and Flemish translations. Besides Spanish literature, one could read in San Pablo Portuguese authors like Vieira, Italians like Dante, Petrarch and Platina; Frenchmen like Racine, Molière, Corneille, Bossuet and Bourdaloue (of course, not in Spanish translations but in their original languages). The library also kept the best theatrical works of the classics and of modern Spanish and foreign playwrights.[22]

History

It had been said that the Spanish people of the age of the empire had a sort of obsession with history. In those decades of an expanding Europe, history was not only made, it was also written with artistic precision and it was read with passion. The Jesuits of Lima were caught up in the spirit of the times and they gathered in their library at San Pablo an impressive collection of historical writings. There were treatises on historiography like Luis Cabrera's De Historia, para Entenderla y Escribirla published in Madrid in 1611, a four-volume work in French on the elements of history, and Mabillon's classic work De Re Diplomatica Libri VI (the foundation of scientific palaeography), which was published in France in 1681. The library had also a good sample of general histories written by historians of different nationalities and periods. Even a very quick glance at the shelves would reveal John Botero's Relaciones Universales del Mundo, the three volumes of Antonio de Herrera's Historia General del Mundo published in Madrid between 1601 and 1612, El Gran Diccionario Histórico written by the French historian Louis Moreri in ten volumes, whose Spanish translation appeared in Paris in 1753, and Salmon's Lo Stato Presente di Tutti i Paesi e Popoli del Mondo in seventeen volumes and printed in Venice in the first half of the seventeenth century.[23]

Besides the general works, one could easily find in the Jesuit library at Lima good histories of every period and every region of the globe, including those most recently discovered. The historians of Greece and Rome were naturally present in a library which did not lack any of the classics, but ancient history was represented not only by them. San Pablo also had ''modern'' histories of antiquity, and one could read the fourteen volumes in French of Charles Rollin who covered the histories of the Egyptians, Carthaginians and Assyrians, as well as Antonio Balerini's work on the ancient Romans, and Anselmo Banduri's *Imperium Orientale sive Antiquitates Constantinopolitanae*, published in Paris in 1712. The works of Spanish historians filled several shelves in the library, and the reader could turn to the sixteenth-century chronicles of Miguel Carbonell who wrote in his native Catalan, to the works of Esteban de Garibay, or to more systematic and modern authors like Antonio de Herrera in his five volumes of the *Historia General de los Hechos de los Castellanos*. The Jesuits and their lay friends could also read in San Pablo the *Historiae de Rebus Hispaniae Libri XX* of the Jesuit Juan de Mariana, whose political ideas were considered dangerous in certain European circles, and who merited having one of his books burned by order of the French *Parlement*.[24] They could consult the sixteen volumes of Juan de Ferrera's *Synopsis Histórica Cronológica de España*, a popular work reprinted several times and translated into German and French, or they could study Francisco Estrada's book on the political and religious conflicts which erupted into the wars of the Low Countries. On the shelves of the library also rested that magnificent example of baroque history, Antonio de Solís' *Historia de la Conquista de México*.[25]

The Jesuits of Lima did not look at the world solely through Spanish eyes, and non-Spanish historians occupied as much space as domestic authors. They could read in their comfortable library good histories of Italy by the Italians Francesco Guicciardini 'and Ludovico Antonio Muratori, histories of France in the original French, like Pierre Mathieu's *Histoire Générale des derniers Troubles Arrivés en France*, printed in Paris in 1622, and histories of Portugal and her empire written by Portuguese authors. There were available upon request histories of Hungary,

Sweden, England, Germany, Russia (or Moscovia, as it was then called), all of them written by non-Spanish historians. The regular users of San Pablo's library could look even to the papacy not through pious medieval eyes, but through the new eyes of Bartolome dei Sacchi, the versatile Italian better known to history as Platina.[26]

The ships which moored every year at Callao brought to Lima more than new immigrants, European articles, and silk and spices from the Orient. These ships also brought news of an expanding world and of the birth of new nations, and at times they brought on their masts and sails the fresh scars of their encounters with Dutch and English men-of-war. The library at San Pablo reflected the life of the epoch, and the Jesuits had in it histories of the deeds of merchants and missionaries in the Philippine Islands, China and Japan, Charlevoix' works on the history of New France, books on the foreign encroachments in the new world, narratives of the Portuguese settlements along the coast of Africa and in Brazil, a naval history of the Dutch nation, and a good collection of *mémoires* of European travelers, which offered to the Jesuits of San Pablo the raw substance of contemporary history.[27]

If the Jesuit library had multi-volume works covering the general history of the world, and the histories of nations, it also kept an abundant supply of historical treatises which focused on rather limited subjects. Into this classification fell regional histories, and histories of famous cities. San Pablo had the histories of Rome, Madrid, Paris, Toledo, Venice and her commercial enterprises, Seville, Lima and Jaén, among others. In the same section of the library the reader could locate histories of religious orders and their founders, military histories like a history of the French army and navy, books on heraldry and genealogies, and works on the religious thought of different nations and groups. Among the latter one could find several histories of world religions by French authors, and R. P. Lebrun's *Historia Crítica de las Superticiones Prácticas que Han Engañado a los Pueblos* translated into Spanish in 1745, and whose French original rested on the shelves of the Jesuit library of Lima.[28]

[89]

Civil Administration

From the earliest days of the Order, the Jesuits provided confessors and advisors to European royalty and the black robe of the Order could be seen at times in the private chambers of kings and royal counselors. In Peru this tradition was kept, and there was a long list of Jesuits all through the colonial period who saw the mighty viceroys kneel in humble confession before them, or who were consulted by the *alter rex* in problems concerning the government of the viceroyalty. Those Jesuits approached the difficult task of advising the civil administrators by wide reading in the literature available on political theories, relations between nations, law, and on the new, ever-growing body of royal orders and regulations touching upon the administration of the Spanish Empire. The library at San Pablo had not only the Spanish authors who had written about government and politics, but also Italian, French, Portuguese, and German writers. In the Jesuit library one could read Suarez' *De Legibus*, in which the Andalusian genius laid the cornerstone of international law and de-emphasized the divine right of kings, pointing to the people as the direct source of political power. The reader could browse through the twenty-eight volumes of a work on the common, universal laws of nations, or consult the brilliant Fleming Justus Lipsius, who wrote *Politicorum sive Civilis Doctrinae Libri Sex*, the French Berulle or the Italian Botero, whose *Diez Libros de la Razón de Estado* had been available in Spanish translation since 1592.

The reader interested in politics and government could also find in San Pablo's library Mariana's *De Rege et Regis Institutione*, Baltasar Gracián's *El Príncipe* and *El Cortesano*, works of deep political insight cloaked in some of the best literature of the seventeenth century, and Andrés Mendo's *Príncipe Perfecto y Ministros Ajustados*, published in Salamanca in 1657. From the shelves of the library many other political works tempted the reader with their suggestive titles: *The Ambassador, The King's Secretary, Advice to Princes, Thesaurus Politicus, The True Politics, Politicus Christianus; Historical Essay on the Government of Holland.* Every work dealing with the civil administration of the Spanish Empire had, of course, a very prominent place in San Pablo's library, where the reader could find among others Torquemada's *Monarquía Indiana*, Avendaño's *Thesaurus Indicus*, Antonio León Pinelo's extensive writings, and Solórzano Pereira's *Política Indiana*, the first edition of which, printed in Madrid in 1629, was already in the Jesuit library in 1630.[29]

Economics and Geography

The Jesuit library of Lima also had a few surprising corners for those who might have gratuitously presupposed that the colonial clergy was only interested in useless scholastic disquisitions and perhaps in the humanities. Not far away from Aristotle, Aquinas and the scholastic philosophers and theologians with their ponderous, multi-volume Latin works, there was an entire section of the library filled with French books printed in France and in the Low Countries. If the curious visitor, amazed to see so many French works in a colonial library, would examine some of those volumes, he might become even more amazed at their contents, a world apart from scholastic disquisitions. For a moment the visitor might even think that he was in the library of some agrarian or commercial school. Right there on the shelves rested a four-volume French dictionary of economics, and a three-volume encyclopedia of commerce, also in French. Together with these works, there were general treatises on agriculture, commercial routes, and monetary transactions.[30]

The men who owned and used San Pablo's library had spread a wide net of haciendas through the entire viceroyalty, and had worked to harness the virgin lands with European crops, and European domestic animals. The Jesuits of San Pablo owned extensive herds, produced the best wines of Peru, transformed patches of coastal desert by artificial irrigation into green oases, and made in their *obraje* or colonial factory of San Bernardo some of the most delicious bread of Lima. In their college library they had a good number of French treatises which taught them how to go about their agricultural and commercial activities with a scientific touch. The library had French books on how to build farmhouses, how to tap hidden sources of water, how to open new roads, and how to plant and take care of vegetable gardens and orchards.

[91]

There were several works, also in French, which taught the current theories of cattle-breeding, chicken-raising, breeding of horses, the care of mules and dogs, the planting of white mulberry trees and the proper methods of feeding the precious silkworms. One could find in the library treatises ranging from general works on how to become a good farmer or a good hunter, to specialized works on the fine techniques of stone- and wood-cutting, and on the dyeing process for different kinds of textiles.[31]

The occasional visitor to San Pablo's library might have become even more startled to find there a two-volume French work entitled *The Perfect Merchant*, and treatises explaining the art of shipbuilding, the management of shipyards, and the latest techniques on maneuvring sea-going vessels, together with several histories of navigation. For men who kept close contact with Europe via Panama, and with other Jesuit foundations along the Peruvian coast, and who worked in missions lost in a tangle of rivers, ships and navigation were more than a hobby— they were a necessity. The Jesuits of Lima had covered the viceroyalty with an extensive web of colleges, haciendas and missions, and communications were vital to keep the fabric together. Waterways were the only efficient routes available in many places, and it is no wonder that the Jesuits gathered together in the library at Lima, nerve center of the network, treatises on navigation and on the art of building and maneuvring ships.[32]

Many of the Jesuits, who studied and worked at San Pablo, traveled extensively in Peru and fell in love with the geography of the virgin lands. They gathered in their library at Lima geographic studies and maps of the new regions, from California in the north to Paraguay and La Plata in the south. The great rivers must have exercised a very special fascination, and many a San Pablo Jesuit enjoyed reading José Gumilla's *El Orinoco Ilustrado y Defendido*, as well as first-hand descriptions of the Amazon, the Marañón and the Paraná. As in the case of historical writings, the college library had a good number of geographic works on different regions of the world, geographies of Spain, France, Italy, Central Europe, a French description of the African continent, and narratives on the regions of the Far East. The reader could consult there a curious treatise comparing the old geographic theories with the new ideas, and the six volumes of a French dictionary, Martinier's *Dictionnaire Geographique*.

The men interested in geography or astronomy had certainly a wide range of choice in the library at San Pablo. One could read the Greek Strabo's *Geography* in seventeen books, the masterpiece of antiquity on the subject, or study the geographic ideas of the Egyptians in the works of Ptolemy. Nicholas Copernicus' great breakthrough in the understanding of the cosmos, as reflected in his *De Revolutione Orbium Caelestium*, was also available to the Jesuit readers who had in their library the works of Johannes Kepler and the scientific writings of that Italian genius, Galileo Galilei, including his masterful defense of the Copernican system. Besides these classics, one could also consult different sets of tables for astronomical observations, and practical treatises on how to build and use telescopes, how to measure latitude and longitude, and how to study eclipses and earthquakes.[33]

The Age of Reason

The scientific interest of the Jesuits of San Pablo was not limited to economics, agriculture, geography and astronomy. In the faraway and sleepy colonial city there was a group of men interested and informed on the latest scientific developments taking place in Europe. The world, or rather man's understanding of it, was dramatically changing, and a new intellectual dawn was breaking everywhere. Colonial Lima was not left in darkness. The Enlightenment had begun, and men in Europe were as excited as children with new toys. The new lights were also flooding the Jesuit library of San Pablo, and the Jesuits of the colonial city, their students and friends, shared the intellectual excitement of men across the seas.

In England, in the shadow of the Royal Academy of London, Isaac Newton had been shaking the old scientific foundations of the world and recasting them in new frames, since 1668. Newton's *Opera Omnia* rested on the shelves of San Pablo's library. In France the *Academie des*

Sciences, founded in 1666 during the reign of Louis XIV, gathered some of the best French minds and published a good amount of scientific findings. In faraway Lima, the Jesuits of San Pablo received and read these French publications. They had in their library fifty-four volumes in French with a detailed history of the *Academie des Sciences*, plus five additional volumes containing an alphabetical index of all the subjects in the multi-volume work. One could also find in the Jesuit library twelve volumes of the scientific memoirs presented to the French Academy, and a separate collection of papers on mathematics. San Pablo also owned the descriptive list of all the machines approved by the French Academy, a six-volume work, and a special publication in seven volumes describing the instruments and machines which had won scientific awards in Paris. The Jesuits of Lima were also aware of the existence and activities of the *Akademie der Wissenschaften* which had functioned in Berlin since 1711 under the presidency of Gottfried Wilhelm von Leibniz. The library had a three-volume history of the German Academy, and a collection of memoirs and papers read at its gatherings. The scientifically bent reader also had at his disposal fifty-eight volumes in Italian of a work entitled *New Collection of Scientific Pamphlets*.[34]

Together with these official publications, the reader could find in the college library many of the authors who wrote on scientific subjects during the seventeenth and eighteenth centuries. Treatises on mathematics and geometry abounded. Some of them were multi-volume works, written in Latin, Spanish, French, or Italian, covering the entire history and evolution of those disciplines up to the second half of the eighteenth century. The library kept a collection ranging from *Veteres Mathematici* and the writings of Euclid to modern works like Pedro Ciruelo's *Cursus Quatuor Mathematicarum*, and the works of Caramuel, Descartes and Newton. Books on metallurgy were not rare in San Pablo, and beginning with Alonso Barba's *Arte de los Metales*, widely read in the European schools of the eighteenth century, one could find in the Jesuit library treatises on how to work metal ores, how to purify silver and gold, and how to make steel out of iron. The library owned, besides, specialized works on hydraulics, botany, optics, mechanics, physics and electricity.[35]

The Jesuits of San Pablo had more than speculative interest in science and by the middle of the eighteenth century they had formed in the back room of their library a small scientific laboratory. There they were able to test, in "mathematical and physical machines" imported from Europe, the new scientific theories. Several telescopes, one of them described as "a Newtonian telescope of reflexion," were used by San Pablo's students to pursue the traditional Jesuit interest in scanning the heavens to study the stars. Two rather large "electric machines" rested on a bulky table in the middle of the room. One of them was a modern machine "made in England," and was equipped with all sorts of additional instruments. The other one was an older model "made in Italy," which, by 1767, had been somehow damaged by constant use. San Pablo owned some pneumatic machines and pumps imported from England, which were used at the college to experiment in drawing water and air. In the small Jesuit laboratory there was also an assorted collection of machines designed to weigh liquids, to measure centrifugal forces, to test hydrostatic laws and to make other physical experiments. The royal officials who confiscated the library noticed that most of these machines were in need of repair, possibly indicating that the Jesuits had made frequent use of them.[36]

The philosophical cast of mind of those men who read the scientific writings of the day and were familiar with modern scientific machines could not have remained solidly frozen within the molds of a rigid and blind Aristotelianism. As early as the last decades of the sixteenth century, José de Acosta had broken away from the old master whenever his own scientific observations proved Aristotle wrong or unreliable. The spirit of Acosta lived on in San Pablo, whose professors were always in touch with the new philosophical currents of Europe. The works of Suarez and his many disciples had arrived at the common library of San Pablo fresh from the printing shops of Europe, and in them the Jesuits of Lima could study a new kind of philosophy.

In the first half of the seventeenth century, René Descartes, a Jesuit alumnus of the College of La Flèche, started a Copernican revolution in philosophy with his book *Discours de la Méthode*. After him, a new body of philosophers, with the brand of Cartesianism clearly marked on their new systems, flourished all through Europe. They were men like the Frenchman Malebranche, the German Leibniz, and the Englishman Locke, who opened new, still-uncharted routes for the philosophical thought of Europe. In San Pablo the reader could find the works of Descartes and Locke, and studies and commentaries on the post-Cartesian philosophers. In philosophy, as in many other disciplines, the Jesuits of Lima closely followed the evolution and progress of Europe.[37]

The Age of Reason had begun, and, in Spain, a frail monk, Fray Benito Gerónimo Feijoo y Montenegro, was preaching the new intellectual gospel. Feijoo's *Theatro Crítico* and *Cartas Eruditas*, published between 1726 and 1760, brought to San Pablo the new winds of the Enlightenment. Feijoo's works were to be found not only in the common library, but also in the private libraries of some professors, a sign of their acceptance and popularity with the Jesuits of San Pablo. The Jesuit college at Lima, so near the day of its extinction, still reached through the writings of Feijoo to see not only the breaking dawn, but almost the full midday of a new intellectual era.[38]

When the College of San Pablo was confiscated by the Viceroy Amat in September of 1767, the doors and windows of the common library were sealed. On the 25th of January, 1768, the University of San Marcos, old academic foe of the Jesuit college, planning to form the library it still lacked, petitioned the king to grant the university the books of the exiled Jesuits. The generous king graciously acquiesced and granted the university, "as a gift from his liberal hand," the library of San Pablo and all the books confiscated in the other Jesuit houses of Lima. The Jesuits sailed away, but more than forty thousand of their books were left behind in the College of San Pablo: the wake of a great institution which had sunk below the horizons of history.

V

MEDICINE AT SAN PABLO

Between the years 1547 and 1557 Ignatius Loyola, now master of arts of the University of Paris, drew up in the Jesuit *Constitutions* the main guidelines for all future Jesuit colleges and universities. Influenced and inspired by Diego Lainez, the greatest intellectual of the fledgling Society of Jesus, Ignatius described in the fourth part of his *Constitutions* the aim of Jesuit education, the administrative system, the kinds of books to be read by the students, and the courses to be offered in the colleges of the Order. Toward the study of medicine Ignatius had a rather reserved attitude. He had accepted for Jesuit colleges the study of the humanities, ancient and modern languages, philosophy and theology, mathematics and the natural sciences, but he explicitly excluded the study of medicine from the curriculum of Jesuit universities, as a subject foreign to the aims of the Order. If medical studies should prove to be convenient somewhere, Ignatius ruled, they could be accepted in Jesuit universities but taught by lay professors and never by the Jesuits themselves.[1]

This piece of legislation, which discriminated against medicine as a formal part of the Jesuit curriculum, did not reveal the entire mind of Ignatius who was perhaps unique among religious founders in his preoccupation with medical problems. He ordered a ''prefect of health'' in every Jesuit college to watch over the community and the student body, to ensure that their health was preserved or restored when needed. All the Jesuit colleges should also have a regular doctor to be consulted and obeyed in determining the kinds of food, the amount of sleep, or the types of medicines needed in each region. Besides the prefect of health and the doctor, Ignatius wanted an infirmarian or nurse in every college, chosen from among the most capable Jesuit lay brothers, to run the college's infirmary and have the immediate care of the sick.[2]

Those two currents of Ignatius' thought would influence the medical activities in the Jesuit college at Lima. San Pablo would never offer any formal courses in medicine, and yet it became an important medical center for the viceroyalty, even before the first chairs of medicine were established in San Marcos in 1634 by the Count of Chinchón. The Jesuits who arrived in Lima in 1568 brought with them a supply of medicines collected in Seville to meet possible emergencies on the long trip, and those medicines were the humble seeds from which would grow, with the passing of the years, the best pharmacy of the Viceroyalty of Peru. In 1592 Father Hernando de Mendoza, brother of the then Viceroy of Peru Don García Hurtado de Mendoza, became rector of San Pablo. The new rector, respected and feared in Lima as "el padre que todo lo puede" because of his closeness to his brother the viceroy, built an entirely new infirmary for the college to take proper care of the sick. He spent so much money on the construction that at the end of his term of office, and in spite of the help given by his brother the viceroy, San Pablo was burdened with serious debts.[3] In December of 1600 the Provincial Rodríguez de Cabredo summoned to San Pablo a group of Jesuit representatives to elect a man to be sent to Europe, charged with the duty of informing the Father General on the affairs of the Order in Peru, and of recruiting new European Jesuits to work in America. The chosen man was Diego de Torres Bollo, whose trip to Europe would prove instrumental for the development of the infirmary and pharmacy of San Pablo.[4]

Augustino Salumbrino

Torres Bollo, the Peruvian representative, worn out by the long and dangerous trip from Lima to the Holy City, became sick in Rome and retired to the Jesuit infirmary of the Roman college under the care of the Italian lay brother Augustino Salumbrino. Salumbrino had joined the Jesuits in Rome in 1588 and after taking his vows in 1590 he was sent to the Jesuit college at Milan as an infirmarian. To fulfill his new duties with competence, Salumbrino turned to the study of pharmacy, and in Milan he became an accomplished pharmacist and nurse. A few years later he was called back to Rome to place his medical knowledge at the service of the many Jesuits then living in the Holy City. When Torres Bollo fell sick in Rome at his arrival from Peru, Augustino Salumbrino was there to nurse him back to health. During the long hours of convalescence the Peruvian Jesuit talked to Brother Salumbrino about Peru, the great College of San Pablo, and the Jesuit missions in the new world. Like many other Europeans of his time, Salumbrino felt the mysterious call of the world beyond the seas, and he volunteered for Peru. In 1605, lost among the forty-six Jesuits brought by Diego de Torres Bollo to Peru, the Italian pharmacist and infirmarian entered the cloisters of San Pablo for the first time. For thirty-seven years Brother Salumbrino would live in the college at Lima and become recognized by all as the father and founder of the pharmacy of San Pablo.

Salumbrino was a real professional and a tireless worker. He improved the infirmary of San Pablo, but he soon realized that the infirmary was not sufficient to take proper care of the sick in Lima. He needed a steady supply of medicines, and they were hard to get in colonial Lima. Brother Salumbrino made up his mind. He would build a pharmacy in San Pablo, and he would do it in the grand manner, not only to supply the college at Lima, but also the haciendas and the other Jesuit colleges spread throughout the viceroyalty. Relying on knowledge and experience acquired in Milan and Rome, Salumbrino taught another Jesuit the science of pharmacy, and with him as his collaborator they soon began experimenting in the college's garden with different kinds of medicinal seeds. It was not an amateurish pastime, but a professional effort to start a pharmacy where none had existed before.[5]

Many of the medicines used by Salumbrino in those first years were the spontaneous product of nature, but others were "compounds" which had to be prepared in a laboratory following strict pharmaceutical rules. In San Pablo Brother Salumbrino had some of the European pharmacopoeias, the official pharmaceutical guides used in pharmacies to fill medical prescriptions, and with their help he began a laboratory at the Jesuit college. Among the pharmacopoeias used during those first decades of the seventeenth century were Luis de Oviedo's *Methodo de la Collection y Reposición de las Medicinas Simples y de su Corrección y Preparación*, printed in Madrid in 1581, and Juan del Castillo's *Universa Medicamenta in Officinis Pharmaceuticis Usitata*, printed in Cádiz by Joanne de Burg in 1622. The Spanish doctor Castillo was quite familiar with medical developments in France, and through his work the pharmacist of San Pablo became aware of them as early as the year 1628.[6]

Before his death in 1642, Augustino Salumbrino had extended his influence beyond the walls of the college and the limits of the City of the Kings. His pharmacy, emulating the college's library, became a distributing center of medical information and medicines for other Jesuit institutions through the viceroyalty. Salumbrino supplied with medicines those Jesuits who left San Pablo on long missions among the Indians of the Andes, and sent medicaments to the other Jesuit colleges and haciendas. In 1629, for instance, he prepared a shipment of drugs for the college at Arequipa, and in 1630 he furnished another college with three boxes of *caña fístula*, a Peruvian wild cane which had certain astringent effects. Also during Salumbrino's tenure as head of San Pablo's pharmacy, the college began sending to Europe some of the medical products of the new world.[7]

In the fleet of 1630, consigned to a certain Jesuit brother, Antonio Robles of Spain, was a shipment of Peruvian *besoardicus lapis* from the college of San Pablo. The *besoardicus lapis*, or bezoar stone, was a calculus of calcic and carbonic phosphate formed in the intestinal tract of the llama and the vicuña, highly prized in Europe as a powerful antidote. After the first decades of the seventeenth century the demand for the Peruvian bezoar stones rose in Europe, and the Jesuits of San Pablo sent across the seas thousands of them to be sold or distributed among friends and benefactors. Felipe de Paz brought with him two shipments of bezoar stones when he sailed from San Pablo in 1667 as procurator to Rome. He died in Havana, but his companion Alonso Gómez took charge of the shipments and made sure that the stones from San Pablo's pharmacy arrived safely in Seville in 1668. In 1669, another Jesuit from Peru, Nicolás de Miraval, declared to customs authorities at Rome more than three hundred *libras* of bezoar stones to be distributed in the Roman Curia and among the Jesuit houses of Italy. It is unknown how many poisoned Europeans were restored to health by the calculus of the Peruvian llama and vicuña, but one cannot help thinking with discomfort of the hundreds of precious animals which must have been sacrificed in the highlands of the Andes to meet the European demand for bezoar stones.[8]

The college of San Pablo made a greater contribution to medical history when in the 1630s, still during Salumbrino's lifetime, it became the distributing center of quinine, the febrifuge, bitter bark of certain Andean rubiaceous trees. Salumbrino's pharmaceutical knowledge must have been instrumental in establishing the medicinal virtues of quinine, and Bernabé Cobo, an alumnus and professor of San Pablo, was certainly the first European to describe for the world the famous "árbol de las calenturas," as he called the quinine tree in his well-known *Historia de Nuevo Mundo*.[9]

Regardless of the very dubious story that the Countess of Chinchón was cured by the Jesuits of San Pablo with the febrifuge bark, there is no doubt that the Jesuit college at Lima had a sort of monopoly on quinine in that first half of the seventeenth century. San Pablo distributed quinine through the other Jesuit colleges in the viceroyalty, and introduced it into Europe. The citizens of Lima soon began calling the street in front of the Jesuit infirmaries "calle de la cascarilla," street of the bark, a name which would remain up to the republican period as a public testimony to San Pablo as the distributor of the precious bark. After Father Alonso Messia Venegas brought samples of quinine to Rome in 1631, every Jesuit procurator who left San Pablo for the Holy City as representative of the Peruvian Jesuits, an occurrence which took place every three years, brought to Europe new supplies of the febrifuge bark. In 1667 Felipe de Paz took with him a trunk filled with "corteza de las calenturas," and in 1699 Nicolás de Miraval arrived in Rome with six hundred thirty-five *libras* of quinine, probably having left a similar amount in Spain.[10] Soon the quinine was known throughout Europe as "the Jesuits' bark," and was attacked in certain Protestant circles as a new and dangerous jesuitical fraud. Many years later, a Jesuit pharmacist in Mexico would write that the Peruvian quinine ". . . because of the many experiments conducted up to our own day [and those experiments were begun by the Jesuits of San Pablo] is the best and safest medicament to cure all kinds of colds and fevers. . . ."[11]

New Developments

The impetus given to the college's pharmacy by the Italian Salumbrino increased with the years, and in the second half of the seventeenth century the Jesuits' administrators were almost overrun by the growing size of the enterprise. It was no longer the small pharmacy serving the college and the brethren working in the haciendas or out in missions among the Indians. Now there was a continuous stream of lay persons coming to San Pablo to buy from the brother pharmacist all kinds of purgatives, ointments, syrups and drugs. Little by little the Jesuit pharmacy became a wholesale center for other pharmacies of Lima, and received orders from as far away as Chile, Paraguay, Potosí, La Plata, Quito and Panama.

When in November of 1656 Leonardo de Peñafiel, fulfilling his duty as Provincial of Peru, visited the College of San Pablo, he recognized the existing situation in the college's pharmacy, and made an effort to regulate its affairs. On the 24th of November he gave orders to the rector and to the brother pharmacist to avoid selling medicines to individual citizens on a retail basis, and he also tried to moderate the wholesaling of medical products through San Pablo's pharmacy. Peñafiel allowed the Jesuit pharmacist to act as a wholesaler for the pharmacists of Lima, and to ship medicines to Potosí and other parts of the highlands when requested, but only on the condition that the brother pharmacist would never accept investments from lay persons to expand the scope of the pharmacy. The provincial insisted also on the principles of sound administration, giving orders to the brother to keep his account books faithfully, and to enter in them the buying and selling prices of each medical shipment. The pharmacist was also reminded that he should never embark on any major operation without first requesting the provincial's permission.[12]

Four years later, in October of 1660, the meticulous Andrés de Rada was in San Pablo as an official Visitor from Rome, and he made a careful tour of inspection of all the dependencies of the college, leaving behind a vast amount of instructions and regulations which, because of their size and meticulousness, were probably never fulfilled. The pharmacy, as it had developed by that second half of the seventeenth century, posed many problems to the conscientious Visitor who took his time inspecting everything before he sat down in his office to write a report to Rome and long instructions to the brother pharmacist of San Pablo.

Rada became aware, as had Peñafiel years before, of the great number of individuals coming to San Pablo to buy medicines and, like Peñafiel, the Visitor was not too happy with the existing situation. On the 24th of October, 1660, Rada gave orders to the administrator of the pharmacy to stop selling medicines as a retailer, allowing but few exceptions to this command. The pharmacy could, of course, sell to other Jesuit institutions in or outside the city, to close friends or benefactors of the Order, and to persons of high rank, whose requests could not be easily ignored. The pharmacy should also provide medicines to the poor and needy who could not afford to buy them from the regular merchants. Andrés de Rada made a final exception when he allowed the retailing of medicine to any person, regardless of social quality or numbers, in the event that those medical products were available only in the Jesuit pharmacy, a seemingly not rare occurrence. With so many conditions and loopholes attached to it, Rada's orders were obviously helpless to stop the retailing of medicines in San Pablo.

The Visitor, an intelligent man, recognized the unique role played by San Pablo's pharmacy in preserving and restoring bodily health not only in Lima, but all through that wide net of haciendas, missions, parishes and colleges run by the Jesuits in the Viceroyalty of Peru. Rada encouraged the brother pharmacist to keep constantly informed about new medicines and drugs coming onto the market, and to order them in time to have an abundant supply in San Pablo. The pharmacist should estimate the yearly demand, taking into account the needs of all the Jesuit institutions in Peru, and be sure to have a surplus of medicines at the end of the year rather than a deficiency of them. He could, of course, place his orders with the European pharmaceutical centers, but he should be aware of the long trips in which many delicate medical products could easily be spoiled. To avoid this Rada suggested relying more and more on the American pharmacopoeia by ordering medicines from Chile, Paraguay, Nuevo Reino and the provinces of Peru.

The Visitor frowned upon the idea of San Pablo's pharmacy being a wholesale center for the pharmacies of Lima, and he commanded the brother pharmacist to keep the volume of his medical orders within the limits needed to supply his Jesuit customers. Surpluses could be sold to the lay pharmacists of the city, but the volume of orders should not be expanded to meet their demands. The question of prices also occupied the attention of the Roman Visitor who made clear to the administrators of San Pablo that they could not run the Jesuit pharmacy as a business enterprise. San Pablo could sell medicines at a moderate profit, but just sufficient to cover expenses and pay the salaries of the lay staff who worked in the pharmacy. In the Visitor's mind the pharmacy of San Pablo should be a community service, rather than a business.

Andrés de Rada's final remarks in his instructions to the brother pharmacist showed how seriously the Visitor took the affairs of the pharmacy, and the great hopes he entertained for the future of that unique dependency of San Pablo. The Visitor imposed upon the college's rector the duty of having an annual professional inspection of the pharmacy at the beginning of September. The rector should entrust this professional inspection to the best lay pharmacist in the city, giving him authority to take the required measures to improve the college's pharmacy and laboratory. Every Saturday the brother pharmacist should present the account books of the pharmacy to the general administrator of the college to have him check the weekly activity of the pharmacy. With this sytem of checks and inspections, Rada intended to avoid economic pitfalls in the administration and hoped to maintain the Jesuit pharmacy as the great and efficient institution it was in that second half of the seventeenth century.[13]

Although Jesuit superiors were obviously concerned with the pharmacy's relations to the world outside San Pablo, they did not forget that the main purpose of its foundation was to serve the needs of the college and its infirmaries. San Pablo's population had been steadily climbing and requiring more medical attention with the passing of the years. The eighty Jesuits living in the college in 1603 had been increased to ninety-nine by 1606. San Pablo had one hundred fifteen Jesuits in 1609, one hundred thirty-three in 1610, and by the year 1635 there were one hundred sixty-three Jesuits studying, teaching, writing and working in the college at Lima.[14] They had come to Peru not only from Spain, but also from different regions of Italy and central Europe. San Pablo was for them the first arena in which they struggled to adapt themselves not only to the cultural but also to the physical environment of the Indies' food, climate and habitat.

To help the newly arrived Jesuits in that painful process of physical adaptation and to meet possible contingencies, Brother Salumbrino had improved the infirmary of the college and had started the pharmacy. By the second half of the seventeenth century San Pablo's infirmary was a clean and quiet courtyard in the southeast corner of the college. Besides the infirmarian's office and a first-aid room, the Jesuit infirmary had about fifteen private rooms, all of them facing a fountain which enlivened the center of the courtyard. Across the street from the main building, the brother infirmarian had a house adapted to serve as infirmary for the Negro slaves of the college. Those in charge of the patients not only administered medicines to them, but also ran an independent kitchen to prepare special food for the sick. Since the first decades of the seventeenth century, several provincials had ordered time and again that the infirmarians spare neither money nor work to cook even delicacies and European-style dishes to nurse the patients back to health. To carry out these orders and to help them break the monotony of the diet, the infirmarians of San Pablo had at their disposal a cookbook printed in Spain and called *El Arte de la Cocina*.[15]

The Medical Library of San Pablo

Since the 1610s, when the Italian Salumbrino began training his collaborators in the pharmacy and filling prescriptions in his burgeoning laboratory, medical and pharmaceutical literature became a necessity in San Pablo. The college's administrators did not spare any expense to order the best medical books available from Europe, and during the seventeenth century the Jesuits of Lima built a notable medical library, housed partly in the common library of the college, and partly in the office of the brother pharmacist.

Pharmacopoeias naturally occupied a prominent place in the Jesuit collection, and they were an essential tool in running their efficient pharmacy. The pharmacopoeias were works describing chemicals, drugs, and medicinal preparations, issued regularly with the approval of medical authorities and recognized as standard manuals in every pharmacy. San Pablo had in its collection the pharmacopoeias of Luis de Oviedo and Juan del Castillo, already noted above, which were widely used in seventeenth-century Spain. Besides these two classics, the Jesuit pharmacists of Lima could consult and follow in filling prescriptions a work called *De Compositione Medicamentorum*, printed in Venice in 1590 and written by the Italian doctor Girolamo Mercuriale, who from his chairs in the Universities of Padua, Bologna and Pisa exercised a profound influence in medical circles all through Europe. Other pharmacopoeias of San Pablo's medical library showed by their titles that they were issued by local or regional authorities and specialized in local drugs and chemicals. Among them the Jesuit library had the *Pharmacopeia Parisiensis*, *Pharmacopeia Valenciana*, *Pharmacopeia Matritensis* and *Botánica Americana*. During the eighteenth century the brother pharmacists used as a vademecum Félix Palacios' *La Farmacopea Triunfante*, printed in Madrid in 1713. It was so highly regarded and so frequently referred to that the brother pharmacist had written inside its cover: "For the daily use of this pharmacy."[16]

The Jesuit pharmacists of San Pablo, besides running the pharmacy, also had a certain duty to help the infirmarians in the daily care of the sick. It was only natural that, besides strictly pharmaceutical works, they gathered in their collection books on several other branches of medicine, anatomy, osteology, treatises on different kinds of fevers and their remedies, descriptions of contagious diseases and infections, and the methods of combating them. Surgery seems to have been a favorite subject, and one could easily find on the shelves of San Pablo's library Bartolomé Hidalgo's *Thesoro de la Verdadera Cirugía y Via Particular contra la Común*, printed in Seville in 1604, and Juan Calvo's *Primera y Segunda Parte de la Cirugía Universal del Cuerpo Humano*, which was reprinted many times during the seventeenth century and was still used in the eighteenth. The brother pharmacist owned, besides, a work called *El Sueño Quirúrgico*, dealing perhaps with problems of anesthesia, and two volumes with the titles *Operaciones Quirúrgicas* and *El Cirujano en Prática*.

As in other branches of human knowledge, the Jesuits of San Pablo showed a remarkably universal spirit in medicine. Their library had the ancient classics, Galen and Hippocrates, and voluminous Latin commentaries on the two masters by the medieval doctors, as well as an impressive array of contemporary medical authors. Among contemporaries, the works of the Italians Girolamo Mercuriale, Giovanni B. Cortesi, of the College of Doctors of Bologna and one of the best anatomists of his time, Gabrielle Falopio, professor of Padua, Michele Mercati, the personal doctor of Popes Gregory XIII and Clement VIII, and Girolamo Cardano, a Milanese of true genius, doctor, philosopher, physicist and mathematician, one of the main builders of the new scientific concept of nature, were available. French medical works were not rare in the Jesuit library where the reader could find a French work on new medical prescriptions, another two volumes describing new medical products, and Jean Riolan's work on anatomy. Riolan was well known in seventeenth-century Europe through his famous polemic with William Harvey on the circulation of the blood. Another known author,

French by adoption although Danish by birth, was Jakob Benignus Winslow, whose *Exposition Anatomique de la Structure du Corps Humain*, in five volumes, was used by the brother pharmacist of San Pablo and kept in his office.[17]

The Spanish doctors whose works were in the Jesuit library of San Pablo or in the office of the pharmacist understandably outnumbered foreign authors, and covered the period from the sixteenth century up to the middle of the eighteenth. Among them were Antonio Aguilera, who wrote *Preclarae Rudimentorum Medicinae Libri Octo*, Juan Fernández, author of a *Universa Medicina*, Bernardo Montano, and the two Catalans Jacinto Andreu, professor in Barcelona, who wrote *Practicae . . . pro Curandis Humani Corporis Morbis*, and José Fornés, an expert on epidemic fevers. Fornés had been sent to Marseilles by the Spanish authorities to study the plague which ravaged that French city in 1720. His book on the subject, *Tractatus de Peste . . . in V Partes Divisus*, published in Barcelona in 1725, rested on the shelves of San Pablo's library. But perhaps one of the most illustrious Spanish doctors of the eighteenth century whose works were at San Pablo was Juan de Dios López, the founder of the Spanish Royal Academy of Medicine and of the Royal College of Surgeons. López published in Madrid, between 1750 and 1752, four volumes of a work entitled *Compendio Anatómico*, which reached the library of San Pablo before the expulsion of the Jesuits in 1767.[18]

The Eighteenth Century

The Jesuit medical library was the result of the constant efforts made during two centuries by the many men who had been the successive pharmacists and infirmarians of San Pablo. The Italian Salumbrino began the work in the first years of the seventeenth century, and men of several nationalities carried on after him. In the first decades of the eighteenth century a group of outstanding German Jesuits, all of them professional pharmacists, came to America and with them the pharmacy of San Pablo would know the beginnings of its golden years. By the year 1700 the Jesuits had extended throughout the vast continent of South America a wide network of infirmaries and pharmacies, and a good number of them were manned by German Jesuits. Those German pharmacists would always look to San Pablo, because of its location at the heart of the viceroyalty, as the center of the network and the main supplier of European medicaments.

In 1702 Heinrich Peschke was in Córdoba as pharmacist of the Jesuit college there, and was serving as link to supply medicines to the Jesuits working in Tucumán, La Plata and Paraguay. The Bohemian known as Juan de Esteyneffer ran the Jesuit pharmacy in Mexico City, and by 1712 he had written a book which would exert its influence in San Pablo and in other Jesuit colleges of Peru. Esteyneffer's book, called *Florilegio Medicinal de Todas las Enfermedades*, was a practical compendium divided into three sections—general medicine, surgery and pharmacy. It was meant to be distributed throughout the network of Jesuit infirmaries in missions and haciendas as a brief, basic manual to help the man in the field who was usually far from extensive libraries to cope with medical emergencies. Esteyneffer's work was also well known and frequently used in the pharmacy of San Pablo by his fellow countrymen Franz Zimmermann, Johann Sheretter, pharmacist and surgeon who died only three years after his arrival at San Pablo, and Joseph Mayer. Mayer had come from Germany in 1724 as a professional pharmacist to practice his profession in Lima, but in San Pablo his outstanding talents were soon recognized, and he was ordered to quit pharmacy and to follow the courses in philosophy and theology. After a few years, Mayer was ordained a priest and sent to the missions. The college of San Pablo thus lost one of its best German pharmacists.[19]

Toward the middle of the eighteenth century the Spaniard Juan Francisco Toro took over from the Germans as head of San Pablo's pharmacy. Toro was a tireless worker and a very efficient administrator, who improved the pharmacy and laboratory, increased the volume of sales, and through his profits made a substantial contribution to support the entire college, where lectures were still tuition-free. In February of 1752, Baltasar de Moncada, Jesuit Provincial of Peru, came in his official capacity to visit the College of San Pablo. The provincial, following a regular procedure, inspected all the college's dependencies, and among them the pharmacy and infirmaries. He studied the account books presented by the pharmacist Toro and by the administrator of the college, Miguel Garrido, and was pleasantly surprised. From August of 1748 up to February of 1752, the pharmacy had realized under Toro's management a gross profit of some 60,678 pesos. From that amount the brother pharmacist had spent more than 23,000 pesos on ordinary and special expenses to run the pharmacy, and 6,490 pesos for the maintenance of the college's infirmary, the infirmary of the Negro slaves, and its branches in the haciendas. During that period of three and a half years, San Pablo's pharmacist gave the college 30,000 pesos to help maintain students and professors. At the time that Moncada checked the account books, February of 1752, the pharmacy had a floating capital of more than 8,000 pesos invested in buying new medicines from Spain and Panama.

Baltasar de Moncada was impressed and satisfied with the economic soundness of the pharmacy of San Pablo. Unlike his predecessors of the seventeenth century, Leonardo de Peñafiel and Andrés de Rada, Moncada did not make any suggestions to limit the volume of business or to discourage the retailing of medicines to the citizens of Lima. Not only that, in the final report of his visitation the provincial was not sparing in his praise for the work accomplished in the pharmacy by Brother Toro, and thanked him publicly.[20]

Three years after Baltasar de Moncada visited the pharmacy, the College of San Pablo was privileged to receive the visit in 1755 of the German Jesuit Joseph Zeitler, pharmacist of the Jesuit college in Santiago de Chile and perhaps the greatest medical authority the Jesuits ever had in South America. His knowledge of medicine, pharmacy and chemistry was so notable for his time and so vital for the citizens of Santiago that when the Jesuits were expelled from South America in 1767, the Chileans prevented Zeitler from leaving the country, in spite of the king's strict orders to the contrary. Joseph Zeitler was in Lima in 1755 and remained at San Pablo for about a year. His advice and technical help gave a fresh impetus to the flourishing pharmacy of San Pablo with which he would maintain close professional contacts in the years ahead. During the remaining decade of its existence, the pharmacy would be under the management of another Spanish Jesuit, but it would feel the strong influence of the German Zeitler in faraway Santiago de Chile.[21]

The Pharmacist José Rojo

Brother Joseph Zeitler had returned to his homebase in Chile, when superiors in Lima began searching for a new, competent administrator to be placed at the head of that sizable enterprise which was now the Jesuit pharmacy of San Pablo. The superiors realized in that second half of the eighteenth century that the pharmacy required nothing less than the best man available, and they found that man in the imperial city of the Incas, in the Jesuit college at Cusco. In the winter of early 1757 a courier left San Pablo with a sealed envelope from the provincial. After a painful trip on mule back over steep Indian trails, the messenger reached Cusco and handed the envelope to Brother José Rojo, the pharmacist of the local college. It was a summons to Lima to take charge of San Pablo's pharmacy. Brother Rojo, with Jesuit obedience, began packing, and in a few weeks he was on his way down the sierra toward the dry coastal plains.

When José Rojo was installed as the new pharmacist of San Pablo, in September of 1757, no one suspected that he was to be the last administrator of the pharmacy. Ten years later, almost to the very day, armed soldiers would occupy the college and confiscate the Jesuit pharmacy, but in September, 1757, Rojo had still a decade ahead of him to prove that the Jesuit superiors had not been mistaken in placing in his hands the all-important pharmacy of San Pablo. During his first weeks in Lima, Rojo became aware of his central position and of his obligations toward the other Jesuit pharmacies, and he faithfully maintained close contact with all of them. Rojo wrote and exchanged medical products and information with the German Andreas Lechner, pharmacist of the Jesuit college in Quito, and years later with Lechner's successor, the Italian Ignacio Lyro. He also sent medicines to the Jesuit brothers who ran the infirmaries in the haciendas, bought from and sold medicaments to his own successor in Cusco, and even maintained professional contacts with the German Georg Schult, Jesuit pharmacist in Mexico City.[22]

In this web of interrelations which connected the Jesuit pharmacies in America, perhaps the strongest thread ran from Lima to Santiago de Chile. The memory of the great Joseph Zeitler was still very much alive in San Pablo, and soon the German Zeitler and the Spaniard Rojo were corresponding and became friends. In the very month he took charge of the pharmacy of Lima, Rojo sent to Zeitler seven hundred pesos to be invested in Chile to buy medical products of those regions. It was only the first installment of a long, mutual account, which would remain open until the expulsion of the Jesuits.

On the 12th of February, 1760, Joseph Zeitler wrote a letter from Santiago to his friend Rojo, who received it in Lima on the 12th of March. Zeitler thanked the pharmacist of San Pablo for a shipment of medicines which had arrived safely at Santiago, and placed a new order with Rojo. Zeitler requested Peruvian quinine of good quality, *caña fístula*, sponges and saffron. Because of its connections with the infirmaries and the need for special diets for the sick, the pharmacy of Lima supplied upon request spices of all kinds, *e.g.*, saffron, cloves, nutmeg and pepper, as it also supplied tobacco—considered an excellent medicament to dry up certain malignant fluids in the head and stomach. In other letters Zeitler repeated his orders for *caña fístula*, and asked Rojo to send new products such as tar and galipot, the secretion exuded from certain types of pines in southern Europe; a special oil called *aceite María*; vermillion, the mercuric sulphide which Rojo could easily obtain from the neighborhood of Huancavelica; and turpentine, the yellowish oleoresin extracted from the terebinth, and received in Lima from the east coast of South America.

San Pablo's pharmacist not only supplied Zeitler with all these different products, but at times depended on his friend in Chile for medicaments and articles which were scarce or too expensive in Lima. On the 30th of July, 1764, Rojo sent an order to Chile requesting mutton tallow and butter made of pure cow's milk, a request which makes it clear that cattle and ships were more abundant in the southern regions. José Rojo also inquired in that letter into the possibility of acquiring good cathartic salts in Chile. The demand for aperient and cathartic salts was great in San Pablo's pharmacy, and brother Rojo had to find new sources of supply to keep a good stock. Zeitler wrote back to Lima on the 19th of September, 1764. He informed Rojo of the existence in Chile of fountains and springs where salts of different types coagulated, but all of them mixed with vitriol and other harmful substances. The German pharmacist had made all possible efforts to purify those salts in his laboratory to obtain medically usable ones, but up to that September he had always failed. For this reason, Zeitler explained, he could not even send samples to Rojo, but he promised to ship the mutton tallow and the butter requested by his friend in Lima as soon as possible.[23]

This closely knit network of pharmacies and infirmaries and the need to exchange medical products among them gave rise to an ever-growing volume of business transacted through San Pablo's pharmacy. By the last months of 1757, brother Rojo had spent 1,177 pesos in medicines bought in Chile and Alto Peru. On the 20th of January of the following year, 1758, the ship *San Martín* moored at Callao carrying in her hold fourteen boxes of medicines from Europe, consigned to San Pablo. The merchandise was valued at 1,281 pesos, and brother Rojo had to pay 1,000 pesos in freight charges to the shipmaster. In January of 1759, San Pablo's pharmacist remitted to Spain 2,000 pesos to buy new European medicaments, but aware of the contingencies at sea he divided his remittance between two ships, the *San Martín* and the *San Borja*. In November of 1760, eight new boxes arrived from Europe in the ship *Nuestra Señora del Pilar*, and in February of 1761, Rojo sent an additional 2,000 pesos to Seville, this time in the ships *La Esperanza* and *San Juan Bautista*, only to be followed by 1,000 pesos more in January of 1762. In July of that year, crossing the soaring ridges of the Andes on mule back, ten cases of medicines arrived at San Pablo from La Plata. And all through those years, between 1757 and 1762, José Rojo made regular remittances of money to pay his bills in places like Mexico, Panama, Quito, Cusco, Chile and La Plata.[24]

The efforts of Brother Rojo to continue the great tradition of San Pablo's pharmacy were recognized and praised in the summer of 1762, when the Provincial Pascual Ponce de León came to visit the college. Ponce de León was a creole born in Lima in 1707. He knew well the great Jesuit institution flourishing in his home town, and now, going as provincial through the dependencies of San Pablo, he felt proud of the college's accomplishments. In the pharmacy the Provincial Ponce de León took his time talking with Rojo, examining the stock of medicines and the laboratory where the brother pharmacist and his officials filled prescriptions, and he carefully studied the account books. The provincial was satisfied and, like his predecessor in 1752, he also left in writing his praise of the brother, and his conviction of the great usefulness of the pharmacy, whose renown in the city he was also happy to verify. But Ponce de León went even a step further, serving notice on the rector and the administrator of the college neither to interfere with brother Rojo's busy schedule nor to request his services outside of the pharmacy. The provincial explained that Rojo needed all his working hours to attend to customers, Jesuits and laymen, and to be in the laboratory preparing special medicines.[25]

The Provincial Ponce de León had every reason to feel deeply satisfied in that summer of 1762. The pharmacy had grown, and the volume of work kept busy, now on a full-time basis, the Jesuit brother, a Spanish layman called José Emeregildo Guerrero, and three Negro slaves trained at the college. The infirmary of the college and those of the haciendas were well provided with medicines and articles needed for the sick. San Pablo had maintained communication with the rest of the Jesuit pharmacies and infirmaries, and there was a constant ebb and flow of medical products and information passing through the college. The pharmacy proper was beautifully furnished. In the center hung a large painting of Augustino Salumbrino, the founder of the pharmacy, and the walls were covered from floor to ceiling with solid oak shelves laden with bottles and flasks. Tables and chairs were made of wood imported from Chile, and in the middle of the room there was a long and wide mahogany counter with its beautiful reddish-brown color. On top of the counter, in contrast to the heavy mahogany, rested four delicate scales.

The laboratory of the pharmacy was a forest of glazed earthenware and shiny instruments, some of them made of pure silver. The three Negro employees of the pharmacy worked under the supervision of Guerrero in that laboratory filled with large jugs, scales, all kinds of stills used in distilling liquids, glass and metal funnels of all shapes and sizes, retorts and "matrasses," gridirons and hand mills, pumping engines and ovens, condensers and cauldrons, handsaws and sieves. The provincial might have been uncomfortable in that room with the fumes and the strong, unpleasant odor of medicines, but he was certainly happy to realize that in San Pablo's pharmacy and laboratory he had the means to preserve and restore the health of his men working in the coastal plains, in the high sierras, and in the forests of America.[26]

Encouraged by the attitude and words of the Provincial Ponce de León, José Rojo continued improving and expanding the scope of the pharmacy. In 1763, he sent to Spain twelve hundred pesos to renew his stock of European medicaments, and in September of 1764 he received almost the same amount from the college at Ica, which thus canceled its bill with San Pablo's pharmacy. Quito and the Jesuit novitiate in Lima also paid their debts to Rojo at the same time as Ica. The year 1764 saw feverish activity in the pharmacy of San Pablo. In March, José Rojo and his helpers worked to get a special shipment ready on time to be sent to Rome. Father Diego Jurado was leaving for the Holy City, and Rojo took advantage of his departure to send to the Jesuit pharmacy and infirmaries of Rome some American products. He carefully packed several libras of quinine, both bark and powder, balsam imported from Guatemala, some medical resins, vanilla—the flavoring extract made from the capsules of certain tropical American plants—and finally chocolate and cocoa, delicacies highly regarded in Jesuit European infirmaries, and which the Jesuits helped to popularize throughout Europe.

The following month, April of 1764, Rojo made a new remittance of medicaments to his friend Joseph Zeitler in Chile, and he got two boxes of medicines from the Jesuit pharmacist in Mexico City. In August the ship *El Gallardo* entered Callao, and brother Rojo rushed to the port to bring home nine boxes filled with medicines sent by his supplier in Spain. In February of 1766, San Pablo's pharmacy received a medical shipment from its agent in Guatemala, and in September of the same year, when the frigate *Nuestra Señora de los Dolores* dropped anchor at Callao, Rojo was notified that twelve new boxes had arrived from Europe consigned to his pharmacy. In December, to replenish his European stocks, Rojo sent to Cádiz in the ships *Ventura* and *Águila* 2,216 pesos. Months later, without suspecting that the money carried by those two ships was his last expenditure in Europe, Brother Rojo went through his books, and after some computations he wrote in his *Libro de Botica* with a feeling of understandable pride: "Up to this year I have sent to Spain to buy pharmaceutical products 13,130 pesos with seven *reales* and a half, without counting the amounts spent here in America."[27]

The End of the Pharmacy

While the ships *Ventura* and *Águila* crossed the seas towards Spain, heavy, menacing clouds gathered on the horizon and the stillness which always precedes a tropical storm could be felt in the air. In a few more months the storm would break in such a wild and violent manner that it would entirely shipwreck the Jesuit pharmacy of Lima, the College of San Pablo, and the whole Society of Jesus, uprooting all the Jesuits from South American soil.

Rojo's 2,216 pesos arrived safely in Cádiz, and San Pablo's Spanish agent spent a few months buying the medicaments and preparing their shipment. Finally twenty-three boxes were ready and, tightly stowed in the hold of a vessel named *La Concordia*, they began their long journey to Lima. But another ship, fitted out in haste and sent away in secrecy, left the Spanish coast sooner and was now proceeding under full sail towards the estuary of La Plata. A royal messenger, who carried for the viceroy of Peru sealed documents with high secrets of state, scanned the horizon tensely, impatient to set foot on land and to begin his trip across the Alto Peru to the viceregal capital. A few weeks before *La Concordia*, with its shipments of medicines for San Pablo, dropped anchors at Callao, the royal messenger had arrived at Lima, and the suppression of the Jesuits had been proclaimed. Brother José Rojo, for crimes still not clearly explained, was now a prisoner of the king, condemned to exile, and royal officials confiscated the twenty-three boxes of medicines brought by *La Concordia*.[28]

It was September of the year 1767. Viceroy Amat named Don Juan Isidro de Rivera y Zapata, the proto-pharmacist of Lima, to conduct an inspection and make an inventory of the pharmacy and laboratory of San Pablo. As many Jesuit provincials had done before him, Don Juan Isidro carefully inspected the pharmacy to report to the authorities of the state. He admired the efficiency of administration, and was impressed by the amount and quality of medicines. After several months of work he valued San Pablo's medical stock at some 44,734 pesos. An amount of almost seven thousand pesos in cash was found in Brother Rojo's office, and his books showed that two thousand of them belonged to the bishop of La Plata, two hundred to the bishop of Arequipa, and more than one thousand to the Jesuit college in the latter city. They were regular customers of San Pablo's pharmacy, and the money was meant either to buy new medicines from Brother Rojo, or as an investment in his thriving pharmacy.[29]

José Rojo, the last Jesuit pharmacist of Lima, was on his way into exile, already herded with his brethren onto royal ships, when the civil authorities back in Lima began discussing the future of the pharmacy of San Pablo. Doctors and pharmacists were summoned to give their opinion as experts on the Jesuit pharmacy, and their testimonies would have made Brother Rojo cry with gratitude. Their unanimous opinion was that the pharmacy had to be kept open at all costs, because it was the best in Lima, and because without its services not only the common citizens would suffer, but also all the other pharmacies in the city, ". . . whose limited supplies could not be compared by far with those in the pharmacy of San Pablo's College. . . ." Other expert witnesses gave their testimony at the public inquiry with still higher words of praise:

We must establish as a principle [in discussing the future of the pharmacy] that the Pharmacy of San Pablo was, of course, the wealthiest and best in this city; its wealth consisted in the considerable funds invested in it by the Jesuits . . .; its reputation originated in its supply of medicines . . ., in the care taken to replace the stock and in the particular watchfulness of the brother pharmacist to make sure that the public was properly served. . . .[30]

Following the experts' advice, civil authorities decided to keep open the pharmacy of San Pablo, although reducing greatly the volume of its transactions. The network of Jesuit colleges, haciendas, infirmaries, missions and parishes had been broken, and with them San Pablo's customers and suppliers had disappeared from the American continent. Don Rafael Velada, a medical doctor of repute who held the important position of chief surgeon of San Andrés' Hospital, was named the first non-Jesuit administrator of the pharmacy with a yearly salary of one thousand pesos. But the civil authorities, who had found it so easy to expropriate the pharmacy, did not find it equally easy to run it efficiently. They understood very soon that one could not sever the head and mutilate the body, and still keep the heart beating. The Jesuit pharmacy had been an integral part of an extensive institutional body, vitally linked with other cells and tissues of that body, and placed at the very heart of the vast Jesuit organization in America. It could not possibly survive, torn from its natural connections. In 1770, less than three years after the Jesuits had abandoned San Pablo, Don Rafael Velada resigned as administrator. The pharmacy was then entrusted to another private religious group, the Fathers of St. Philip Neri (Oratorians), but not even they could recapture the spirit of the Jesuits, and the pharmacy declined and finally disappeared. But the people of Lima did not forget an institution which had rendered great services to the city and the viceroyalty. Well into the republican period, they still called the street in front of the old Jesuit pharmacy *Botica de la Compañía*.

VI

A BAROQUE WAY OF LIFE

San Pablo's teachers, writers, and administrators, joined by hundreds of their students and friends, gathered periodically to worship in the college church. Located in the corner of San Pablo facing the *Plaza Mayor*, the church was a symbol of the college and of its teachers. Built early in the seventeenth century according to blueprints brought from Rome by Nicolás Durán, it was conceived and realized as a neo-classic structure along the lines of the Roman church of the *Gesu*. But those were baroque times in Peru and the architecture of San Pablo's church was caught in the whirlwind of the American Baroque, which covered the neo-classic lines with a superb ivy-like ornamentation. The artistic metamorphosis of the church was but the luxurious outgrowth of a whole style of life. If the Jesuits of San Pablo built that outstanding baroque monument, if they preached in a baroque manner and produced a baroque theater and literature, it was because theirs was a baroque way of life.

The regular channels through which a college life usually runs (teaching, studying, and writing) overflowed many times at San Pablo. The academic structures of the Jesuit college burst out time and again into hundreds of social and religious activities, which were an outlet for the men of San Pablo in their eagerness to influence colonial society. Students, teachers and administrators traveled around the viceroyalty preaching the Christian gospel to the natives. They organized religious

[119]

sodalities for the Lima nobility, the intellectuals, the merchants, the young people, the Indians and even the Negroes. They played the role of chaplain in the fleet and in the armies, conducted spiritual retreats, acted as confessors and counselors, and delivered sermons in the streets and on the plazas of Lima. As the baroque revolution of shapes and colors had transformed the college church, so did the social and religious activities of teachers and students give to San Pablo a unique physiognomy which has to be described for a full understanding of the institution.

Temporary Missions

While the first Jesuits of Lima struggled in the colonial city laying the foundations of San Pablo, King Philip II of Spain wrote to the Jesuit General in October of 1568 requesting new members of the Order to work in Peru. His Most Catholic Majesty, perhaps aware of the Jesuit tendency to be absorbed in educational work, reminded the General in his letter that the aim of Jesuit activities in the new lands should be to engage primarily in "the instruction and conversion of the natives." This wish of the king, to make Christians of the Indians of Peru, was very much alive in the hearts of the men who built San Pablo. Even before leaving Spain, they had begun studying the Indian language. In instructions received from Rome in March of 1567, before their departure for Peru, the founders of San Pablo were told to give themselves to the training and conversion of the Indians. The Roman instructions cautiously warned the Jesuits not to disperse their forces, but rather to build a central headquarters from which to move among the Indians in temporary missions, returning always to their homebase.[1]

Colonial realities taught the Jesuits to modify somewhat Roman policies and to accept permanent *doctrinas* among the Indians, but the original instructions of 1567 were never forgotten. The College of San Pablo soon became, and remained for two centuries, the bustling headquarters of hundreds of temporary missions among the Indians of Peru. San Pablo's administrators planned and executed those missions, choosing from the college community the men better prepared in the Indian languages. The first apostolic mission organized in San Pablo was entrusted to Alonso de Barzana, one of the most capable men in the college and subsequently the best Jesuit linguist in Peru. Barzana, pioneer of a long army of missionaries, left San Pablo about the middle of December, 1569, together with a young companion. Both of them visited the Indian villages in the valley of Lima preaching to and instructing the natives. Barzana sent reports back to San Pablo, a regular procedure with Jesuit missionaries, explaining to the brethren in Lima his experiences among the Indians. Those reports spurred the missionary spirit among San Pablo's students and teachers, who began importuning the rector to be sent in Barzana's footsteps. By the beginning of 1571 ten Jesuits of San Pablo had already left the college to engage for a certain period in ministering to the Indians. [2]

Those first missions were organized at San Pablo following the general norms contained in the Roman instructions of 1567, which exhorted the Peruvian Jesuits to stress "instruction" rather than "conversion," and requested of them a serious intellectual effort to understand Indian society and its religious implications. How well they carried out these directives is shown in a letter of Bartolomé Hernández, rector of San Pablo in 1570, to the all-powerful president of the Council of the Indies, Juan de Ovando. Writing on the 19th of April, 1572, the former rector explained to Ovando the prevailing opinion at San Pablo about the Indian problem, which was considered paramount. Some of the Jesuits, drawing from the experiences gained in their roving missions, had begun thinking that the Christian faith had been imposed on the Indians through pressures, stressing "conversions" and not so much "instruction." Bartolomé Hernández reacted against this trend, and twice in his letter to Ovando affirmed the Jesuit conviction that before trying to convert the Indians, they should be helped to lead a fully human life within a well organized socio-political structure. Then the former rector of San Pablo went on to explain the civilizing mission of urban life (a true Renaissance way of thinking), and the need to "reduce" the scattered Indians to villages and towns to help them to become fully men—"men" as understood by sixteenth century Europeans.[3]

Eight days after Bartolomé Hernández wrote his letter to the president of the Council of the Indies, José de Acosta arrived in Lima to become professor and, later, rector of San Pablo. The arrival of Acosta was perhaps the single most important event in the intellectual history of the Jesuit college at Lima. Father Acosta, an intellectual giant whose works are read with profit even today, became immediately entangled in the problem of how to adapt this exotic culture and race to the Christian standards of Europe. After a year of teaching at San Pablo, José de Acosta was chosen to go to Upper Peru on a mission which would last for a year and a half. It was a golden opportunity for a man with an unquenchable curiosity to study and observe for himself Indian realities He left San Pablo towards the end of May, 1573, spent four months in Cusco, still the center of Indian life in Peru, and then descended towards the Pacific coast to visit Arequipa. From Arequipa, Acosta went back again through the high sierras, visiting Indian communities and reaching La Paz at the end of January, 1574. On the 30th of April he was in Chuquisaca, where he resided for two months and joined as chaplain Viceroy Toledo's expedition against the Chiriguano Indians. Later, he was the first Jesuit to enter the fabulous silver city of Potosí, and he saw the wretched condition of the Indians forced to labor in the silver mines.[4]

When José de Acosta, the thinker who knew so well the intellectual climate of Coimbra, Salamanca, Valladolid and Alcalá, returned to San Pablo in Lima at the end of 1574, he was a man staggering under the weight of the "Indian problem." He agreed with the prevailing clerical idea, so well developed by the Dominican Las Casas, that Spain had been chosen by divine providence to bring the Christian faith to the Indians. The Jesuits had founded San Pablo in Lima, Acosta knew, as a tool to establish a Christian society in America, but how could that tool be best used to Christianize the Indians? For two years Acosta stubbornly faced this question in his cell at San Pablo.

More scholar–teacher than missionary, Father Acosta thought that the college faculty should contribute a solution to the Indian problem more on the theoretic level—through ideas which might later influence missionary action. Acosta persuaded Roman authorities to accept permanent *doctrinas* besides continuing the temporary missions organized and directed from the college. In 1576 he supported and helped in the organization of the five missions which left San Pablo for Chachapoyas, Huarochiri, Huanuco, Ica, and the district of Chancay, but personally he spent his leisure time during that year writing a book on the Indian question. The book, the first to be written by any Jesuit in any part of America, was a rational approach to the problem of how to Christianize the Indians. It became a blueprint for action for the men of San Pablo, and it was so well received in Europe that in 1588 it was published in the university city of Salamanca under the title *De Procuranda Indorum Salute*. The book, studied and analyzed many times, reflects the optimistic vision of a Christian humanist. The Indian, for Acosta, is a full human being, capable of the greatest Christian perfection, although still in an infantile stage of development. His shortcomings are not the result of birth or environment, but the tragic consequences of a lack of proper education. Instruction is the key to solve the Indian problem, but instruction which implies rational persuasion and abhors all pressure. Christian ways cannot be imposed by force or violence, and faith has to be accepted in a free manner.[5]

José de Acosta was in line with the Roman instructions of 1567 and with the ideas of San Pablo's former rector, Bartolomé Hernández. Thanks to men like Acosta and Hernández, the Jesuit college at Lima had developed by the 1570s its own policy towards the Indian missions. That policy was upheld by professors and administrators until the end of the century, and was put into practice by the college missionaries. When in 1582 a provincial convention of the Peruvian Jesuits met at San Pablo, a resolution was unanimously passed not to lead a cloistered life within the walls of the college, but to foster a steady increase in the temporary missions among the Indians. Prospective missionaries were instructed to go to tribes and communities not yet evangelized, even if they were at extremely great distances from Lima, and to spend long periods living among the natives. The convention also emphasized,

[123]

once again, the need to master the Indian languages to carry out efficiently the missionary task.

In Rome, the Jesuit General encouraged these apostolic activities as they developed at San Pablo. Writing to Lima on the 8th of April, 1584, Father General Aquaviva stressed the convenience of human instruction by teaching the natives how to read and write. He also insisted on the need for peaceful persuasion, for avoiding violence and pressure, and he ordered the Jesuit missionaries never to enter Indian territories in the company of armed soldiers. The Jesuit General considered the roving missions so important that he gave them priority over the administration of the Order in Peru. Those who knew the Indian language and were capable should be engaged in Indian missions, Father General ordered, and not be bogged down in administrative positions.[6]

These instructions were not so much dead paper at San Pablo. During the remaining years of the nineteenth century the college was the busy headquarters of many temporary missions. The college missionaries were always on the move, and wove a tangled labyrinth of paths and trails which crossed from Panama to Chile and from the coasts of Peru to the forests of Paraguay and the plains of Argentina. In 1584 San Pablo organized four missionary expeditions, of which one lasted for a year and a half. During the same year the ubiquitous José de Acosta, who always retained his deep concern for the missions in spite of academic and administrative assignments, suggested that San Pablo's missionaries be sent to the most crucial points of America. Acosta singled out two of those regions: Panama, the busy thoroughfare of the Spanish Empire, and Chile, the rough frontier in a constant state of war.[7]

In 1585, perhaps heeding Acosta's advice, two men left San Pablo for Panama. They were Juan Gómez and Diego Baena, who were ordered to remain for a year on the isthmus. The following year Quito was chosen as a target, and San Pablo sent some of its best men to the ancient birthplace of Atahualpa. Baltasar de Piñas, former rector of San Pablo, headed the expedition and was joined by, among others, Diego Gonzalez Holguín, an expert in Quechua and Aymara, and by Juan de

Hinojosa, professor of the humanities at San Pablo. During the 1580s, the Jesuit college at Lima sent its men to Chachapoyas, Ica, Huancavelica, Tucumán and Santa Cruz de la Sierra, in a feverish crisscrossing of the Peruvian Viceroyalty. In 1593 the college saw the departure of the first Jesuit expedition to the Captaincy of Chile, led like the one to Quito years before by Baltasar de Piñas. In 1596 twenty-two Indian towns were visited by San Pablo's Jesuits while Nicolás Durán evangelized with Juan Font the Andean valley of Jauja.[8]

Religious Hysteria

The seventeenth century did not slow down the tempo of the missions organized by the administrators of San Pablo, although it brought a change in approach which would have saddened men like Bartolomé Hernández and José de Acosta. In the 1610s the Jesuit college was caught in a mass religious hysteria, which opened a painful chapter in the missionary history of San Pablo. In the winter of 1609 a secular priest of Huarochiri, by the name of Francisco de Avila, discovered to his horror that many so-called Christian Indians were in fact adorers of idols and ancient deities. Knowing the Jesuit reputation as missionaries, he wrote in distress to the rector of San Pablo requesting help to crush Indian idolatries. The discovery of Indian idolaters after so many years of evangelization, a fact not surprising at all, was a painful shock felt throughout the entire structure of colonial society. Viceroy and bishop joined forces to root out the evil. Gatherings of civil and ecclesiastical personalities were held to discuss the emergency. Clerical visitors were appointed to go among the idolaters as prosecutors and judges. The administrators of San Pablo were prevailed upon to detach a team of about ten missionaries to accompany the visitors, and to bring the poor Indians back to the straight path of orthodoxy.

Before the departure of visitors and missionaries from Lima, an *auto de fe* was solemnly held in the *Plaza Mayor* only three blocks from San Pablo. Francisco de Avila had brought to Lima six cart-loads of idols, sacred objects and Indian mummies in an effort to impress the viceroy and bishop with the gravity of the situation. On the 20th of December religious Lima packed the *Plaza Mayor* to witness the punishment of an Indian idolater, who suffered 200 lashes and other indignities, and who was sentenced to exile in Chile under the care of the Jesuits. The multitude also saw in silent fear how a huge bonfire reduced to ashes hundreds of idols and mummies. While the Indians of Lima were forced to watch the destruction by fire of many objects which were living symbols of their history and their culture, the intellectuals of San Pablo remained silent and no voice was heard to protest the harsh measure.

The second decade of the seventeenth century saw the Jesuits helping the official visitors to hunt idols and idolaters, destroying the former and trying to reduce to orthodoxy the latter. It was a sad decade indeed in the religious history of Peru. On the 27th of May, 1619, in a letter to the king, the viceroy could triumphantly summarize, to edify His Most Catholic Majesty one may suppose, the results of the holy crusade against idolatry: 20,893 Indians had acknowledged the sin of idolatry and were duly absolved; 1,618 sorcerers were imprisoned, judged and sentenced; 1,768 great idols and 7,288 minor ones were destroyed; 1,365 mummies were discovered and burnt to ashes. To assure that these results would last, the viceroy imprisoned the most dangerous sorcerers, about forty of them, and placed them under the care of the Jesuits in a house not far from San Pablo. *La Casa de la Santa Cruz*, as the house was called, was a sort of jail–school–factory where the Indians were kept forcibly under instruction while working at the looms to support themselves.[9]

Religious hysteria cannot be maintained for long, and eventually sanity and common sense are bound to prevail. San Pablo did not have to wait too long to rediscover its traditional approach to the Indian problem. In August of 1626 San Pablo's rector, Diego de Torres, chose two members of the college to go on a mission among the pagan Indians of Huanuco. Torres wrote instructions for the two missionaries, ideologically based upon the sixteenth-century writings of Alonso de Barzana, Bartolomé Hernández and José de Acosta. In his instructions the rector of San Pablo began by affirming his conviction that the temporary missions to the Indians were among the most important works undertaken by the Jesuit college. He stressed the intellectual approach so dear to Acosta by ordering the two missionaries to gather data on the geographical features of the region, population patterns, native culture, habits and customs, and to report in detail to the college in Lima. The rector also revived two old principles. The Indian language should be mastered as soon as possible, and the missionaries should not enter Indian territories in the company of Spanish soldiers. Finally, "instruction" was placed high above "conversion" when the two missionaries were ordered in the rector's precepts neither to build churches nor to baptize the natives without first sending their findings to San Pablo and waiting for further directives. Torres' words, which reflected the theological wisdom and human common sense of a Christian gentleman, were echoed by the college administrators in the following years to encourage the men appointed to the missions.[10]

New missions were organized in the 1630s, and several men left San Pablo during that decade to preach the gospel in Pachacamac, Cañete, and to cross in all directions the provinces of Huailas and Chinchaycocha in the highlands of the Andes. By the middle of the seventeenth century the Indian missions had become such a remarkable characteristic of the College of San Pablo that more than one observer would overlook the academic and intellectual accomplishments of the institution to admire only the missionary work of the Jesuits. One of those observers was Diego de Córdoba y Salinas who wrote about 1650 his *Teatro de la Iglesia Metropolitana de la Ciudad de los Reyes*, where he described the Jesuit college among other colonial institutions. Salinas suffered the same optical phenomenon experienced today by the visitor to the college church whose eyes are caught by the glittering baroque ornamentation and who seldom pays attention to the neo-classic shell of the building. Salinas saw San Pablo in 1650 as a busy beehive of missionary activities, and knew little or nothing about the great college library, the pharmacy, and the work of teachers and writers.[11]

The volume and complexity of those missionary expeditions were so great in fact that the rectors of San Pablo had to appoint a prefect of missions to be their permanent delegate in planning and executing the missions among the Peruvian Indians. Many men had held that position when in 1689 Juan de la Serna was put in charge of all the missions organized at San Pablo. Juan de la Serna and his successors were meticulous administrators who kept detailed records, thanks to which we learn that not a single year went by from the 1680s to 1767, the year of the Jesuit expulsion, without several missionaries leaving the College of San Pablo to evangelize the Indians. The pattern was unchanged, and again one can follow San Pablo's missionaries north and south along the Pacific coast, to all points of the Andes, and into the plains and forests on the other side of the mountains. Alonso de Barzana had opened the missionary trail for the men of San Pablo back in 1569, and hundreds of Jesuits had followed him over the span of two centuries. The last two men to walk that well-trodden path were José Ignacio de Arevalo and Sebastián Zorrilla, who left the college in 1767, the year the Jesuits were expelled from America and San Pablo closed forever.[12]

Financing the Missions

Traveling in America during colonial days was neither comfortable nor cheap. The men roaming among the Indians preaching the gospel had to face the problem of financing their trips and supporting themselves during the missions before leaving San Pablo. The college rectors, following an old regulation written into the *Constitutions* of the Order by the founder himself, strove not to impose any financial burden on those ministered to by the Jesuits, and forbade the missionaries to demand any financial reward from the Indians. Some rectors even went as far as to forbid the missionaries to beg alms or to accept room and board in the towns in which they preached. This Jesuit policy was acknowledged in 1579 by two *oidores* of the *Audiencia* of Lima, who wrote to the king defending the Jesuits against Viceroy Toledo and who commended in passing the lack of greed on the part of San Pablo's men.[13]

This economic policy placed the burden of financing the missions on the shoulders of San Pablo's administrators. Friends and wealthy benefactors of the college provided at times the money to meet the expenses, covered on occasion by using part of the revenues of the college haciendas. There were bishops and viceroys, like Don Gonzalo de Ocampo, the Prince of Esquilache, and the Count of Lemos, who admired the Jesuit missions and gave the funds required to finance some of them. There were also lay benefactors like the gentleman mentioned in the *Carta anua* of 1656, who left the college the capital required to cover the expenses of an annual mission to the town of Ica. By the middle of the seventeenth century San Pablo had solved the problem of supporting its own missionaries without depending on occasional donations alone. It was during the administration of the Provincial Nicolás Durán in the 1630s that a permanent solution was found. Durán was an old hand at missionary work who went as a missionary in 1596 to the village of Jauja and later headed the famous Jesuit missions of Paraguay. As provincial of Peru he upheld the old policy of not begging alms during the missions, and tried to find other permanent sources of support. He succeeded in his wishes when two young Jesuits, Francisco Ramírez de Olivos and Antonio Aguirre, took their last vow of poverty and renounced their possessions in favor of San Pablo with the specific purpose of supporting the Indian missions. Durán accepted the generous proposal of the young Jesuits and applied their capital to the mission fund of San Pablo. Francisco Ramírez de Olivos signed a legal instrument before the notary Diego Sanchez Vellido, and transferred his property to San Pablo on the 7th of May, 1630. Antonio Aguirre followed his example and in 1633 turned over his property to the college to be used in financing the missions.[14]

The capital formed with the donations of Ramírez de Olivos, Aguirre and some lay benefactors was producing handsome interest in the second half of the seventeenth century. In 1666, the Provincial Luis Jacinto Contreras had to take steps to regulate the administration of the mission fund, and ordered the treasurer of the college to pay faithfully to the prefect of missions all the interest on the capital. The money received from the treasurer could not be diverted to other purposes, the provincial made clear, but had to be expended entirely on the missions. To avoid any exceptions to this rule, the money was placed in a safe locked with two keys, one kept by the prefect of missions and

[129]

the other by the rector himself. Contreras ordered the rector to have as many missions every year as could be supported by revenues from the mission fund, always making sure that the missionaries were well provided with everything needed before leaving San Pablo. At the end of 1672 a new provincial checked the regulations established by Contreras and was satisfied with the way the college administrators were managing the mission fund. By 1689 the capital derived from the properties of Ramírez de Olivos had climbed to 24,500 pesos, which, deposited with San Pablo's treasurer at an interest of 4% per annum, was giving to the prefect of missions 980 pesos every year.[15]

The missions took weeks of preparation and planning. As soon as the rector made public the names of new missionaries and the places they would visit, the college became a beehive of activity with constant comings and goings of Negro slaves and Indian servants. It is not easy to travel even today through the Andean region and the forests of South America, and in colonial days it was quite a challenge. The Jesuits of San Pablo did not leave anything to chance and spent weeks preparing to meet the challenge of the mighty rivers, the mountains, and the jungles. The prefect of missions went out accompanied by some of the college slaves to purchase riding equipment, and hardy mules which could climb the steep slopes of the sierra. He visited the mule-dealers of Lima, who imported animals of the best quality, bred on the plains of faraway Córdoba and Tucumán. In the second half of the seventeenth century the prefect of missions was paying 200 and even 300 pesos for a good riding mule, an excessive price to which the Visitor Gonzalo de Lira objected in 1687.[16]

Riding equipment was only the beginning of the long preparations. The prefect of missions provided the missionaries with shoes, clothing and bedding for different altitudes and climates, and with large tents of canvas together with the ropes and poles needed to encamp under the open skies. He also provided cooking equipment and provisions to last for weeks, a portable chapel and altar, and all kinds of medicines from the college pharmacy. The missionaries also received tools and supplies to reshoe the horses and mules on the way, parasols and umbrellas, soap and candles, paper, ink and pens to keep records and to write to San Pablo, religious articles to distribute among the prospective converts, and even a small library of spiritual and theological books for personal reading and for the preparation of sermons. All these articles had to be purchased in different parts of the city and brought on the shoulders of the slaves to one of the large courtyards of the college. Friends and relatives of the men leaving for the missions also brought to San Pablo all kinds of gifts to be added to the already abundant supplies. Some cash for emergencies were finally given to the missionaries: 20 pesos to the men going to Huamanga; 55 pesos to those who went as far as La Paz, 60 or 70 if they proceeded ahead to Oruro and Potosí, and 80 pesos to the missionaries going to the region of Chuquisaca.[17]

The departure day was filled with the color and noise of a *fiesta*. The pack mules had been loaded at dawn by the Negro slaves. A few Indian servants, wearing the bright ponchos kept for festive days, waited holding the halters to accompany the fathers. Jesuits, students, friends and relatives gathered in the college church to pray for the success of the mission and to receive the rector's blessing. In a variegated, noisy group they marched towards the outskirts of Lima, their voices mingling with the horseshoes of the mules resounding on the stony pavement of the streets. Outside the city they halted briefly for a last embrace in the Jesuit tradition, and the missionaries marched on towards the sierra and the world of the Indians, leaving behind their own people and the comforts of the viceregal capital.

The Sodalities

The Jesuits who stayed behind at the college, envious perhaps of the roaming missionaries, could not contain their lives within the rigid frame of the academic structures, either. From its beginnings, the College of San Pablo broke out time and again into a bewildering flurry of activities, which, together with the missions, entangled and sometimes even hid the academic life of the college. Diego de Bracamonte, the first rector of San Pablo in 1568, went through the city teaching Christian doctrine to the children and organizing with them noisy processions along the main streets of Lima. Gerónimo de Portillo became a thunderous preacher and used to lead a group of young Spaniards into the hospitals to minister to the poor. Luis López was the friend of the Negroes, and on Sundays he would bring to the college church as many as 1,000 slaves for a weekly religion class. Others taught the Indians and regularly visited the city jail to bring comfort to the prisoners.[18] Many of these priestly activities were institutionalized with the passing of the years and gave rise to San Pablo's lay sodalities, one of the most eye-catching ''ornaments'' of the Jesuit college at Lima.

The sodalities of San Pablo were lay associations formed for the religious development of the members and for charitable purposes. Following the example of their Roman college where a sodality had existed since 1563, the Jesuits of Lima organized at first a students' sodality. A select group of seniors from San Pablo's school of humanities was invited in the 1580s to join the sodality, and the college rector together with the Viceroy Martín Enríquez presided over the foundational solemnities and the first reception of members. This sodality became not only an arena for the moral training of the students, but moreover a tool used by the Jesuit masters to produce academic excellence. The sodality not only demanded that its members maintain a high level of academic competency, but also organized literary competitions which were attended by the best society of Lima and were presided over most of the time by civil authorities. The written works of the young scholars were read to the public, who were also entertained by the students themselves with excellent songs and music. A jury of Jesuits and lay experts awarded prizes to the winners of the academic competitions.[19]

The students' sodality, a colonial fraternity with religious overtones, proved so successful that before the end of the sixteenth century the Jesuits of San Pablo were applying the same formula outside the college to other groups in the city. The Jesuit mestizo Bartolomé de Santiago was the founder of a new sodality for the Indians of Lima, and Juan Sebastián organized another one for the city clergy. San Pablo's Rector Hernando de Mendoza, brother of the Viceroy García Hurtado de

Mendoza, and Luis de Estella were instrumental in 1596 in starting a sodality for Spanish gentlemen, which under the popular name of *Nuestra Señora de La O* would in time become one of the most important welfare agencies in colonial Peru. Those working for the religious development of the Negro slaves also began a Negro sodality before the end of the century. The younger children were organized by the Jesuits into a religious group known as *La Decuria*, a word with strong Roman and classical connotations. By 1600 five sodalities were active in the College of San Pablo.[20]

The seventeenth century, a deeply religious century in colonial Lima, saw an increase in the lay associations operating in the Jesuit college. About 1614 the students' sodality divided into two: one for the school of humanities, the other for the major faculties of philosophy and theology, which was also open to the students and professors of San Marcos University. Since the sodality of *La O* had become a rather exclusive association for Spaniards of a certain social rank, a new sodality was created for young Spanish men who were neither students nor socially prominent. About 1630 Bernabé Cobo, one of the great writers of San Pablo, wrote in his well-known *Fundación de Lima* that nine sodalities were active in San Pablo. A few years later a very curious phenomenon took place within the structure of these nine sodalities, a phenomenon which speaks to the modern reader of the social and racial tensions in the colonial city.[21]

From the very beginning the men of San Pablo had accepted the social patterns of the city and had organized their lay sodalities by classes: Spaniards, Indians, slaves, students, and clerics. Before the middle of the seventeenth century racial and social tensions cracked the initial structures and the sodalities split further along color lines and social positions. The Negro sodality, for instance, expanded into three different associations. The "criollo" and "ladino" Negroes, born in Peru and well assimilated in language and customs to the Spanish culture, demanded their own sodality apart from the "bozales" Negroes born in Africa who could understand neither the Spanish language nor the Spanish way of life. A new sodality of native Peruvian Negroes was therefore created, only to split once again when racial tensions developed between the pure Negroes and the "pardos" or mulattoes. The historian Jacinto Barrasa, who lived for years at San Pablo and was personally involved in the work of the sodalities, gave the reasons for this further division in a short sentence: ". . . [the Jesuits] becoming aware *that the diversity of color* gave rise to incompatibility of spirit. . . , it was judged prudent to divide in two the sodality of the 'criollo' Negroes . . ."[22] (my italics). This racial tension would also sunder the children's *decuria*, one being reserved for Spanish children and the other for "negritos."

A similar process of social differentiation was also in progress among the Indians in the first half of the seventeenth century. The Jesuits of San Pablo detected that process and divided the initial Indian sodality into three different confraternities. One was reserved for "ladino" Indians and Indians who served in the militia. The second sodality was the regular religious association for Peruvian Indians, while the third was formed in 1659 by Father Rafael Venegas for Indians of the Kingdom of Chile. A document of the times informs us that "it was acknowledged that many Indians from the kingdom of Chile had moved to this city [Lima], some of them slaves and others free men, and they were uprooted and lost, without going to the sacrament of penance or caring for the other things needed for their salvation."[23] In trying to help them and because of the impossibility of fusing them with the Peruvian Indians, Venegas created a new group known as the "Sodality of the Indians of Chile."

According to San Pablo's catalogues of 1659 and 1670 there were thirteen sodalities operating at the college, divided into the following groupings: clerics, Spanish gentlemen of the upper class, young Spanish merchants, university students, students of the humanities, "ladino" Indians, Peruvian Indians, Indians of Chile, "criollo" Negroes, mulattoes, "bozales" Negroes, Spanish children, and Negro children. The Jesuits had allowed, or rather fostered, this luxurious baroque proliferation of sodalities, moved by the social and racial conditions of Lima. About twenty Jesuits of San Pablo, under the general direction of the college rector, were directly involved, serving as mentors and leaders of the thirteen sodalities, and they seem to have enjoyed this great variety of associations. Once a week the Jesuit directors gathered all the members of the sodalities in the college, making the academic halls burst with all kinds of religious activities, solemn processions, sermons, meditations, reception of the sacraments, religious novenas, and even public penitential scourgings. The Jesuits throve in this dynamic religious environment, and they worked constantly outside the college to attract more and more persons to their sodalities. The clergy sodality, which began with only a few pious priests, had about 50 members by 1598 and 150 in the first years of the seventeenth century. *La O*, the sodality for Spanish gentlemen, had gathered 250 men before the end of the sixteenth century and in the first two years of the new century had almost doubled the number of its members. There were almost 700 members in *La O* in 1615, and the number fluctuated between 800 and 1,000 by the middle of the seventeenth century.[24]

Non-Religious Roles of the Sodalities

The popularity of San Pablo's sodalities and the Jesuit interest in them can hardly be explained by religious reasons alone, even if the deep religious feeling of the era be taken into account. The Jesuit sodalities proliferated and attracted so many persons because they fulfilled certain roles in colonial society, which had nothing or very little to do with the religious or supernatural aspects of life. Due to their division along social and racial lines, membership in one of the sodalities was a symbolic means of identification with a certain colonial class. The origin of the sodalities for "ladino" Indians and "criollo" Negroes and their further subdivisions cannot be fully explained otherwise. The creation of a Spanish sodality for young merchants and young office-holders, keeping *La O* as an exclusive association for white persons of a higher social status, also postulates a similar explanation.

The sodality of Our Lady of *La O* had become an exclusive, aristo-cratic association before 1650, and membership in it a status symbol in

[135]

colonial Lima. Viceroys, *oidores*, military men of high rank, titles of nobility, and wealthy landowners could be counted among the members of *La O*, and they surrounded the sodality with a social glow which attracted many others. Perhaps nothing illustrates better the role of *La O* as a status symbol than the solemnities held at San Pablo in 1688 while Father Fernandez Tardío was director and Captain Alonso Jiménez Vela prefect of the sodality. On the 25th of December of that year, the sodality passed a resolution accepting into the brotherhood of *La O* His Holiness Innocent XI and all his successors in the Chair of Peter, and the imbecile King of Spain, Charles II, "the Bewitched," and all his successors on the throne of Spain. The resolution was executed by the director and president of *La O* and accepted in the name of His Holiness by the Archbishop of Lima, Melchor de Liñan, and by the Viceroy the Duke of La Palata in the name of His Majesty. On that 25th of December the archbishop and the viceroy ascended the altar in the Church of San Pablo and signed the legal documents, which conferred upon the vicar of Christ and the king of Spain the honor of membership in the colonial sodality of *La O*.[25]

San Pablo's sodalities were not static confraternities engaged only in pious exercises. They were permeated by the dynamic spirit of the baroque, which animated the Jesuits themselves. The members of the sodality, following a path opened to them by the men of San Pablo, knew how to turn any religious festivity into a gaudy social affair. The Jesuit correspondence of the period and the diarist Suardo, who entered in his diary all the important social events in the Lima of the 1630s, speak time and again of the solemnities held by San Pablo's sodalities. The viceroy was present most of the time with the *caballeros* of his court, the *oidores* and the senior clergy. Society ladies, whose husbands and sons were members of the sodalities, filled the college church to attend the services. The cloisters and halls of the college were decorated for these special occasions by the best families of Lima with their jewelry, silks and brocades. Carriages and finely draped horses and mules under the care of Indian and Negro slaves waited outside for their masters, forming a colorful wreath around the imposing walls of San

Pablo. It is easy to understand how this type of religious festivity became also a fine occasion to meet important people, interchange social pleasantries, and display jewels, ornaments and robes.[26]

Taking advantage of their periodic solemnities, the sodalities of San Pablo offered to the public some of the best entertainment available in the colonial capital. The literary competitions and plays presented by the students' sodality had undoubtedly an entertaining aspect, besides being of academic value. Music and singing were an essential part of the religious services, and many would go to San Pablo just to enjoy the music and hear the fine choir of the college. San Pablo had a very unique band of Negro performers, slaves of the college and trained by the Jesuits. The Jesuit Miguel Castro was their director for the first half of the seventeenth century, and under his care the Negroes had become accomplished players of clarinets and *chirimias*, the Spanish version of the Scottish bagpipe. These Negro musicians performed at the festivities organized by the sodalities and became so famous that they were in great demand even outside the college. Besides clarinets and bagpipes, one could listen at San Pablo to trumpets, drums, flutes, and to the more delicate music of string instruments like guitars, lutes and *rabeles*. If the Negro slaves were well known as musicians, the Jesuit-trained Indians had formed a choir that could sing religious and secular compositions in Latin, Quechua and Spanish, and could be heard at times even in the cathedral. Their fine singing was certainly another attraction of San Pablo's religious festivals. On occasion some venturesome Jesuits joined the lay musicians and singers in their public performances, to which the Provincial Juan de Frías objected in a letter to the rector of San Pablo on the 11th of November, 1623.[27]

Religious processions, so much in favor with all the sodalities, also had an obvious character of popular entertainment. Many times they exuded the gay atmosphere of a parade with light music and singing, and they always gave everybody an opportunity to wear his best clothing and join neighbors and friends along the crowded streets of the city. The evening processions had the added attraction of fireworks, which thrilled the gasping multitude and filled the Lima skies with lights and noise. The frequency, size and complexity of these fireworks had become so great that by the second half of the seventeenth century the college was expending a notable amount of money on this form of popular entertainment. In May of 1661 the rector of San Pablo received a warning from his superiors, and was told simply to tone down the pyrotechnic fervor of his community. Andrés de Rada, who issued the warning, did not understand that the noisy processions and the luxurious display of fireworks from the college towers sprang from the same spirit which animated the thunderous oratory of the college preachers, the affected poetry of the school of humanities, and the baroque theater presented on the college stage. Fireworks were never discontinued at San Pablo, and the common people kept coming to the Jesuit college not just to honor the saints, but to contemplate in awe the towers of San Pablo erupting in a cataract of lights and colors.[28]

Besides their roles as symbols of social status and sources of popular entertainment, the sodalities of San Pablo also became agencies of public welfare. Colonial welfare was in the hands of religious confraternities, and the Jesuit sodalities were among the most active in the field. Through donations and periodic offerings of the members, the sodalities acquired a certain amount of wealth which was partly used to meet the needs of the poor. The Indian sodality, for instance, began accumulating property in the last decade of the sixteenth century, and used it for works of charity. Wealthy Indians made their wills in favor of the sodality, which could later assist the most destitute members of their community. In May of 1591, the Indian Alonso Vilcatanta left his land to the sodality. In August of 1606 an Indian lady, called María de Jesús and identified as "ladina," bequeathed to the college a house, a fruit garden, and two slaves from her property. In 1626 another Indian woman, Juana Pazna, gave a house to the sodality requesting that ten Masses be said for her every year. In 1631 Alonso Tulca donated his land "for the good of his soul," and in 1634 an Indian named Juan Cristobal applied to the sodality the interest from 330 pesos owed him by another Indian called Francisco Quispi.[29]

By the end of the seventeenth century San Pablo's Indian sodality owned six houses and two stores in Lima, one house in Callao, tracts of land in the districts of Late and Chancay, and a good plot in the Jesuit hacienda of San Juan not far from the city. In the eighteenth century the Indian sodality acquired new properties, and in 1752 the administrator could report to the Jesuit provincial an income of almost 500 pesos from three new houses in Macambo Street, from an orchard and vegetable garden, and from a vacant lot near the convent of *La Buena Muerte*. Although part of this capital was consumed by the elaborate religious festivities, the remaining capital was used to help the Indian hospital, to assist needy members of the sodality, and to cover the expenses of baptisms, weddings and burials of the poor.[30]

The sodality of *La O* was naturally more wealthy and therefore more active than the Indian sodality in the field of welfare. The gentlemen of *La O* volunteered in turns to serve in the hospitals of San Andrés and Santa Ana, visited the city jail, and tried to free through their monetary contributions the Spaniards imprisoned there for debt. Once a year they contributed six new beds to San Andrés' Hospital, and twice a year they gave a banquet, worthy of a Renaissance prince, to the patients of the Spanish and the Indian hospitals. These banquets and the exuberant ritual surrounding them are a further proof, if further proof is needed, of the baroque structures of life so much loved by the Peruvian Jesuits. A meal of the most delicate dishes was prepared in the convent of San José. The wealthy families lent for the occasion their gold and silver tableware, and trays and bowls of pure Potosí silver to carry the food. Rich baskets filled with all kinds of fruits, sweets, pastry and cakes dipped in wine were donated by the members of the sodality. The Spanish gentlemen of *La O*, led by the oldest and best known members of San Pablo's faculty, carried the food through the streets of Lima towards San Andrés' Hospital, while the Negro musicians of the Jesuit college filled the city with the sounds of their trumpets and bagpipes. The poor and the curious crowded the sidewalks, and the balconies along the route were occupied by the wives and daughters of not a few of those who passed carrying the food. It was, as Jacinto Barrasa wrote, "a solemn and ostentatious procession stretching three city blocks." On arrival at the hospital, and while the Negro musicians still played, the Spanish gentlemen and the Jesuits washed the hands of the patients and waited on them, serving the delicate dishes prepared by the nuns.[31]

Among the welfare services of *La O*, those derived from the so-called *contrato espiritual* or spiritual contract afford a good example of a religious device turned into a tool of great economic consequence. From the beginning of the sodality the custom was established of collecting money at the death of one of the members to offer Masses for his soul. To avoid wasting time in collecting the money, a fund was created a few years later to cover the expenses of funeral Masses as soon as the death of a member was announced. In the 1620s the practice was somewhat modified, opening the way for a rapid increase in the capital of *La O*. A resolution was passed in July of 1622 to enter into a "spiritual contract" with any person, member of the sodality or not, who would like to partake of the spiritual benefits of the Masses offered for the departed members of *La O*. The contract was bilateral. The individuals had to donate 72 pesos to the fund of *La O*, and in turn the sodality placed their names on the roster of those for whom Masses would be offered at the hour of death.

The piety of the times plus the social prestige of being associated with *La O* made the spiritual contract one of the great financial successes of colonial Lima. There were years when the sodality, without taking into account other sources of revenue, received 60,000 pesos from individuals entering into the contract. The prominent of Peru gave the 72 pesos and signed the contract, and the common people followed them by the hundreds. In the records of the spiritual contract one finds the names of viceroys, like the Count of Santisteban, the Count of Cañete, the Duke and Duchess of La Palata, the Archbishops Diego Morcillo and Diego Ladrón de Guevara, the Marquis of Castelfuerte and many others. Together with them, hundreds of unknown persons gave 72 pesos to *La O* which, although an exclusive association, did not hesitate to receive that money even from Indians and Negroes.[32]

This fund of *La O*, which had a yearly increase of several thousand pesos, became a sound source of support for some members of the colonial clergy. The capital could cover the expenses of 6,000 or 7,000 Masses every year, and obviously not all of them could be celebrated by the Jesuits of San Pablo. The administrators of *La O* had to look for "poor and virtuous" priests of the viceroyalty to whom to offer the hundreds of Masses which could not be said in the Jesuit college. Each priest received from *La O* six pesos for every Mass he offered, and in this manner the fund created "to alleviate the souls of the departed" helped to support the priests working in the poorest section of the viceroyalty. Soon the Jesuit director and the lay administrators realized that not even several thousand Masses a year could consume the income available, and they began thinking of new means to use that capital.

Since hospital work had been traditional in the sodality, part of the revenues of the contract were channeled in that direction. The great banquets already described were reduced, and more money was invested in "a kind of financial support more profitable and enduring." New beds, medicines, clothing and food were bought with the money of *La O* and donated to the hospitals. The accumulated capital was also used in another traditional service, to cancel the debts of poor Spaniards imprisoned for insolvency. A good amount of that capital was applied by the administrators of *La O* to meet a peculiar need of colonial society. Those were still the days when marriage arrangements involved the two families concerned and included delicate discussions about a proper dowry. Many marriageable girls, who were either orphans or from very poor families, found it difficult to marry because they lacked a satisfactory dowry. The gentlemen of *La O*, concerned with the problem of Christian families, invested part of their capital to provide dowries for poor girls who showed promise of being good wives and mothers.[33]

Besides the capital derived from the contract, the sodality of *La O* owned rural and urban properties whose revenues were spent in religious solemnities and in alms and gifts for the poor. In the last years of the seventeenth century, when Don Juan de Murga, the *Alcalde Ordinario* of Lima, was treasurer, the sodality enjoyed a net revenue of 59,739 pesos and two reales. By the middle of the eighteenth century,

La O owned in Lima alone 27 houses, seven stores, and two *callejones* or alleyways which gave an annual rent of 10,116 pesos and seven reales, most of it used in charities. When the Jesuits were expelled in 1767, the *Tribunal de Temporalidades* absorbed all the properties and revenues of *La O*. After the independence of Peru in the nineteenth century, the Bureau of Public Welfare took over those properties and administered them up to our own day for the benefit of the sick and the poor.[34]

Chaplains in Peace and War

The work of the Indian missions and the proliferation of the thirteen sodalities did not exhaust the boundless energies of the men of San Pablo. Missions and sodalities were the socio–religious contributions of the college to colonial society. They were highly organized and directed by the rectors, and the moral responsibility of the entire institution. Besides the missions and the sodalities, the individual Jesuits still found many occasional outlets for their desire to influence a world in the making. The college preachers, bursting with the grandiloquence of a baroque era, delivered sermons to packed audiences in San Pablo's church, the cathedral, and other curches of Lima. There were years in the seventeenth century when the Jesuits of San Pablo managed to preach more than 250 formal sermons during the weeks of Lent alone. But the city churches were not quite enough. The Jesuit preachers, as the college playwrights and actors had also done, left San Pablo to deliver their sermons throughout the streets and plazas of Lima, wherever a noticeable group would have gathered.

A Jesuit preached every day in Quechua to the poor Indians, who waited in line at the college door to collect the leavings from the Jesuit table. Another man of San Pablo also went every day to the corner of the *Plaza Mayor* to preach to the Negroes and mestizos, who waited there to be hired as day-laborers. The public market was one of the places regularly visited by the Jesuits. The Indian merchants and their customers, sitting on the ground among the scattered wares, had all the time in the world to listen to the preachers of San Pablo. On Friday mornings the fish market was the center of action. Fish dealers broke the stillness of dawn shouting their offerings from the morning catch. Servants of the wealthy houses and middle-class housewives went around, looking for their favored fish and bargaining for lower prices. Indian and Negro slaves were bent under the dripping boxes just arrived by mulepack from Callao. Every week, in the middle of that confusion, appeared the preachers of San Pablo, bell in hand, and for a while transactions were suspended and a short sermon delivered.[35]

The regular visit to jails and hospitals, to comfort the inmates and patients and to catechize them, was a foundational tradition of the Jesuit Order. In Lima, the Jesuits of San Pablo carried on that tradition in collaboration with the lay sodalities. Once or twice a week, depending on their free time and zeal, some teachers and students from the Jesuit college spent a few hours in the hospitals of San Andrés, Santa Ana, and San Bartolomé y Espíritu Santo. In 1659 the Visitor Andrés de Rada acknowledged and praised the existing tradition, ordered its continuation, and appointed four Jesuits to act as assistant chaplains of the four hospitals. Besides this work in jails and hospitals, the Jesuits of San Pablo began in the seventeenth century to make regular visits to the *obrajes* of the city, where Indians and Negroes were driven to exhaustion by white overseers and where the workers lived in virtual imprisonment. On Thursdays young Jesuits, students at San Pablo, used to visit ten *obrajes* in the district of San Lazaro, catechizing the Indians and Negroes, and trying to alleviate their wretched condition. A pottery located near San Bartolomé's Hospital, the city mint, and several textile factories were also occasionally visited by priests from San Pablo.[36]

Of more romantic appeal than the visits to hospitals, jails and *obrajes* was the Jesuit service as chaplain with the fleets and in the armies. José de Acosta was one of the first men of San Pablo to serve as chaplain when he joined the expedition organized by Viceroy Toledo in 1574 against the Chiriguano Indians in Upper Peru. In 1577 English pirates threatened Panama, and the viceroy sent Spanish ships from Callao to check the English encroachment. Father Miguel Fuentes, the first professor of the humanities at San Pablo, went as chaplain on that occasion. In 1594 news arrived that the pirate Richard Hawkins had penetrated into the *Mar del Sur*, and was razing and plundering the coasts of the Empire. Lima was excited and so were the Jesuits. Ships were fitted out in haste and sent in pursuit of the pirate. When the Spanish ships sailed from Callao, two Jesuits were on board as chaplains, Father Diego de Paz and Brother Gaspar Antonio. Diego de Paz wrote later from Panama to the brethren of San Pablo to inform them that God had been once more at the side of Spain with a great victory over the pirates.[37]

The threat of pirates was so great that it became imperative to arm the coastal cities. In 1592 the Viceroy García Hurtado de Mendoza sent a ship across the Pacific Ocean to China, to buy metals in the Orient to cast the cannons needed to defend Callao. At the request of the viceroy two Jesuits were appointed to act as chaplains in that long, solitary crossing of the Pacific. They were Father Leandro Felipe, who had taught the humanities at San Pablo since 1584, and Brother Gonzalo de Belmonte. Their trip to the Orient proved to be an odyssey of eight years, most of them spent in the Jesuit college at Goa where they were confined by Portuguese authorities. They returned to Lima around 1600, probably making the crossing to Acapulco in the Manila Galleon. Being the good Jesuits they were, Felipe and Belmonte did not come back to San Pablo empty-handed. They brought home, as souvenirs of their long sojourn in the Orient, rich brocades and sacred vestments, and draperies made of silk from China, which adorned the college church on solemn occasions.[38]

The Jesuits of San Pablo did not interrupt their services as chaplains during the seventeenth century. When the arrival of new pirates shocked the quiet colonial city, some Jesuits were always among the first to rush to Callao ready to join the crews sent to patrol the Peruvian coasts. In 1615, for instance, Dutch pirates struck at the heart of the viceroyalty, bombarding Callao and sinking the Spanish flagship moored at the docks. Terror spread through Lima, and the Viceroy the Marquis of Montesclaros rushed with the militia and a multitude of volunteers to defend the port city. Several Jesuits left San Pablo to join Montesclaros' men, and the Jesuit provincial delivered a sermon to the troops exhorting the soldiers to crush the enemies of Spain, the Dutch heretics who were also the enemies of God. In 1624 eleven Dutch men-of-war again threatened the Peruvian coast, and again the Jesuits provided the chaplains for sailors and soldiers. The men of San Pablo served again in the same capacity in the 1680s in the ships sent by the Duke of La Palata to clear the Mar del Sur of pirates, and they were available once more in the 1690s every time patrol ships left Callao.[39]

For two centuries the Jesuits of San Pablo kept open the missionary trail. San Pablo served as headquarters and home base for hundreds of men who conquered the Andes and met the challenge of the forests and rivers in a continent still new. The Jesuits went forward in their missionary excursions year after year, soldiers of a silent conquest, to return months later to San Pablo with fantastic tales about new peoples and new horizons. They fired the imagination of the young students, and they kept the college always oriented towards the world of the Indian. Planted almost at the center of the city, San Pablo was also a crossroads of colonial life, constantly busy with the comings and goings of noble-men, merchants, students, Indians, children and slaves. The college's thirteen sodalities, like the arms of a gigantic octopus, reached into every level of society. Elaborate religious solemnities, works of charity and welfare, ostentatious processions and a ceaseless crisscrossing of the city to visit hospitals, *obrajes* and jails, were the outer signs of an ex-uberant spirit, which could not be contained within the walls of the college.

San Pablo was not only an outstanding academic institution, but, to use the words of a colonial observer, "a great and complex machine." That complex machine revolved like a huge spinning wheel constantly in-creasing its velocity, weaving around the academic structures of the col-lege the yarn of hundreds of socio-religious activities. Many interpreta-tions could be given to explain the exuberance and luxuriousness of life at San Pablo, but none would be satisfactory unless one takes into account the religious fervor of the Counter Reformation and the dynamic tensions of a baroque era. The winds of the baroque, blowing so strongly in America, covered the college church with the most exquisite orna-mentation in colonial Lima. The winds of the baroque shaped the way of

[145]

life at the Jesuit college. San Pablo became a baroque institution and the Jesuit professors baroque intellectuals whose lives could not be contained within the academic channels, and overflowed time and again into all fields of colonial society.

VII

THE END OF A COLONIAL INSTITUTION

During the last days of February, 1767, life went on as usual in the cloisters of San Pablo. The Jesuit school of humanities was still the only school of its type in Lima, and the best youngsters of the city crowded its classrooms and patios. After 200 years, San Pablo was still training the future students of San Marcos University. The courses in moral theology were taught and the public seminar on problems of conscience was still in session at the Jesuit college. The Jesuits of San Pablo, heirs to the great tradition established by José de Acosta, Esteban de Ávila, Diego de Avendaño and Pedro de Oñate, were still publicly asking some embarrassing questions and trying painfully to find some of the answers. St. Thomas and Suarez still led the young Jesuits into the realms of philosophy and theology, although the old monolithic systems were being challenged by new philosophers whose works were read at San Pablo. The college's pharmacy had grown, and in those first months of 1767 it was the pride of Jesuit administrators. Men like Zeitler, Esteyneffer and Rojo were spreading medical knowledge throughout America.

In those closing days of February, 1767, nobody in San Pablo suspected that His Most Christian Majesty, Charles III of Spain, had signed on the 27th a decree banishing the Jesuit Order from all his dominions.

San Pablo's professors, who toiled daily teaching hundreds of youngsters, would have smiled bitterly at the irony, had they known that the execution of the royal decree had been entrusted to a former Jesuit pupil, the Count of Aranda.

A royal courier entered the viceregal capital of Lima on the 20th of August, and handed the King's dispatches to Viceroy Manuel de Amat who, alone in his private chambers, broke the seals and eagerly began reading the documents. The sovereign appealed to Amat's love and fidelity to carry out without delay the orders transmitted by the Count of Aranda, persuading himself that those orders were of "great importance for the royal service and the security of the empire." Amat carefully put aside the documents and summoned two men to his presence: the chamberlain Don José, his most trusted counselor, and Don Antonio Elexpuru, his private secretary. They were the only two persons in Lima to share with the viceroy the tremendous secret of the expulsion of the Jesuits.[1]

The arrival of the royal courier in Lima was like a stone thrown into the middle of a pond. Wild rumors spread to the four corners of the city, and on the 21st of August everybody in Lima talked about the news of the day, the arrival of secret dispatches from Buenos Aires. Civil officials whispered the rumors in the halls of the viceregal palace and in the tribunals of the *Audiencia*. The news broke through the thick walls of the cloisters and priests and monks made conjectures. Women had a new topic of conversation on their way to the markets and fountains. Soldiers thought of war, and merchants feared new taxes. Even slaves and Indians felt, with the sensitivity of wounded animals, the new excitement gripping the city.

Viceroy Amat, at first amused, but then afraid that somebody might suspect the true content of the royal orders, decided to mislead public opinion. On the 22nd of August, he sent a messenger to Callao with orders to get the ship *San José* (popularly known as *El Peruano*) ready, so that it would be seaworthy as soon as possible. These orders leaked out as Amat had intended, and soon the *limeños* thought that they had the key to solve the mystery contained in the secret dispatches: some sort of military expedition was at hand, and the viceroy had been ordered to equip the best ship available in Peru.[2] When Amat heard the new rumors, he smiled and began feverish preparations for the expulsion of the Jesuits. It had taken Viceroy de Croix twenty-five days to execute the royal decree in Mexico; it would take Amat only slightly longer than two weeks to destroy what the Jesuits had built in two centuries.

The Closing of San Pablo

On the 8th of September, 1767, religious Lima filled the churches to celebrate the Nativity of Our Lady. In the afternoon the companies of soldiers posted in the city, wearing their best uniforms, went to the church of the Benedictines to honor their patroness, Our Lady of Monserrat. Lima society gathered there for the singing of vespers, and the viceroy presided at the solemnities from his throne in the sanctuary, although that afternoon his mind was not on the religious services. Only three persons in Lima knew about the impending expulsion of the Jesuits, and in a few hours the viceroy would need hundreds of disciplined men to execute the royal decree. Amat was worried; while the monks chanted in the choir, his excellency turned his eyes time and again toward the four hundred soldiers who occupied the main body of the church. At dawn he would strike with all the might of the *alter rex*, and the Jesuits would be swept from Peru forever.

Amat left the church while the soldiers stood at attention. Although he had carefully planned all the events of the day, the viceroy sounded casual when he told the captain of the militia that he was pleased and would like to entertain the soldiers that evening in the courtyard of his palace.[3] An hour later more than four hundred armed men assembled in front of Amat's palace ready to spend a pleasant evening. In years past they had celebrated the *fiesta* of their patroness, but this was the first time that they had been invited to the viceregal palace. Some of them were surprised at the generous gesture, but nobody suspected that the invitation had anything to do with the mysterious dispatches that had arrived two weeks before from Buenos Aires. At dusk, fires were lit in the courtyard and dinner was served. The host was generous that night

[149]

and had ordered two calves slaughtered and a delicious stew prepared with potatoes, *zapallos* and rice. Bread was abundant, and two large jars of wine and one of *aguardiente* made the meal more convivial. Music was played and thirty-six new decks of cards were distributed among the soldiers.[4]

While the four hundred soldiers ate, sang and played cards, Don Manuel de Amat stole silently from the palace and went to the theater to see Calderón's play *El Mayor Monstruo Los Celos*.[5] Almost at the same time the eighty-eight Jesuits living at San Pablo had finished their evening prayers and were retiring to their rooms for the night. The brother-in-charge put out the candles in the halls and patios, and the college was wrapped in darkness and silence. In sharp contrast, the theater was flooded with lights and the audience cheered and applauded. The viceroy was enjoying himself, but that night not even the great Calderón could make him forget the soldiers singing in the patios of his palace or the Jesuits sleeping in the cloisters of San Pablo. When the viceroy left the theater and returned to the palace, the soldiers had finished their meal and were now quietly playing cards by the fires. Only eight hours were left to execute the expulsion of the Jesuits, and only three persons in Lima knew the best-kept secret of the century. Even those chosen by Amat to be executors of the royal decree were ignorant of the viceroy's plans. They had retired as usual and were now resting in their homes in different parts of the city.

Time was running short, but Don Manuel de Amat was in no hurry. Slowly he mounted the stairs, entered his private chamber and sat at his desk ready to spend a sleepless night. His secretary, Antonio Elexpuru, brought in lights, paper, pens and ink, and the viceroy of Peru began writing short notes:

In the Palace, September 8th of 1767—At 11 o'clock P.M. Without any excuse whatsoever, because none will be accepted, come immediately and quickly to the Palace through the gate facing the *Desamparados* [a Jesuit church at the back of Amat's palace]. You will find the door slightly ajar. I need you for matters of great service to the King, and I warn you to come so secretly that not even those of your household would realize that you have gone out.

Amat[6]

When the viceroy had written a good number of these notes, messengers were dispatched to deliver them immediately. They went into the night, and very soon long shadows could be seen moving rapidly toward the back gate of the viceregal palace. They were the most important men in Lima—nobles and *oidores*, judges and lawyers, members of the *cabildo* and of the *consulado*, rich merchants and professors of the university. Some of them blessed themselves with the sign of the cross and muttered a short prayer to Our Lady of the *Desamparados* when they crossed in front of the Jesuit church. They had been awakened in the middle of the night and summoned to the palace, and they were apprehensive and afraid. The Rimac, only a few feet away, could not be seen in the darkness, but the sound of its waters running under the stone bridge was easily heard from the palace's back gate. Some of the men shivered and rushed into the building. Inside the palace their faces showed surprise, shock and fear. They did not like the noise coming from the courtyard crowded with soldiers, and they talked to each other in whispers.

When Don Manuel de Amat entered the reception hall, he felt hundreds of eyes questioning him in silence. It was already the 9th of September, 1767, the day chosen to execute the decree of expulsion in Lima, and the viceroy broke for the first time the secret kept so well since the 20th of August. Amat spoke slowly but firmly, while watching intently the impact of his words on the men who crowded the hall. Most of them avoided looking straight at the face of the viceroy, and stood expressionless in silence. Not a few among those men had studied under Jesuit masters in the cloisters of San Pablo; many had gone frequently to the religious services of the college, some had Jesuit confessors, and others were linked to them through commercial enterprises. There were in the palace that night the best lawyers and judges of the viceroyalty, men who shared the judicial power of the state and who knew that no man should be condemned unless proven guilty in a proper judicial action. All of them bent to the despotic will of Charles III, and no word was said in defense of the Jesuits.

By about four A.M. Amat had everything ready. He personally assigned the troops to go to the different Jesuit houses and named the civil executors of the royal decree. The viceroy knew that San Pablo was the heart of all Jesuit institutions in Peru, and he chose the *oidor* Don Domingo de Orrantia and the *alcalde* Don José Puente de Ibañez to lead the soldiers who would occupy the Jesuit college. Of the seven hundred men who left the *Plaza Mayor* to execute the royal wishes, more than three hundred followed Orrantia and walked in silence the three blocks separating the palace from San Pablo. Between four and five o'clock on the morning of the 9th of September, royal troops with their weapons ready surrounded the Jesuit college at Lima. A few Indians passing by rushed away in fear. Indoors the Jesuit community had not yet awakened.[7]

Domingo de Orrantia, alumnus of San Pablo, knew the college and the Jesuit customs well. He went over to the heavy wooden door next to the church entrance and banged the large bronze knocker several times. When he heard steps approaching the door from the inside, the *oidor* requested in a loud voice a confessor to administer immediately the last rites of the Church to a dying person. The Jesuit door-keeper swung the door open only to be pushed aside by guns and bayonets. In a few minutes the Jesuit college was in a state of chaos. Armed soldiers occupied courtyards and stairways and the frightened Jesuits were rounded up and herded into the chapel. Prayers came easily to their lips and many thought they were going to die. Domingo de Orrantia, standing near the altar, was deeply moved at the sight of his former teachers and could not bring himself to read the royal decree. He asked the notary Francisco Luque to read it to the fathers. Luque, a former Jesuit scholastic himself, broke into sobs and tears and had to be excused. Domingo de Orrantia, alumnus of San Pablo, did not have a choice, and personally had to fulfill the painful duty of reading to his teachers and friends the despotic decree of Charles III.[8]

San Pablo, a center of learning for two centuries, served during

September and October of 1767 as a temporary prison for the Jesuits. During the last weeks of September, members of the Order from Pisco, Ica, Nazca, Huancavelica, Huamanga and Trujillo arrived under heavy guard at San Pablo where many of them had begun their apostolic lives in America. By the 20th of October, almost two hundred Jesuits waited in the college at Lima for the hour of exile, which came on the night of the 27th when the Jesuits were taken to Callao. The ship *El Peruano* moved slowly away from the pier while the eyes and hearts of the exiles clung desperately to the receding coastline.

————————

The colonial institution known as *Colegio de San Pablo* came to an end in September, 1767, by the mighty will of an absolute monarch. The buildings of the college, empty shells of the old Jesuit institution, survived for one hundred and sixty years more in the heart of colonial Lima. In 1943, a fire destroyed the old school of humanities of San Pablo, which was serving at the time as the National Library of Peru. A few years later, a new enlightened ruler leveled the main cloisters of the college to make room for a parking lot. Only the superb college church, a jewel of colonial architecture, and the adjacent cloister are all that remains today of the glory which was once San Pablo's.

NOTES

INTRODUCTION

1. José de la Riva Agüero (ed.), *Los Cronistas de Convento* ("Biblioteca de Cultura Peruana" vol. IV, Paris: Desclée, De Brouwer, 1938), p. 64. Bernabé Cobo, S.J., *Fundación de Lima* ("Biblioteca de Autores Españoles" vol. XCII, Madrid: Ediciones Atlas, 1956), pp. 289–90, 302.

2. *Ibid.*, pp. 291, 305.

3. Roberto Levillier, *Don Francisco de Toledo, Supremo Organizador del Perú: Su Vida y Su Obra, 1515–1582* (3 vols., Buenos Aires and Madrid: Espasa y Calpe S.A., 1935), I, 108–09.

4. Arthur F. Zimmerman, *Francisco de Toledo, Fifth Viceroy of Peru: 1569–1581* (Caldwell, Idaho: The Caxton Printers, Ltd., 1938), pp. 18–22. Rubén Vargas Ugarte, S.J., *Historia de la Iglesia en el Perú* (5 vols., Lima: Imprenta de Santa María, 1953), I, 162.

5. Cobo, *op. cit.*, pp. 309, 314, 347–48.

6. *Ibid.*, pp. 417–21; Zimmerman, *op. cit.*, p. 25.

7. Vargas Ugarte, *Historia de la Iglesia*, I, 342.

8. *Ibid.*, I, 328 n. 3.

9. Guillermo Lohmann Villena, *El Arte Drámatico en Lima durante el Virreinato* (Madrid: Artes Gráficas, 1945), p. 11.

10. Rubén Vargas Ugarte, S.J., *Historia del Perú* (5 vols., Lima: Talleres Gráficos A. Baiocco y Cia., 1949), I, 71.

11. Antonine Tibesar, O.F.M., *Franciscan Beginnings in Colonial Peru* (Washington, D.C.: Academy of American Franciscan History, 1953), p. 28; Vargas Ugarte, *Historia de la Iglesia*, I, 328.

12. *Ibid.*, I, 331–32; idem, *Historia del Perú*, I, 71.

13. Cobo, *op cit.*, p. 403. Vargas Ugarte, *Historia de la Iglesia*, I, 337-42.

14. Fray Domingo de Santo Tomás, O.P., *Grammática o Arte de la Lengua General de los Indios de los Reynos del Perú* (Raul Porras Barrenechea, ed., Lima: Edición del Instituto de Historia, 1951).

CHAPTER I

1. Borgia himself informed the Jesuit General of this trip from Plasencia to Oropesa. Cf. *SFB* III, 255–56.
2. Borgia was summoned to Yuste by the Count of Oropesa. *SFB* III, 271–73.
3. *SFB* III, 479.
4. *Relación de lo que Toca a los Colegios de la Compañía de Jesús en la Provincia de Castilla la Nueva: 1564–1565* (Madrid: Imprenta de Gabriel López del Horno, 1907), p. 12.
5. *SFB* III, 200–01, 255, 501; IV, 226. *MP* I, 80–2, 93–4.
6. *MP* I, 130.
7. *MP* I, 129. AVP: Jacinto Barrasa, s.j., "Historia Eclesiástica" MS, I, 28.
8. *MP* I, 130.
9. AVP: Barrasa, "Historia," 30–6. *MP* I, 166–67.
10. *MP* I, 198–200. *SFB* IV, 631–32. Levillier, *op. cit.*, I, 27.
11. *Ibid.*
12. *SFB* IV, 619–20, 641–43. *MP* I, 223–25.
13. *MP* I, 238–41.
14. *MP* I, 250, 320.
15. *MP* I, 138, 248–49.
16. *MP* I, 182–90.
17. *MP* I, 248–51.
18. *MP* I, 264–65.
19. *MP* I, 253–73.
20. *MP* I, 274. AVP: Barrasa, "Historia," I, 45–9.
21. *MP* I, 278–84 contains the complete first catalogue of the Peruvian Jesuits.
22. *MP* I, 310, 317. AVP: Barrasa, "Historia," I, 170.
23. *MP* I, 351–52.
24. *MP* I, 353.
25. AVP: Barrasa, "Historia," I, 68–9. Emilio Lissón, *La Iglesia en el Perú: Colección de Documentos para la Historia de la Iglesia que se Encuentran en Varios Archivos* (5 vols., Sevilla: Editorial Católica Española s.a., 1943–1956), II, 502–15. *MP* I, 373–77.
26. *MP* I, 387–400, 407–09.
27. *MP* I, 448–53. After that summer of 1572, Toledo's relations with the Jesuits, as shown in his correspondence with the king, went from bad to worse. Cf. *MP* I, 453–54, 622–23. For a complete history of Toledo's clash with the

Jesuits, see Antonio de Egaña, s.j., "El Virrey D. Francisco de Toledo y los Jesuitas del Perú: 1569–1581," *Estudios de Deusto* IV (Enero–Junio, 1956), 117–86.

28. *MP* I, 499–502.

29. *MP* I, 529–33. AVP: Barrasa, "Historia," I, 102.

30. *MP* I, 533–44, 644.

31. *MP* I, 607–09, 648. Father Bracamonte, former rector of San Pablo, informed the Father General in a letter of February, 1574, about the Visitor's fears and doubts. Cf. *MP* I, 613.

32. These ideas are contained in a letter from Plaza to Mercurian in *MP* I, 583–86.

33. *MP* I, 620–21. AVP: Barrasa, "Historia," I, 551–52. *MP* I, 631, 649.

34. *MP* I, 635. Martínez already appears in the Jesuit catalogue of 1572 as a lecturer in philosophy. Cf. *MP* I, 511.

35. *MP* I, 630, 632, 659.

36. Acosta's frame of mind when he volunteered for Peru is reflected in the letter which he wrote to the Jesuit General in 1569. Cf. *MP* I, 299–303.

37. *MP* II, 43, 45.

38. León Lopetegui, s.j., *El Padre José de Acosta S.J. y las Misiones* (Madrid: Consejo Superior de Investigaciones Científicas, 1942), 151–78.

39. AVP: *LC*, "Congregación Provincial del Perú. en Lima año de 1576. en enero–en Romance." Egaña has published the Latin version of the original Spanish acts in *MP* II, 54–102.

40. *Ibid.*

41. *MP* II, 133–34, 214–17.

42. The original Spanish acts of the Jesuit convention held in Cusco are in AVP: *LC*, "Congregación Provincial del Perú. en el Cuzco en otte. del año de 1576–en Romance."

43. *MP* II, 109–10. Acosta's concept was simple. He merely wanted freedom to teach, but undoubtedly that concept was unacceptable within the legal framework of an absolute, theocratic government in which the source of all rights, including that of teaching, was always and solely the king. With Acosta's specifying his conditions, the seeds were sown for a new and more serious clash between the viceroy and the Jesuits.

44. *MP* II, 214–16.

45. *MP* II, 613–14.

46. *MP* II, 485–87.

47. Toledo's action was logical within the legal framework of the absolute Spanish monarchy, and was partly caused by the inflexible attitude of the Jesuits. For the complete text of the decree see *MP* II, 484–91.

48. *MP* II, 491–93, 756–60, 774.

49. Several friends of the Jesuits wrote to the king protesting Toledo's violent measures against San Pablo. The letters written by Fray Juan de Ocampo, an influential Franciscan, and by the *Oidor* Ramírez de Cartagena have been preserved and can be seen in transcript in *MP* II, 640–42, 697–703. Acosta's report to Piñas is in *MP* II, 771–77.

50. *MP* II, 743, 802–04.

CHAPTER II

1. Dr. Luis A. Eguiguren has collected the main documents related to this legal battle in his works *Diccionario Histórico Cronológico de la Real y Pontificia Universidad de San Marcos y sus Colegios* (3 vols., Lima: Torres Aguirre S.A., 1940–1951), and *Alma Mater: Orígenes de la Universidad de San Marcos, 1515–1579* (Lima: Torres Aguirre S.A., 1939).

2. Lissón, *La Iglesia en el Perú*, III, 41.

3. *MP* III, 20–2.

4. The provision of the Viceroy Cañete was given on the 6th of May, 1595, and confirmed in Madrid on the 4th of February, 1604. Cf. Eguiguren, *Diccionario*, I, 281–82, 293; II, 49–57, 108–10.

5. *Ibid.*, II, 96–7, 690; III, 498–99. In 1670 the Jesuit provincial gave orders to the rector of San Pablo not to grant a university entrance certificate to any student who had not completed the full course in the humanities at San Pablo. Cf. AVP: *LO*, f. 223.

6. *Ibid.*, ff. 53, 95–6, 161–62.

7. *Ibid.*, ff. 211, 221, 226. CV: Papeles Varios MSS, XXXIX, Doc. 16, No. 10. "Libro de Usos y Costumbres del Colegio de San Pablo," chap. 25. This last book was kept in the manuscript collection of the Biblioteca Nacional in Lima, but was destroyed in the fire of 1943. I have examined the microfilm copy owned by the editor of *MP*.

8. Francisco Mateos, S.J. (ed.), *Historia General de la Compañía de Jesús en el Perú: Crónica Anónima de 1600 que Trata del Establecimiento y Misiones de la Compañía de Jesús en los Países de Habla Española* (2 vols., Madrid: Consejo Superior de Investigaciones Científicas, 1944), I, 215. *MP* I, 425; II, 6, 215, 615.

9. *MP* III, 218, 625, 674–75.

10. Cobo, *op. cit.*, 413. Diego de Córdoba y Salinas, O.M., *Teatro de la Iglesia Metropolitana de la Ciudad de los Reyes: Anales de la Catedral de Lima* ("Biblioteca Histórica Peruana," vol. VII, Lima: Tipografía Peruana, 1958), 91. CV: Cartas Anuas de la Provincia del Perú, XLVII, Anuas 1648–1650.

11. "Ministerios que ejercita la Compañía de JHS en la capilla de Ntra. Señora de los Desamparados en esta ciudad de Lima"; this report was written by Padre Francisco Del Castillo in 1666 and gives the earliest information about the Jesuit elementary school in Lima; published in Rubén Vargas Ugarte, S.J., *Historia de la Compañía de Jesús en el Perú* (3 vols., Burgos: Imprenta de Aldecoa, 1963–1965), II, 151–53. For additional information on the school cf. CV: Cartas Anuas, XLVII, Anuas 1685–1688, 1697–1699.

12. *MP* I, 348. In 1568 Lima had a population of about 10,000 Spaniards, 12,000–15,000 Negroes, and about 20,000 Indians. Bernabé Cobo estimated in the 1630s that the population of the city had grown to 25,000 Spaniards and 30,000 Negroes.

13. AVP: Libro de Ordenaciones, f. 112.

14. *Ibid.*, ff. 612–63, 193.

15. AVP: *LI*, "Ordenaciones Varios de Ntro. Padre Tyrso González . . . 1692," No. 24.

16. CV: Papeles Varios MSS, XXXIX, Doc. 17, No. 6.

17. *Ratio atque Institutio Studiorum Societatis Jesu* (Antverpiae: Apud Joannem Meursium, 1635), 134. I have been able to use the same copy of the *Ratio Studiorum* which was in the Jesuit library during colonial days.

18. *MP* II, 670. AVP: *LO*, f. 60.

19. José de Arriaga, S.J., *Rhetoris Christiani Partes Septem Exemplis cum Sacris tum Philosophicis Illustratae* (Lugduni: Sumptibus Horatii Cardon, ex typographeis Joannis Arnad, 1619).

20. Gramatica Latina MS [1672]. The original of this grammar is in the manuscript collection of the Colegio de la Inmaculada, the present-day Jesuit high school in Lima.

21. Besides the two editions of 1734 and 1839, the 1777 and 1791 Lima editions are in CV. For further information concerning José Rodríguez, see Pedro Cano Pérez, "Jesuitas Peruanos Humanistas," *Mercurio Peruano* CLXIII (September, 1940), 576–84.

22. Enrique Torres Saldamando, "El Colegio Mayor de San Pablo," *Revista Peruana* IV (Enero, 1880), 474. AVP: Barrasa, "Historia," I, 560–61.

23. The *Poema Heroyco* was published after the death of Valdés by his cousin Francisco Garabito de León y Messia, rector of the Cathedral of Lima.

24. Samples of the different kinds of poetry written in San Pablo can be found in Joseph de Buendía, s.j., *Parentación Real al Soberano Nombre e Inmortal Memoria del Católico Rey . . . D. Carlos II . . .* (Lima: Joseph de Contrera, 1701), 120–34, in Alexo Alvítez, *Puntual Descripción Fúnebre Lamento . . . Exéquias de la . . . Señora Mariana Josepha de Austria* (Lima, 1765), 118–25, and in CV: Papeles Varios mss, XII, Doc. 25.

25. AVP: Barrasa, "Historia," I, 60, 560.

26. *Ibid.*, I, 214. Mateos, *Historia General* I, 215, 284.

27. *MP* II, 9.

28. *MP* I, 351–52, 426.

29. CV: Cartas Anuas, XLVII, Anuas 1660–1661. This form is clearly allied to the debate poems (*conflictus*) of medieval Latin literature, growing out of the Eclogues of Virgil. Cf. Hans Walther, *Das Streitgedicht in der lateinischen Literatur des Mittelalters* (Munich: Beck, 1920) [Editor's note].

30. The text of this short play has been published by Rubén Vargas Ugarte, s.j., *De Nuestro Antiguo Teatro: Colección de Piezas Dramáticas de los Siglos XVI, XVII y XVIII* ("Biblioteca Histórica Peruana," vol. IV, Lima: Compañía de Impresiones y Publicidad, 1943), 218–27.

31. Comedies written by lay authors were forbidden in 1604 by the Provincial Esteban Páez, in 1641 by the Provincial Nicolás Durán, in 1687 by the Visitor Gonzalo de Lira, and in 1692 by the Jesuit General himself. AVP: *LO*, ff. 108, 228; *LI*, "Ordenes Varios de Ntro. Padre Tyrso Gonzalez . . .," No. 8.

32. AVP: Barrasa, "Historia," I, 561–63.

33. Lohmann Villena, *El Arte Dramático*, 23–4.

34. CV: Cartas Anuas, XLVII, Anuas 1667–1674. AVP: Libro de Ordenaciones, "Ordenaciones del P. Gonzalo de Lira," No. 45. Bernabé Cobo, s.j., *Historia del Nuevo Mundo* (2 vols., "Biblioteca de Autores Españoles," vols. XCI, XCII, edited by Francisco Mateos, s.j., Madrid: Ediciones Atlas, 1956), II, 272–73.

35. *MP* II, 104.

36. Vicente D. Sierra, *Los Jesuitas Germanos en la Conquista Espiritual de Hispano-América* (Buenos Aires: Talleras Gráficos de Padilla y Contreras s.r.l., 1944), 75–6, 169–79. CV: Perú, Varios mss, LXXIX, Doc. 14.

37. *MP* I, 252–53, 258, 354.

38. *MP* II, 118–19. For a complete list of Barzana's outstanding linguistic productions, see José E. de Uriarte and Mariano Lecina, s.j., *Biblioteca de Escritores*

de la Compañia de Jesús, pertenecientes a la Antigua Asistencia de España: Desde sus Orígenes hasta el Año 1773 (2 vols., Madrid: Viuda dé López del Horno, 1925–1930), I, 434–36.

39. *MP* III, 396–97, 401. Vargas Ugarte, *Historia del Perú*, I, 341–43. Antonio de Herrera, *Historia General de los Hechos de los Castellanos* (2 vols., Madrid: Academia de la Historia, 1934), I, 145.

40. AVP: *LO*, f. 224. *MP* II, 316, 400, 456, 476, 655–56.

41. AVP: *LC*, "Congregatio habita Arequipae . . . 1595," No. 4; "Respuestas dadas en Roma en octubre 1596," No. 4. AVP: *LI*, "Ordenes Varios de Ntro. Padre Tyrso González," No. 3.

42. ARSJ: FG 1488.

43. ANP: Compañía de Jesús, Varios, Legajo 2, "Libro de Viáticos y Almacén del Colegio de San Pablo, 1628–1631" MS, f. 24.

44. *Ibid.*, f. 42.

CHAPTER III

1. Mateos, *Historia General*, I, 147, 268, 432–39.

2. *Ratio Studiorum*, 71–3. This was an outgrowth of the *Casus conscientiae*, a traditional feature of Jesuit communities.

3. Lopetegui, *José de Acosta*, 145, 148. AVP: Libro de Ordenaciones, ff. 54, 101–02; Libro de Instrucciones, "Ordenes Varios de Ntro. Padre Tyrso González," No. 19.

4. *MP* II, 166–67.

5. José de Acosta, s.j., *De Natura Novi Orbis Libri Duo et de Promulgatione Evangelii apud Barbaros, sive de Procuranda Indorum Salute* (Salmanticae: Apud Guillelmum Foquel, 1589), 349–54.

6. *MP* II, 299–302.

7. Luis A. Eguiguren, *La Universidad en el Siglo XVI* (2 vols., Lima: Imprenta de Santa María, 1951), I, 399–411.

8. Rubén Vargas Ugarte, s.j. (ed.), *Pareceres Jurídicos en Asuntos de Indias: 1601–1718* (Lima: Compañía de Impresiones y Publicidad, 1951), 89–93.

9. Vargas Ugarte, *Historia de la Compañía*, II, 272–74.

10. Pedro de Oñate, s.j., *De Contractibus* (3 vols., Romae: Ex Typographia Francisci Caballi, 1646–1647, Apud Angelum Bernabo, 1654).

11. CV: Papeles Varios MSS, XXXIX, Doc. 3, "Caso 137: De las minas de Huancavelica." Vargas Ugarte, *Pareceres Jurídicos*, 140–53.

12. This line of thought was an early version of the pan-American principle of "America for the Americans" and contained the seeds of an emancipation philosophy.

13. Uriarte and Lecina, *op. cit.*, I, 365–68.

14. Diego de Avendaño, s.j., *Thesaurus Indicus seu Generalis Instructor pro Regimine Conscientiae, in iis quae ad indias Spectant* (2 vols., Antverpiae: Apud Jacobum Meursium, 1668), I, 298, 328–29, 335–41.

15. *Ibid.*, 24–7. Compare the testimony of Oñate and Avendaño on the horrors and deaths which occurred in Huancavelica with the conclusions reached by Guillermo Lohmann Villena, *La Minas de Huancavelica en los Siglos XVI y XVII* (Sevilla: Escuela de Estudios Hispano–Americanos, 1949), 173–77, 210–12.

16. Quoted by Jorge Basadre, *El Conde de Lemos y su Tiempo* (second ed., Lima: Editorial Huascarán s.a., 1948), 111–12.

17. Vargas Ugarte, *Pareceres Jurídicos*, 154–65.

18. Francisco de Contreras, s.j., *Información sobre que los Electos para Obispos no Pueden Consagrarse, ni Tomar la Posesión de sus Obispos sin que Primero Reciban las Letras Apostólicas de Su Santidad . . . (s.l., 1647).*

19. Vargas Ugarte, *Pareceres Jurídicos*, 137–39.

20. Avendaño, *Thesaurus*, I, 27, 266–67.

21. Oñate, *De Contractibus*, III, 28–30.

22. Avendaño, *Thesaurus*, I, 11–3, 20, 71–8, 81–8, 119–20, 270–72. The entire first volume deals with problems related to the civil administration of the viceroyalty.

23. Antonio Astrain, s.j., *Historia de la Compañía de Jesús en la Asistencia de España* (7 vols., Madrid: Sucesores de Ribadeneira, 1902–1909, Razón y Fe, 1913–1925), IV, 115–385.

24. In ANP: Compañía de Jesús, Sermones, Legajo 3, I have found a detached Latin manuscript leaf, misplaced among the Jesuit sermons, reading in translation: "The morality of human acts is essentially rooted in freedom, which is partly intrinsic and partly extrinsic to those human acts . . ." See also LCI: Tractatus de Actibus Humanis Agens ms [1692].

25. LCI: Breve Tratado Misceláneo de Casos Curiosos y muy Especiales, en Varias Cuestiones de Moral ms, Caso 26. CV: Papeles Varios mss, XLI, Doc. 9.

26. *MP* II, 456.

27. *MP* III, 4–17, 47–60. AVP: "Relación Brebe del Principio fundación y augmento del collegio de Lyma hasta principio del año de 1589 ms."

28. Some of the legal documents related to the slaves bought by San Pablo are

in ANP: Compañía de Jesús, Varios, Legajo 13 and 17; Compañía de Jesús, Venta de Esclavos, Legajo 16. Thyrsus González approved the existing policy of replacing the sick or deceased slaves by buying new ones. Cf. AVP: *LI*, "Ordenes Varios de Ntro. Padre Tyrso González," No. 12.

29. ANP: Compañía de Jesús, Varios, Legajo 18, "Estado de lo Temporal del Colegio Máximo de San Pablo . : . 1764"; Temporalidades, Colegios (San Pablo), Legajo 85, codex 391, f. 135. Manuel de Amat y Junient, *Memoria de Gobierno* (Edición y Estudio Preliminar de Vicente Rodríguez Casado y Florentino Pérez Embid, Sevilla: Escuela de Estudios Hispano–Americanos, 1947), 148.

30. Avendaño, *Thesaurus*, I, 324–29.

31. Felipe Barreda y Laos gives a highly distorted explanation on pp. 215–19 of his *Vida Intelectual del Virreinato del Perú* (third ed., Lima: Imprenta de la Universidad Nacional de San Marcos, 1964) of the doctrine of probabilism as taught in the colonial schools. His superficial interpretation would make even an amateur theologian smile. For an expert's explanation of the moral theory of probabilism see Marcellinus Zalba, s.j., *Theologiae Moralis Compendium* (2 vols., "Biblioteca Autores Cristianos," vols. CLXXV, CLXXVI, Madrid: Editorial Católica s.a., 1958), I, 387–406.

32. Avendaño, *Thesaurus*, I, 329–30.

33. Oñate, *De Contractibus*, III, 21–4.

34. AVP: *LO*, f. 150; Libro de Instrucciones, "Praeceptos de obediencia de los Padres Provinciales de esta Provincia del Perú." CV: Papeles Varios mss, XII, Doc. 8, Nos. 4, 12, 13.

35. AVP: *LO*, f. 192.

36. The medical activities of the Jesuits of San Pablo are treated in detail in Chapter V.

37. Orders concerning the just treatment of slaves were constantly promulgated during the seventeenth century by the Jesuit superiors: in 1607 by Esteban Páez, in 1648 by Lupercio Zurbano, in 1655 by Antonio Vásquez, in 1659 by Andrés de Rada, and in 1666 by Luis J. de Contreras. AVP: *LO*, ff. 61, 112, 115, 123, 220.

38. The administrative books of the Jesuit haciendas preserved in ANP contain evidence of this care taken of slaves working the farms. See, *e.g.*, ANP: Compañía de Jesús, Varios, Legajo 13, "Libro del Gasto . . . de La Calera, 1709–1758," ff. 40, 125, 126, 130; Compañía de Jesús, Cuentas de Colegio (San Pablo), Legajo 30, "Libro de Cuentas de la Botica," *passim*. The Jesuit

practice of becoming godfathers of the slave children was so general that it had to be restricted by the Provincial Congregation of 1764. AVP: *LO*, "Congregatio Provincialis Societatis Jesu . . . celebrata anno 1764," f. 4.

39. These treatises served as textbooks for the classes on moral theology, and, like the works of Avendaño and Oñate, contain a great deal of information about the social and economic situation of Peru.

40. Both treatises are in the manuscript collection of LCI.

41. LCI: Martín de Jaúregui, s.j., "Tractatus de Restitutione" ms, ff. 188, 190, 191. Barreda y Laos ignored the existence of this and other manuscripts of the Jesuit professor, and his harsh judgment of Jaúregui is based solely on certain pious sermons, and therefore untenable: *idem, Vida Intelectual*, 127–31.

42. The Jesuits, after imposing the duty of restitution on their penitents, tried to avoid handling the restitution itself. Yet there are some cases of restitutions made through the offices of the Jesuits of San Pablo on record in ANP: Temporalidades, Colegios, Legajo 84, codex 380 and AHN: Clero (Jesuitas), Libro 363-J ms, f. 658.

CHAPTER IV

1. Cándido de Dalmases, s.j. and Ignacio Iparraguirre, s.j. (edd.), *Obras Completas de San Ignacio de Loyola* (second ed., "Biblioteca de Autores Cristianos," vol. LXXXIV, Madrid: Editorial Católica s.a., 1963), 94–108, 117–32.

2. *Ibid.*, 496. George E. Ganss, s.j., *Saint Ignatius' Idea of a Jesuit University* (Milwaukee: Marquette University Press, 1954).

3. *MP* I, 250–51, 350.

4. *MP* I, 597, 599–603, 671–76, 723–24; II, 1–2.

5. *MP* I, 696.

6. *MP* II, 169. Plaza's words imply that the Jesuits had a rather sizable library and that it was frequently used even by some lay friends of the college—a supposition confirmed by later evidence.

7. *Ratio Studiorum*, 19, 36, 92–3. AVP: *LO*, f. 125. The information on the house left by the brothers Perlín is contained in ANP: Temporalidades, Colegios (San Pablo), Legajo 85, codex 391, ff. 58 and 69, and in CV: Papeles Varios mss, XL, Doc. 18.

8. AVP: Barrasa, "Historia," II, codex 60.

9. Cobo, *Fundación*, 425.

10. Obviously misplaced among the Jesuit Sermons in ANP: Compañía de

Jesús, Sermones, Legajo 3, are the following manuscripts relating to the shipment of books to San Pablo: "Memoria de los libros que envía el P. Hernando Morillo a la Proa. del Piru," "Contrato entre el Capitán de Navío San José, D. Ordoño de Salazar, y el P. Cristóbal García Añez [1629]," "Cuentas del Procurador, 1662–1667," "Cuentas del P. Alonso Gómez, 1665."

11. ANP: Compañía de Jesús, Varios, Legajo 1, "Libro de Viáticos y Almacén, 1626–1627"; Legajo 2, "Libro de Viáticos y Almacén, 1628–1631." In these two manuscripts the administrator of San Pablo has listed all the books and articles taken from the storerooms by the members of the college, or sent to other Jesuit institutions throughout the viceroyalty.

12. AVP: *LO*, f. 180.

13. ANP: Compañía de Jesús, Varios, Legajo 2, "Libro de Viáticos y Almacén, 1628–1631," ff. 92–100, 121–22.

14. AVP: *LO*, f. 103.

15. *Ibid.*, ff. 200–01.

16. *Ibid.*, ff. 147.

17. *Ibid.*, ff. 224–25.

18. AVP: *LI*, "Praeceptos de Ntros. PP. Generales para esta Prov. del Perú." CV: Papeles Varios MSS, XXXIX, Doc. 16, No. 19; Doc. 11, Nos. 15–7; Doc. 17, No. 8; Doc. 19, Nos. 5–6; Doc. 27, No. 7.

19. ANP: Compañía de Jesús, Temporalidades, Colegios (San Pablo), Legajo 85, codex 391, f. 12. AHN: Clero, Jesuitas, Libro 363-J, ff. 658–99.

20. All the information about the common library of San Pablo is based upon the royal inventory of 1767, preserved in AHN: Clero, Jesuitas, Libro 363-J, ff. 409–702. This manuscript document contains the inventory of 9,224 volumes of the common library, 395 volumes of the students' library, and almost 2,000 volumes of several private libraries. For lack of time 32,888 volumes were piled into the large dining room of the college and were never properly described in the inventory.

21. AHN: Clero, Jesuitas, Libro 363-J, ff. 572, 584.

22. *Ibid.*, ff. 410, 413, 420, 592, 595, 677.

23. *Ibid.*, ff. 436, 574, 578.

24. John Laures, S.J., *The Political Economy of Juan de Mariana* (New York: Fordham University Press, 1928).

25. AHN: Clero, Jesuitas, Libro 363-J, ff. 422–23, 435–36, 572, 581.

26. *Ibid.*, ff. 422–26, 428–29, 431–33, 579, 585.

27. *Ibid.*, ff. 423, 424, 427, 434, 438, 574.

28. *Ibid.*, ff. 426, 428–29, 431.

29. *Ibid.*, ff. 422, 424, 429, 431–35, 446–64, 573, 587, 666. Solórzano Pereira's work is listed in ANP: Compañía de Jesús, Varios, Legajo 2, "Libro de Viáticos y Almacén, 1628–1631," ff. 113–14.

30. AHN: Clero, Jesuitas, Libro 363–J, ff. 426, 430, 613.

31. *Ibid.*, ff. 418, 426, 430, 601, 613, 656.

32. *Ibid.*, ff. 600–01.

33. *Ibid.*, ff. 416, 427, 435, 576–78, 582, 598, 600.

34. *Ibid.*, ff. 582–83, 602, 606, 612.

35. *Ibid.*, ff. 597, 599, 600–13.

36. *Ibid.*, ff. 648–49.

37. *Ibid.*, ff. 421, 592, 599, 689.

38. *Ibid.*, ff. 421, 666, 669, 689.

CHAPTER V

1. Dalmases and Iparraguirre, *op. cit.*, 510.

2. *Ibid.*, 478–80, 751–52, 588, 867, 948.

3. AVP: Barrasa, "Historia," I, 28. Mateo, *Historia General*, 366.

4. AVP: *LC*, "Congregatio Provincialis habita Limae anno 1600."

5. *Varones Ilustres de la Compañía de Jesús* (second ed., Bilbao: Administración del Mensajero del Corazón de Jesús, 1887–1892) IV, 210–30. In March, 1764, the Jesuits paid 140 pesos for a large portrait of Salumbrino which bore the legend: "Augustino Salumbrino first founder of this pharmacy of San Pablo" (ANP: Compañía de Jesús, Cuentas de Colegios [San Pablo], Legajo 30, "Libro de Cuentas de la Botica").

6. By that year the Jesuits of San Pablo had, along with other medical works, the two pharmacopoeias referred to in the text. See ANP: Compañía de Jesús, Varios, Legajo 2, "Libro de Viáticos y Almacén, 1628–1631," f. 55.

7. *Ibid.*, ff. 24, 55.

8. *Ibid.*, f. 108. ANP: Compañía de Jesús, Sermones, Legajo 3, "Cuentas del P. Pdor. Felipe de Paz, 1667." CV: Papeles Varios MSS, XXXIX, Doc. 4, "Memoria de los Caxones que de cuenta del P. Miraval llegaron a las Aduanas de Roma, 1699." For more information on the Peruvian bezoar stones see Hermilio Valdizan and Angel Maldonado, *La Medicina Popular Peruana: Contribución al "Folk–lore" Médico del Perú* (3 vols., Lima: Torres Aguirre, 1922), III, 100 n. 516.

NOTES

9. Cobo, *Historia*, 274. Rubén Vargas Ugarte, s.j., "1631–1931. Una Fecha Olvidada. El Tercer Centenario del Descubrimiento de la Quina," *Revista Historica* IX (1931), 291–301.

10. ANP: Compañía de Jesús, Sermones, Legajo 3, "Cuentas Felipe de Paz." CV: Papeles Varios mss, XXXIX, Doc. 4. For the names of the streets in the neighborhood of the Jesuit college, see Juan Bromley and José Barbagelata, *Evolución Urbana de la Ciudad de Lima* (Lima: Editorial Lumen s.a., 1945), 18.

11. Juan de Esteyneffer, s.j., *Florilegio Medicinal de Todas las Enfermedades* (Madrid: Alonso Valvas, 1729), 295.

12. AVP: *LO*, "Ordenaciones de la visita que hizo el P. Leonardo de Peñafiel Provincial de esta provincia visitando este Colegio de San Pablo en 24 de Nov. de 1656," f. 117.

13. *Ibid.*, "Instrucción para el H. Boticario," ff. 152–54.

14. *Annuae Litterae Societatis Jesu* (Duaci: Ex Officina Viduae Laurentii Kellami, 1618), 199–245. Cobo, *Fundación*, 425. CV: Cartas Anuas, XLVII, Anuas 1612–1635.

15. *Colección de las Aplicaciones que se van Haciendo de los Bienes . . . que Fueron de los Regulares de la Compañía de Jesús* (2 vols., Lima: Oficina de la Calle de San Jacinto, 1772–1773), II, 291–95 ("Aplicación de la casa conocida con el nombre de Enfermería de los Negros de los Jesuitas . . ."). AVP: *LO*, ff. 61, 112–15, 220.

16. ANP: Temporalidades, Inventarios, Legajo 2, codex 28, "Inventario de la Botica del Colegio de San Pablo," ff. 22–25. AHN: Clero, Jesuitas, Libro 363-J, ff. 444, 604–05.

17. *Ibid.*, ff. 441, 443–45, 604–05. ANP: Temporalidades, Inventarios, Legajo 2, codex 28, "Inventario de la Botica," ff. 22–5.

18. For a better understanding of the importance and influence of those doctors whose works were used by the pharmacists of San Pablo, cf. Pedro Laín Entralgo, *Historia de la Medicina Moderna y Contemporánea* (second ed., Barcelona and Madrid: Editorial Científico Médica, 1963).

19. Sierra, *Los Jesuitas Germanos*, 174, 291. In 1702, Heinrich Peschke sent a report to Rome: "Papel del H. Peschke sobre las cosas de la botica," printed in Sierra, *op. cit.*, 281–82.

20. ANP: Compañía de Jesús, Varios, Legajo 17, "Visita del Colegio de San Pablo hecha hasta fin de febrero de 1752 por su Ra. el P. Prcial. B. de Moncada."

21. Sierra, *op. cit.*, 280–93. That Zeitler served for a year in San Pablo is confirmed by his successor, José Rojo, in ANP: Compañía de Jesús, Cuentas de

Colegios (San Pablo), Legajo 30, "Libro de Cuentas de la Botica del Colegio de San Pablo, 1757–1767," September, 1757 (instead of correlative numbers, each page of this important manuscript corresponds to a month of a given year).
22. *Ibid.*, April and December, 1764; October, 1758; April and August, 1759.
23. The unpublished letters of the two Jesuit pharmacists are in the National Archives of Chile: Jesuitas–Chile, vol. 76, ff. 81–5.
24. ANP: Compañía de Jesús, Cuentas de Colegios (San Pablo), Legajo 30, "Libros de Cuentas de la Botica." See under the month and year given in the text.
25. CV: Papeles Varios MSS, XXXIX, Doc. 38, "Memorial del P. Pascual Ponce para el Colegio Máximo de San Pablo, 1762."
26. For a detailed account of the furniture and equipment in the pharmacy and laboratory see ANP: Temporalidades, Colegios (San Pablo), Legajo 85, codex 391, ff. 131–32; Legajo 87, codex 433.
27. ANP: Compañía de Jesús, Cuentas de Colegios (San Pablo), Legajo 30, "Libro de Cuentas de la Botica," under the months and years given in the text. The direct quotation is on the page for July, 1767. The testimony of the money carried on the ships *Ventura* and *Águila* is in ANP: Temporalidades, Colegios (San Pablo), Legajo 85, codex 391, f. 97.
28. *Ibid.*, Legajo 84, codex 381.
29. ANP: Temporalidades, Inventarios, Legajo 2, codex 28, "Inventario de la botica del Colegio de San Pablo, hecho a raíz de la expatriación de los Padres de la Compañía de Jesús." ANP: Temporalidades, Colegios (San Pablo), Legajo 85, codex 391, f. 128.
30. *Ibid.*, codex 390, ff. 6, 7, 15, 21.

CHAPTER VI

1. *MP* I, 122, 222.
2. *MP* I, 354–55, 411.
3. *MP* I, 461–75 (for the Indian problem especially 467–72).
4. *MP* I, 706. Lopetegui, *José de Acosta*, xlv–xlvii.
5. Lopetegui, *op. cit.*, 207–378. *MP* II, 218–19.
6. *MP* III, 207–08, 214–15, 381–85.
7. *MP* III, 393, 400–01, 615.
8. AVP: Barrasa, "Historia," I, 603, 858, 871. *MP* III, 570, 581, 648–54.
9. AVP: Barrasa, "Historia," II, *passim.* Vargas Ugarte, *Historia de la Compañía*,

I, 295–301. Pablo José de Arriaga, *Extirpación de la Idolatría del Perú* (Lima: Geronymo de Contreras, 1621).

10. I have found the manuscript of Torres' instructions in the Archivo de la Compañía de Jesús, Quito (Ecuador): Legajo II, 1534–1634, "Ordenaciones del Pe. Diego de Torres Rector del Colegio de la Cia. de Jhs. de Lima para los Pes. . . . que van a la missión de los indios de Guanaco. 20 de Agosto, 1626." AVP: *LO*, ff. 169–76, 190.

11. Córdoba y Salinas, *op. cit.*, 90–01.

12. ANP: Compañía de Jesús, Cuentas de Colegios (San Pablo), Legajo 30, "Libro del Gasto del Colegio de San Pablo relativo a missiones, 1689–1766."

13. AVP: *LO*, ff. 48, 94, 174–75. *MP* II, 697–706.

14. AVP: Barrasa, "Historia," II, chapts. 5–8 inclusive; *LO*, f. 94. CV: Cartas Anuas, Anuas de Julio 1656 and Enero de 1675; Papeles Varios MSS, XVI, Doc. 39: a letter written by the Jesuit provincial in 1621 to the king, explaining that part of the revenue from the haciendas is used in the financing of the missions. The legal papers of the donations made by Ramirez de Olivo and Aguirre are in ANP: Compañía de Jesús, Temporalidades, Colegios (San Pablo), Legajo 87, codex 417; Donaciones, Legajo 6.

15. AVP: *LO*, ff. 219, 229. ANP: Compañía de Jesús, Cuentas de Colegios (San Pablo), Legajo 30, "Libro del Gasto."

16. AVP: *LO*, "Ordenaciones de Gonzalo de Lira," No. 71.

17. All the articles mentioned in the text are listed in ANP: Compañía de Jesús, Cuentas de Colegios (San Pablo), Legajo 30, "Libro del Gasto"; Varios, Legajo 1, "Libro de Viáticos y Almacén, 1626–1627"; AVP: *LO*, "Ordenaciones de Gonzalo de Lira," Nos. 51–2, 64–8.

18. AVP: Barrasa, "Historia," I, 45–9, 162. *MP* I, 256–63, 268, 345–46.

19. *MP* III, 626. AVP: Barrasa, "Historia," I, 557.

20. For a more detailed description of the lay sodalities see Vargas Ugarte, *Historia de la Compañía*, I, 304–11.

21. Cobo, *Fundación*, 425.

22. AVP: Barrasa, "Historia," I, 565–66.

23. ANP: Compañía de Jesús, Temporalidades, Colegios (San Pablo), Legajo 87, codex 422 contains copies of the documents signed by La Palata and Liñan; Archivo de La O, "Libro en que se asientan los Congregantes . . .," contains membership lists from 1632.

26. Juan Antonio Suardo, *Diario de Lima: 1629–1634* (ed. Rubén Vargas Ugarte, s.j., Lima: Vazquez, 1935), 75, 96, 103, 158, 162, 165, 202, 206.

AVP: Barrasa, "Historia," II, codex 52. CV: Perú, Iglesia, IV, Doc. 1; Cartas Anuas, *passim.*

27. AVP: *LO*, ff. 52, 87, 154, 190. *Colección de las Aplicaciones*, I, 18. There is some evidence in the sources that the Jesuits used to hire out their Negro musicians and Indian singers.

28. AVP: *LO*, ff. 52, 115, 190. For a typical example of San Pablo's processions see CV: Perú, Iglesia, IV, Doc. 1, "Relación de la Fiesta que se hizo en la Cia. de Jesús de Lima . . . 1620."

29. The records of these donations, which indicate the existence of an Indian middle class, are in ANP: Compañía de Jesús, Temporalidades, Colegios (San Pablo), Legajo, 87, codex 415; Donaciones, Legajo 1.

30. ANP: Compañía de Jesús, Varios, Legajo 17.

31. AVP: Barrasa, "Historia," I, 271–73; II, codex 52.

32. *Ibid.*, I, 269–79; II, codex 52. ANP: Compañía de Jesús, Temporalidades, Colegios (San Pablo), Legajo 8, codex 422. Vargas Ugarte, *Historia de la Compañía*, I, 309–10.

33. In the Archivo de *La O* there are hundreds of receipts signed by Peruvian priests certifying that they had received stipends from the sodality to say the Masses of the spiritual contract. AVP: Barrasa, "Historia," I, 270–71; II, codex 52.

34. ANP: Compañía de Jesús, Varios, Legajo 13, "Cuentas de La O, 1695–1701"; Temporalidades, Colegios (San Pablo), Legajo 87, codex 423.

35. ANP: Compañía de Jesús, Sermones. AVP: *LO*, ff. 115, 123–25. CV: Papeles Varios MSS, XXXIX, Doc. 16; Cartas Anuas, *passim.*

36. CV: Cartas Anuas, Carta Anua de 1648. AVP: *LO*, ff. 123–24. For a general introduction into the nature of the *obrajes* see Fernando Silva Santisteban, *Los Obrajes en el Virreinato del Perú* (Lima: Museo Nacional de Historia, 1964).

37. Vargas Ugarte, *Historia de la Compañía*, I, 163, 213–15.

38. *Ibid.*, AVP: Barrasa, "Historia," II, codex 47.

39. *Ibid.* CV: Cartas Anuas, Anuas de los Años, 1685–1688, 1690–1696.

CHAPTER VII

1. Amat, *Memoria*, 128–29, 130.

2. *Ibid.*, 130. Rubén Vargas Ugarte, S.J. (ed.), *Relaciones de Viajes* (Lima: Compañía de Impresiones y Publicidad, 1947), 123.

3. *Ibid.*, 123–24. Amat, *Memoria*, 131.

4. I have located the bills charged for the dinner and cards in ANP: Compañía de Jesús, Temporalidades, Cuentas (Colegio San Pablo), Legajo 101, ff. 93, 97.

5. Lohmann Villena, *El Arte Dramático*, 439. Vargas Ugarte, *Relaciones*, 124.

6. One of the original manuscript notes sent by the viceroy to Don Pablo Matute is preserved in AVP: Res Variae MSS.

7. Amat, *Memoria*, 131–32. Vargas Ugarte, *Relaciones*, 125–27.

8. *Ibid.*, 128–29.

APPENDIX A

THE ECONOMIC LIFE OF SAN PABLO

San Pablo was maintained, from its foundation in 1568 to the year 1581, through the free donations of the citizens of Lima and through small, sporadic royal grants. In those early years the Jesuit administrators had to assign one of the most capable lay brothers as the college's official *limosnero*, a man in charge of begging alms daily from the well-to-do families of Lima. The College of San Pablo survived for more than twelve years without charging tuition and without any permanent sources of income, relying totally on the generosity of the *limeños* and on the wits of the brother almoner.

The year 1581 heralded the beginning of a new economic era in San Pablo, soon to become one of the largest landholders of Peru. Extensive rural properties constituted the firm economic foundation of the Jesuit college from the last two decades of the sixteenth century until the expulsion of the Jesuits in 1767. The first haciendas owned by San Pablo were donated to the College in 1581 by Juan Martínez Rengifo and Diego de Porras Sagredo, and were located not far from Lima, near the towns of Chancay and Surco. The hacienda of Chancay, with excellent soil for cultivation, produced wheat which was ground into flour in a mill also owned by the college. By the year 1589, this hacienda had been greatly improved by the college's administrators. They planted about 13,000 new vines and an olive grove, which provided the Jesuits with wine and oil in the years to come. The property of Surco was partly used for grazing eight hundred head of cattle and two hundred and fifty goats, and it was partly reserved for growing sugar cane. A good *trapiche*, or sugar mill, was installed there to produce sugar and honey.

These properties turned out to be a sound business enterprise under Jesuit administration; and the college, which had begged alms for its survival, was investing sizable amounts of money in new rural properties by the end of the sixteenth century. Toward 1589 San Pablo bought a new hacienda thirty *leguas* from Lima and turned it into a grazing land for a herd of 8,486 sheep, which provided the college with wool and meat. During the seventeenth century the Jesuit college increased the number of its landholdings and kept improving the old ones commercially. An example of the former is the vineyard donated in 1620 by Juan de Madrid which could produce more than one thousand jars of good wine. Among the most remarkable improvements introduced by the Jesuits were: the reclamation of marshy lands; the construction of a large reservoir and an aqueduct in the 1620s to increase, through irrigation, the yield of the hacienda San Juan; and the new techniques invented in the 1630s by Brother Bernardo Lete, who made the *trapiches* work faster and produce more, while at the same time decreasing the deafening noise of the mills.

In the eighteenth century the College of San Pablo owned about ten rural properties, some under intensive cultivation and others used as grazing land for cattle, sheep and goats. The college also had the administration of several other haciendas which belonged to different Jesuit houses or to the religious sodalities run by the Jesuits of San Pablo. The following details will give the reader an idea of the economic bulk of those rural properties. An army of 2,000 Negro slaves was employed in the haciendas, which between the years 1762 and 1764 alone gave the college a rent of more than half a million pesos. The vineyards of San Xavier and San Pablo produced, in 1750, more than eleven thousand jars of several kinds of wine which were sold in the public markets of the viceroyalty. Three hundred slaves were engaged full time there picking and pressing the grapes, and producing the well-known Jesuit wines. In 1742 the hacienda Jesús de Pauranga, in the district of Castrovirreina, had 450 head of cattle, 2,492 sheep, 4,000 goats, 54 horses and 92 donkeys. It was leased by the college to a lay overlord for 1,000 pesos a year.

It is obvious, even to a superficial reader of the account books of San Pablo, that the Jesuit administrators did not run their landholdings just to meet the bare needs of the college, but for a growing profit in the fashion of a true commercial enterprise. The tendency, already noticeable in the sixteenth century, of increasing agricultural production to a maximum while diversifying the crops, is a clear sign of this commercial interest on the part of San Pablo's administrators. An even clearer sign of the same were the efforts made to transform the agricultural products: the establishment of mills, sugar refineries and wine distilleries. By the middle of the seventeenth century, some of the haciendas owned by San Pablo were a fusion of farms and industrial plants, which delivered to the Peruvian markets some of the best wines, flowers, sugar, oil and honey available in the viceroyalty.

There is also evidence in the sources to indicate that the Jesuits of San Pablo had transformed some of their properties into *obrajes*, if we accept the word in a rather broad sense. The property *La Calera*, for instance, might fall into this category. It was neither a farm nor a grazing land for cattle, but an incipient factory. As its name clearly shows, *La Calera* was a limestone quarry where the Jesuits had built kilns and ovens to obtain lime and to bake bricks and pottery. These materials were not only used in Jesuit construction, but were also sold to lay contractors. The Jesuits ran, besides, a bakery in Lima where the wheat, produced in the college's haciendas and ground in its mills, was turned into tasty bread. The great abundance of goats, sheep and cattle provided the Jesuits with the raw material for another new industry, a tallow-candle factory. New research would be needed to determine the sizes of the bakery and the candle factory, and to establish whether the products would also be sold to the general public or only to Jesuit institutions.

Besides the rural properties and the *obrajes*, the College of San Pablo also owned a number of urban properties. These properties, mainly houses and empty lots, were rented and their incomes applied to specific needs of the college, like the library, the school of humanities and the chairs of theology. The urban properties accrued to the college as the donations of benefactors and of Jesuits who turned them over to San Pablo when they took their religious vows. The house donated by the brothers Perlín to maintain the library is but one example. Another one is the case of Bartolomé Escobar who donated two houses to the college in 1603 when he took his vows as a Jesuit. At times these donations came from a very unusual source, native Indian owners. On the 16th of August, 1606, an *india ladina* named María Jesús bequeathed to San Pablo a house in the borough of San Lazaro, together with a vegetable garden and two Negro slaves.

Backed by the extensive properties of the college and spurred by the growing demands of the Jesuit colleges and missions throughout America, San Pablo's administrators had already become powerful commercial dealers by the seventeenth century. The *Libros de Viáticos y Almacén*, quoted in our bibliography, give a clear idea of the extraordinary volume of business transacted through San Pablo between 1626 and 1631. San Pablo imported textiles from Spain, France, the Low Countries, Italy and the Philippines, and sold them in Chile, Tucuman, Córdoba, Potosí, La Plata, Cusco and Quito. It provided all the Jesuit schools in the viceroyalty with pens, ink and paper imported from Italy. In 1629 San Pablo sold 3,000 pens to the College of Santiago alone! Farm tools such as plows, sickles and hoes were in great demand. San Pablo provided them together with saddles and harnesses, tallow candles and pottery, shoes and clothing, needles and nails. In 1631 San Pablo sold 2,000 tailors' needles in Arequipa, described as "finas de Sevilla." Between 1628 and 1629, the college sent 12,000 nails to Potosí, 10,000 to Arequipa and 20,500 to Chile. San Pablo also sent American products not only to Spain, but also to Italy, France and England.

The volume of these transactions required that the college maintain its own muletrains to shuttled between Lima and Callao and to climb the Andes at regular intervals. The sources have even preserved the names of some of those animals: La Cabezuda, La Caminante, El Galán. Along the Peruvian coast the Jesuits used the regular commercial ships, but there is at least one instance in 1629 when the college's administrators had to charter a ship in Guayaquil to handle a large cargo of sugar, oil, wine, dried fruits, *estopa* from Chile and *yerba mate* from Paraguay. A stern warning issued in 1687 by the Visitor Gonzalo de Lira proves, as if it were still necessary to do so, that San Pablo was making a handsome profit out of its commercial dealings.

There are also certain grounds, at least as far as the eighteenth century is concerned, for belief that the Jesuit college acted occasionally as a sort of banking house—lending money, accepting deposits and investments, and even assuming the role of a pawnbroker. We know the cases of Tomás Claros, a muleteer on the route to Cusco, and of two ladies of Lima, Josefa Lobatón and Petronila Infantas, who had borrowed cash from San Pablo on the pledge of some personal jewelry and silver objects. Cases of those who borrowed or deposited money, signing only a legal document, are more numerous.

The College of San Pablo had, for two centuries, a solid economic foundation, consisting mainly of extensive rural and urban properties and some well-organized industries. The college's administrators played the role of commercial suppliers for the rest of the Jesuit establishment in America, and acted also as wholesalers for the products of the haciendas. There is no evidence, as far as this writer knows, of any direct Jesuit interests in the thriving mining enterprises of Peru. It would take extensive research to go systematically through all the existing sources on the economic life of San Pablo, to evaluate them, and to be able to present a coherent and complete synthesis.

APPENDIX B

RECTORS OF SAN PABLO*

Diego de Bracamonte	1568	Antonio Vásquez	1638
† ‡*Bartolomé Hernández*	1570	Bartolomé de Recalde	1644
†*Juan de Zúñiga*	1570	Antonio Vásquez	1649
†*Miguel de Fuentes*	1572	Rodrigo de Barnuevo	1649
†*José de Acosta*	1575	Bartolomé Tafur	1653
Baltasar de Piñas	1576	Jerónimo Pallas	1656
Juan de Zúñiga	1577	Diego de Avendaño	1659
§ ‖*Antonio López* (Vice-rector)	1577	Jacinto Garavito de León	1663
		Diego de Avendaño	1666
§*Bartolomé Hernández* (Vice-rector)	1578	Ignacio de las Roelas	1669
		Juan del Campo	1672
§*José Teruel*	1579	Francisco del Cuadro	1675
Juan de Atienza	1581	Jacinto Garavito de León	1675
Juan Sebastián de la Parra	1585	Hernando de Saavedra	1678
Hernando de Mendoza	1592	Martín de Jaúregui	1681
José Teruel	1600	Francisco del Cuadro	1682
Esteban Paez	1601	Juan del Campo	1683
Rodrigo Cabredo	1604	Francisco Javier Grijalva	1685
Diego Álvarez de Paz	1609	Juan Alonso de Cereceda	1688
¶*Martín Pelaez*	1615	Juan Yañez	1691
Francisco Coello	1617	Nicolás de Olea	1692
¶*Juan Sebastián*	1619	Juan de Sotomayor	1695
Andrés Hernández	1622	Francisco Javier Grijalva	1698
Nicolás Durán Mastrilli	1623	Manuel de Herla	1702
¶*Juan Vázquez*	1623	Diego Francisco Altamirano	1705
Diego de Torres Vásquez	1624	José Mudarra de la Serna	1709
Juan de Frías Herrán	1628	Francisco Arancibia	1714
Antonio Vásquez	1632	Francisco de Rotalde	1721
Gaspar Sobrino	1634	Álvaro Cavero	1724

Fermín de Irisarri	1724	* *Bertrand Herbert	ca. 1752
Pedro de Mallavía	ca. 1727	Baltasar de Moncada	1753
Tomás Cavero	1730	Alonso de Lobera	ca. 1756
Diego de Riofrío	1738	Jacobo Pérez	1759
Francisco de Larreta	1742	Antonio Claramunt	1767

*The list of those rectors whose names appear in Roman type is based upon those given in Rubén Vargas Ugarte, s.j., *Los Jesuitas del Perú: 1568–1767* (Lima, 1941), pp. 219–20. Sources of the names of rectors listed in italics are indicated as appropriate.

†*MP* II, 132–33.

‡He was in office only a few months.

§*MP* II, 696.

‖Succeeded Juan de Zúñiga, who died shortly after his second appointment.

¶Eguiguren, *Diccionario* III, 554–58.

* *A Frenchman, Herbert was probably rector between 1749 and 1753, and became provincial of Peru in the latter year. There is a letter in CV: Papeles Varios mss 12, Doc. 16, addressed to ". . . P. B.Herbert, Recteur du Collège de la Compagnie de Jesus à Lima au Peru. Paris, 2 Novembre 1752."

STATEMENT ON SOURCES

The present work is based almost exclusively on manuscript sources kept mainly in three Peruvian archives: the Archives of the Jesuit Vice-Province of Peru, Rubén Vargas Ugarte's Private Collection, and the National Archives of Peru.

In the Archives of the Jesuit Vice-Province, whose holdings for the colonial period are rather scanty, are found some of the best manuscripts for the study of the College of San Pablo. The first in order of importance for the present work is undoubtedly the "Libro de Ordenaciones," a thick manuscript book of two hundred and thirty-three folios. This manuscript contains the acts and memoirs of the official visitations of the college made by the provincials, and covers almost the entire seventeenth century from the visitation of Rodrigo de Cabero in 1601 to the visitation of Gonzalo de Lyra in 1687. There the researcher can find accurate descriptions of life in San Pablo and an account of the official policies followed at the college.

The "Historia Eclesiástica" in two large manuscript volumes written by San Pablo's professor Jacinto Barrasa between 1674 and 1679 is also found in the Jesuit Archives of Lima. Although Barrasa is concerned with the whole history of the Jesuits in Peru, and in spite of his pious and clerical approach, his work nevertheless contains valuable data on the College of San Pablo and on the men who worked there until the second half of the seventeenth century.

The "Libro de Congregaciones" and the "Libro de Instrucciones" are two other important manuscripts in the Jesuit Archives. The first one contains the official acts of all the Jesuit provincial conventions held between 1576 and 1620 to discuss the problems of the Order in Peru. The "Libro de Instrucciones" is a collection of the most important instructions, orders and regulations received from Rome, which were to be observed at the Jesuit college.

The Peruvian historian Rubén Vargas Ugarte has spent almost half a century collecting and classifying manuscripts and rare books relating to the Jesuits in Peru. His private collection has been an indispensable aid in research for the present work. Under the general heading of "Papeles Varios MSS" the collection includes a good number of volumes containing letters of provincials, rectors and professors, acts and memoirs of canonical visitations, Jesuit sermons, economic reports and some of the moral cases proposed and solved at San Pablo. But the real wealth of Vargas Ugarte's collection lies in the rare books that it contains. Many of these books, printed in Europe, were written at San Pablo during colonial days by members of its faculty, and are not easily found today outside Vargas Ugarte's collection. The most important among them are listed in our bibliography.

The largest number of manuscripts relating to the Peruvian Jesuits is located in the National Archives of Peru. When the civil authorities took over the Jesuit properties in 1767, they also seized their private papers. Many of these papers have been destroyed by time, fire and human neglect, but the National Archives still preserves an impressive collection of them. Because the colonial authorities were more interested in Jesuit properties and wealth than in culture and ideological developments, the manuscripts preserved by them deal mostly with economic problems.

The two manuscripts described in our bibliography as "Libro de Viáticos y Almacén" are two large books in which the administrator of San Pablo kept some of his accounts between 1626 and 1631. He entered in them the names of those leaving San Pablo and the money and articles (the *viático*) given them for their long trips. He also noted in the same ledgers all the articles—books, medicines, farming tools, textiles, and food—received into or taken out of the large storerooms under his supervision. The "Libro de Cuentas de la Botica" contains the accounts of San Pablo's pharmacy between 1757 and 1767. These manuscripts could not be located in any catalogue, and it is believed that they have been used for the first time for the present work.

Besides the economic materials, the National Archives has an excellent collection of sermons preached by the Peruvian Jesuits during colonial days. These sermons can be used by the modern researcher to unlock the theological thought of the period and to study the literary style then in vogue in the pulpits of Lima. One can also find parts of philosophical treatises taught at San Pablo, occasional letters or reports and even some theses defended at the college, which have been haphazardly bulked with the sermons.

An essential document, a frequent source of information, is the inventory of San Pablo's library made by royal officials in 1767. This inventory, bound into a thick volume with other manuscripts, is kept in the National Archives of Spain, but a microfilm copy was secured for the present book. In the same manner it was possible to make use of certain manuscripts from the National Archives of Chile, the Roman Archives of the Society of Jesus, and the Jesuit Archives in Quito, Ecuador.

BIBLIOGRAPHY

PRINCIPAL MANUSCRIPT SOURCES

Archivo Histórico Nacional (Madrid):
   Testimonio del segundo cuaderno de diligencias e inventarios actuados en el
   Colegio de San Pablo de Lima y contiene los que se hicieron en la Iglesia,
   Sachristia, Archivos del Provincial y Rector, Congregaciones fundadas en
   él, Biblioteca, Aposentos, libros de los Padres, fábrica material.
Archivo Nacional del Perú (Lima):
   Libro de Viáticos y Almacén, 1626–27.
   Libro de Viáticos y Almacén, 1628–31.
   Libro del Gasto perteneciente a las misiones que están a cargo de este Colegio
   de San Pablo de la Compañía de Jesús. Dase principio a él, desde principio
   de Enero de 1689, en que entró a cuidar de dichas misiones, como Prefecto
   de ellas, el P. Juan de la Serna.
   Razón de Viáticos del Colegio de San Pablo.
   Razón de Patronatos del Colegio de San Pablo.
   Posesiones que tiene este Colegio en la ciudad de los Reyes.
   Estado de lo temporal del Colegio Máximo de San Pablo y entrega que del
   hace su Ra. el P. Jayme Pérez concluido su Rectorado a su Ra. el P. Ror.
   Pascual Ponce en 10 de febrero de 1764.
   Libro de Cuentas de la Botica del Colegio de San Pablo.
   Relacción Sumaria de los ingresos y egresos de las haciendas y fincas del
   Colegio de San Pablo, desde enero de 1762 hasta diciembre del año 1766.
   Razón de las alhajas de oro, plata y pedrería que se inventariaron en el Colegio
   de San Pablo.
   Expediente relativo a las pensiones sobre los fondos del Colegio de San Pablo
   en esta capital.
   Sermones de Jesuitas.
Archivo de la Vice-Provincia del Perú (Jesuitas):
   Relación brebe del Principio fundación y augmento del Collegio de Lyma
   hasta principio del año de 1589.

Jacinto Barrasa, s.j., Historia Eclesiástica. Two vols.

Libro de Ordenaciones.

Libro de Congregaciones.

Libro de Instrucciones.

Cartas y Respuestas de ntros. Pes. Generales Originariamente.

Res Variae.

Fundación, Crecimiento y Utilidades de las Congregaciones de Sacerdotes fundadas en el Collegio de la Compañía de Jesús de Lima . . . Año de 1624.

Colección de Rubén Vargas Ugarte, s.j. (Huachipa):

Cartas Anuas de la Provincia del Perú.

Historia de la Provincia del Perú por el P. Diego Francisco Altamirano.

Papeles Varios Manuscritos (several volumes).

Biblioteca del Colegio de la Inmaculada (Lima):

Córdoba, Juan de, s.j., Tractatus de Gratia Auxiliante.

Tractatus De Restitutione per P. Martinum de Xaureguy Societatis Jesu, in Limensi hoc Max. D. Pauli eiusdem Societatis Collegio meritissimo Moralis Exedrae Professorem.

Menologio de Varones Ilustres.

Pérez Menacho, Juan, s.j., Tratado de la explicación de la Bulla de la Cruzada en conferencias de casos en este collegio de San Pablo de la Compañía de Jesús de Lima a 23 de octubre de 1595.

Tractatus De Restitutione Fortunarum.

PRIMARY PRINTED SOURCES

*Indicates a professor or administrator of San Pablo.

*Acosta, José de, s.j., *De Natura Novi Orbis Libri Duo et de Promulgatione Evangelii apud Barbaros, sive de Procuranda Indorum Salute.* Salamanticae: Apud Guillelmum Foquel, 1589.

—— *Historia Natural y Moral de las Indias.* Barcelona: En la emprenta de Jayme Cendrat, 1591.

*Aguilar, José, s.j., *Cursus Philosophicus Dictatus Limae.* 3 Vols. Hispali: Ex Offic. Joannis Francisci de Blas, 1701.

—— *Sermones Varios predicados en la Ciudad de Lima.* Bruselas: Pro Francisco Tserstevens, 1704.

—— *Sermones Varios de Misión.* Madrid: Viuda de Matheo Blanco, 1716.

*Aguilar, José, s.j., *Sermones Varios Morales*. Madrid: Por Don Gabriel del Barrio, 1723.

—— *Sermones Varios Panegíricos Morales*. Madrid: Por Alonso Balvas, 1731.

—— *Tractationes Posthumae in Primam Partem Divi Tomae*. 5 Vols. Cordubae: In Collegio Assumptionis Societatis Jesu. per Petrum de Pineda, et Valderrama, 1731.

*Altamirano, Diego Francisco, s.j., *Carta a los Padres y Hermanos de la Provincia del Perú sobre la Manera de Gobernar, Lima 1699*. Buenos Aires: De Coni Hermanos, 1899.

*Álvarez de Paz, Diego, s.j., *De Vita Spirituali, Eiusque Perfectione Libri Quinque*. Lugduni: Apud Horatium Cardon, 1608.

—— *De Exterminatione Mali, et Promotione Boni, Libri Quinque*. Lugduni: Apud Horatium Cardon, 1613.

Alvítez, Alejo, *Puntual Descripción, Fúnebre Lamento . . . de la Regia Doliente Pompa . . . Reales Exequias de la . . . Señora Doña Mariana Josepha de Austria*. Lima: 1756.

*Alloza, Juan de, s.j., *A ficción y Amor de San José*. Alcalá: Por María Fernández, 1652.

—— *Flores Summarum, seu Alphabetum Morale, Omnium fere Casuum qui Confessoribus contigere possunt*. Leodii: Impensis Joannis de A. Costa Bibliopolae Ulyssiponensis, 1665.

—— *Convivium Divini Amoris*. Lugduni: Sumptis. H. Boissat et G. Remeus, 1665.

Amat y Junient, Manuel de *Memoria de Gobierno*. Edición y estudio preliminar de Vicente Rodríguez Casado y Florentino Pérez Embid. Sevilla: Escuelas de Estudios Hispano–Americanos, 1947.

Annuae Litterae Societatis Jesu, 1599. Lugduni: Ex Typographia Jacobi Roussin, 1607.

Annuae Litterae Societatis Jesu, 1603. Duaci: Ex Officina Viduae Laurentii Kellami, 1618.

Annuae Litterae Societatis Jesu, 1609. Dilingae: Apud Viduam Joannis Mayer.

Annuae Litterae Societatis Jesu, 1610. Dilingae: Apud Viduam Joannis Mayer.

Annuae Litterae Societatis Jesu, 1611. Dilingae: Ex Typographea Mayeriana.

Annuae Litterae Societatis Jesu, 1612. Lugduni: Apud Claudium Cayne, 1618.

*Arriaga, José de, s.j., *Rhetoris Christiani Partes Septem Exemplis cum Sacris tum Philosophicis Illustratae*. Lugduni: Sumptibus Horatii Cardon, ex Tipographeis Joannis Arnad, 1629

—— *Extirpación de la Idolatría del Perú*. Lima: Geronymo de Contreras, 1621.

[183]

*Avendaño, Diego de, s.j., *Thesaurus Indicus seu Generalis Instructor pro Regimine Conscientiae, in iis quae ad Indias Spectant*. Tomus Primus et Secundus. Antverpiae: Apud Jacobum Meursium, 1668.

—— *Auctarium Indicum seu Tomus Tertius ad Indici Thesauri Ornatius Complementum*. Antverpiae: Apud Jacobum Meursium, 1675.

—— *Auctarii Indici Tomus Secundus seu Thesauri Tomus Quartus*. Antverpiae: Apud Jacobum Meursium, 1676.

—— *Auctarii Indici Tomus Tertius seu Thesauri Tomus quintus*. Antverpiae: Apud Jacobum Meursium, 1678.

—— *Auctarii Indici Tomus Quartus et Thesauri Tomus Sextus*. Antverpiae: Apud Hieronymum Verdussen, 1686.

—— *Problemata Theologica*. 2 Vols. Antverpiae: Apud Engelbertum Gymnicum, 1668.

*Ávila, Esteban de, s.j., *De Censuris Ecclesiasticis Tractatus*. Editio Novissima. Lugduni: Sumptibus Jacobi Cardon et Petri Gavellat, 1623.

—— *Compendium Summae, seu Manualis Doctoris Navarri*. Parisiis: Apud Gasparum Meturas, 1620.

*Barrasa, Jacinto, s.j., *Sermones Varios Predicados . . . en el Reino del Perú*. Madrid: En la Imprenta Real, 1678.

*Buendía, Joseph de, s.j., *Sermones Varios Predicados en la Ciudad de Lima*. Zaragoza: Herederos de Juan de Ybar, 1678.

—— *Vida del Venerable . . . Padre Francisco del Castillo*. Madrid: Antonio Román, 1693.

—— *Parentación Real al Soberano Nombre e Inmortal Memoria del Católico Rey . . . D. Carlos II*. Lima: Joseph de Contreras, 1701.

*Cobo, Bernabé, s.j., *Historia del Nuevo Mundo*. 2 Vols., "Biblioteca de Autores Españobles", Vols. XCI, XCII. Edited by Francisco Mateos, s.j., Madrid: Ediciones Atlas, 1956.

—— *Fundación de Lima*. "Biblioteca de Autores Españoles," Vol. XCII. Ediciones Atlas, 1956.

Colección de las Aplicaciones que se van haciendo de los Bienes, Casas y Colegios que fueron de los Regulares de la Compañía de Jesús. 2 Vols., Lima: Oficina de la Calle de San Jacinto, 1772–73.

*Contreras, Francisco de, s.j., *Información, sobre que los Electos para Obispos no pueden Consagrarse, ni Tomar la Posesión de sus Obispados, sin que primero reciban las letras Apostólicas de Su Santidad*. 1647.

Córdoba y Salinas, Diego de, *Teatro de la Iglesia Metropolitana de la Ciudad de los*

Reyes: Anales de la Catedral de Lima. "Biblioteca Histórica Peruana," Vol. VII. Lima: Tipografía Peruana, 1958.

Dalmases, Cándido de, and Iparraguirre, Ignacio, s.j. (edd.), *Obras Completas de San Ignacio de Loyola.* Second ed., "Biblioteca de Autores Cristianos," Vol. LXXXIV. Madrid: La Editorial Católica s.a., 1963.

Doctrina Christiana y Catecismo para Instrucción de los Indios . . . Compuesto por autoridad del Concilio Provincial, que se celebró en la Ciudad de los Reyes, el año de 1583. Ciudad de los Reyes: Por Antonio Ricardo primero Impressor en estos Reynos del Pirú, 1584.

Egaña, Antonio de, s.j., *Monumenta Peruana.* 3 Vols., MONUMENTA HISTORICA SOCIETATIS JESU, Vols. 75, 87. Romae: Borgo Santo Spirito, 5, 1954–61.

Eguiguren, Luis A. *Diccionario Histórico Cronológico de la Real y Pontificia Universidad de San Marcos y sus Colegios.* 3 Vols., Lima: Torres Aguirre s.a., 1940–51.

Esteyneffer, Juan de, s.j., *Florilegio Medicinal de Todas las Enfermedades.* Madrid: Alonso Valvas, 1729.

*Grijalva, Francisco Xavier, s.j., *Carta que el Padre Francisco Xavier Rector del Colegio Máximo de San Pablo . . . Remitió a los Padres Rectores . . . Dándoles una Breve Noticia de la Exemplarísima Vida y Dichosa Muerte del Venerable Padre Diego de Avendaño.* Lima: Joseph de Contreras, 1689.

Institutum Societatis Jesu. 3 Vols., Florentiae: Ex Typographia a SS. Conceptione, 1892–93.

Instructiones ad Provinciales et Superiores Societatis. Antverpiae: Apud Joannem Meursium, 1635.

*Irisarri, Fermín, s.j., *Vida . . . Del V. P. Juan de Alloza.* Madrid: Diego Martínez Abad, 1715.

Juan, Jorge and Ulloa, Antonio, *Noticias Secretas de América.* Londres: En la Imprenta de R. Taylor, 1826.

Litterae Annuae Societatis Jesu, 1600. Antverpiae: Apud Heredes Martini Nutii et Joannem Meursium, 1614.

Litterae Annuae Societatis Jesu, 1606, 1607, 1608. Moguntiae: Ex Architypographia Joannis Albini, 1618.

Litterae Societatis Jesu, 1613, 1614. Lugduni: Apud Claudium Cayne, 1619.

Lissón, Emilio. *La Iglesia en el Perú: Colección de Documentos para la Historia de la Iglesia que se encuentran en varios Archivos.* 5 Vols., Sevilla: Editorial Católica Española, s.a., 1943–56.

Mateos, Francisco, s.j. (ed.), *Historia General de la Compañía de Jesús en el Perú:*

[185]

Crónica Anónima de 1600 que trata del Establecimiento y Misiones de la Compañía de Jesús en los Países de habla Española. 2 Vols., Madrid: Consejo Superior de Investigaciones Científicas, 1944.

*Medrano, Pedro, s.j., *Rosetum Theologicum Scholasticum.* Hispali: Apud Joannem F. de Blas, 1702.

—— *Gazophylacium Divinae Dilectionis Petra Pretiosior.* Matriti: Ex Typographia Francisci del Hierro, 1720.

*Messia, Alonso, s.j., *Devoción a las Tres Horas . . . Y Méthodo con que se Practica en el Colegio Máximo de San Pablo.* Córdoba: Francisco Villalón, 1758.

*Moncada, Baltazar de, s.j., *Arte de la Santidad.* Sevilla: Joseph Pedrino, 1754.

—— *Descripción de la Casa Favricada en Lima . . . para que las Señoras Ilustres de Ella y demás-Mujeres Devotas . . . Puedan tener en Total Retiro . . . los Ejercicios de San Ignacio.* Sevilla: 1757.

Monumenta Paedagogica Societatis Jesu Quae Primam Rationem Studiorum Anno 1586 Editam Praecessere. MONUMENTA HISTORICA SOCIETATIS JESU. Matriti: Typis Augustini Avrial, 1901.

Odriozola, Manuel de. *Colección de Documentos Literarios del Perú.* 11 Vols., Lima: Establecimiento de tipografía y encuadernación de Aurelio Alfaro, 1863–77.

*Olea, Nicolás, s.j., *Summa tripartita Scholasticae Philosophiae.* 2 Vols., Lima: Sumptibus Josephi Contreras Regio Limani Typographi, 1693–1694.

*Oliva, Anello, s.j., *Historia del Perú y Varones Insignes en Santidad de la Compañía de Jesús.* Lima: Imprenta y Librería de San Pedro, 1895. This book was written in 1631. In that year the Provincial of Peru, Nicolas Durán, after examining Oliva's work, granted permission for the impression.

*Oñate, Pedro de, s.j., *De Contractibus.* 3 Vols., Romae: Ex Typographia Francisci Caballi 1646–47; Romae: Apud Angelum Bernabo, 1654.

Oraciones Traducidas en Lengua del Reino de Angola . . . Impressas primero para el Reyno de Portugal, y aora de nuevo con la declaración en Lengua Castellana. Con Licencia, Lima: Gerónimo de Contreras, junto al Convento de Santo Domingo, 1629.

El Parnaso del Real Colegio de San Martín . . . en Aplauso de la Heroyca Obra del Muelle que en el Puerto del Callao a Fabricado su Excelencia que es la Octava Maravilla. Lima: Imprenta de Joseph de Contreras y Alvarado, 1694.

*Parra, Juan Sebastián de la, s.j., *De el Bien, Excelencias y Obligaciones de el Estado Clerical y Sacerdotal.* 2 Vols., Sevilla: Por Matías Claviso, 1615–1620.

*Peñafiel, Alonso de, s.j., *Cursus Integri Philosophici Tomus Primus et Secundus.* Lugduni: Sumpt. Phil. Borde, Laur. Arnaud, et Cl. Rigaud, 1653.

—— *Tractatus de Incarnatione Verbi Divini.* Lugduni: Sumpt. Joannis Antonii Hugustan et Soc., 1678.

*Pérez de Menacho, Juan, s.j., *Estado de Nuestros Privilegios Temporales.* Romae: 1645.

Ratio atque Institutio Studiorum Societatis Jesu. Antverpiae: Apud Joannem Meursium, 1635.

*Rehr, Juan, s.j., *El Conocimiento de los Tiempos. Ephemerides del Año de 1756, Bissiesto.* Lima: Calle de Palacio, 1755.

Relación de lo que Toca a los Colegios de la Compañía de Jesús en la Provincia de Castilla la Nueva: 1564–1565. Madrid: Imprenta de Gabriel López del Horno, 1907.

*Rodríguez, José, s.j., *Gramática Ilustrada.* Reimpreso en Lima: Casa Real de los Huerfanos, 1777.

Sanctus Franciscus Borgia, Quartus Gandiae Dux et Societatis Jesu Praepositus Generalis Tertius. MONUMENTA HISTORICA SOCIETATIS JESU. 5 Vols., Matriti: Typis Augustini Avrial, 1894–1903; Typis Gabrielis Lopez del Horno, 1908–1911.

Salazar, Juan José de, s.j., *Vida del V. P. Alonso Messía.* Lima: Imprenta Nueva de la Calle de San Marcelo, 1733.

Sommervogel, Charles, s.j., *Bibliotheque de la Compagnie de Jesus.* 10 Vols., Paris: Alphonse Picard, 1890–1909.

Suardo, Juan Antonio. *Diario de Lima: 1629–1634.* Edited by Rubén Vargas Ugarte, s.j., Lima: Imp. C. Vasquez L., 1935.

Suarez, Franciscus. *Metaphysicarum Disputationum Tomus Primus et Posterior.* Coloniae: Excudebat Franciscus Helvidius, 1608.

*Valdés, Rodrigo de, s.j., *Poema Heroyco Hispano–Latino Panegírico de la Fundación y Grandezas de la muy noble, y Leal Ciudad de Lima.* Madrid: Antonio Román, 1687.

Uriarte, José E., and Lecina, Mariano, s.j., *Biblioteca de Escritores de la Compañía de Jesús, Perteneciente a la Antigua Asistencia de España: Desde sus Orígenes hasta el año 1733.* 2 Vols., Madrid: Viuda de López del Horno, 1925–1930.

Vargas Ugarte, Rubén, s.j. (ed.), *De Nuestro Antiguo Teatro.* Lima: Compañía de Impresiones y Publicidad, 1943.

—— (ed.), *Relaciones de Viajes de los Siglos XVII y XVIII.* Biblioteca Histórica Peruana, Vol. 5, Lima: Compañía de Impresiones y Publicidad, 1947.

Vargas Ugarte, Rubén, S.J. *Impresos Peruanos: 1584–1650.* Lima: Editorial San Marcos, 1953

—— (ed.) *Pareceres Jurídicos en Asuntos de Indias: 1601–1718.* Lima: Compañía de Impresiones y Publicidad, 1951.

—— *Impresos Peruanos: 1651–1699.* Lima: Editorial San Marcos, 1954.

—— *Impresos Peruanos: 1700–1762.* Lima: Artes Gráficas, 1956.

—— *Impresos Peruanos: 1763–1805.* Lima: Tipografía Peruana S.A., 1956.

*Zalduendo, Francisco Xavier, S.J., *Los Siete Ángeles del Apocalipsis.* Lima: Joseph Contreras, Impresor Real, 1695.

—— *Sermones Varios.* 4 Vols., Madrid: Viuda de Juan García Infançón, 1717; Don Gabriel del Barrio, 1723.

SECONDARY PRINTED SOURCES

Aspurz, Lázaro de, O.F.M., *La Aportación Extrangera a las Misones del Patronato Regio.* Madrid: Espasa y Calpe S.A., 1946.

Astrain, Antonio, S.J., *Historia de la Compañía de Jesús en la Asistencia de España.* 7 Vols., Madrid: Sucesores de Ribadeneira. 1902–1909; Razón y Fe, 1913–25.

Barrinaga, Augusto, "Documento Nuevo sobre Casos Morales de Indias," *Missionalia Hispanica*, XII, No. 36 (1955), 555–70.

Barreda y Laos, Felipe, *Vida Intelectual del Virreinato del Perú.* Third ed., Lima: Imprenta de la Universidad Nacional de San Marcos, 1964.

Bromley, Juan, and Barbagelata, José, *Evolución Urbana de la Ciudad de Lima.* Lima: Editorial Lumen S.A., 1945.

Bromley Seminario, Juan. "La Ciudad de Lima en el Año 1630," *Revista Histórica*, XXIV (1959), 268–317.

Cano Pérez, Pedro, S.J., "Labor Pedagógica de los Jesuitas en el Vierreinato del Perú," *Mercurio Peruano*, CLXIII (September, 1940), 525–545.

Echánove, Alfonso, S.J., "Origen y Evolución de la Idea Jesuítica de 'Reducciones' en las Misiones del Virreinato del Perú," *Missionalia Hispanica*, XII (1955), 95–144; XIII (1956), 497–540.

Egaña, Antonio de, S.J., "El Virrey Don Francisco de Toledo y los Jesuitas del Perú: 1569–1581," *Estudios de Deusto*, IV (Enero–Junio, 1956), 117–186.

—— "Felipe II y el General Jesuita Mercurian en Indias," *Estudios de Deusto*, VII (Enero–Junio, 1959), 81–138.

Egaña, Antonio de, s.j. "Dos Problemas de Gobierno en la Provincia del Perú en el Año 1579," *Archivum Historicum Societatis Jesu*, XXII (1953), 418–38.

—— "La Visión Humanística del Indio Americano en los Primeros Jesuitas Peruanos: 1568–1576," *Analecta Gregoriana*, LXX (1954), 291–306.

Eguiguren, Luis Antonio, *Alma Mater: Orígenes de la Universidad de San Marcos, 1551–1579*. Lima: Talleres Gráficos Torres Aguirre, 1939.

Farrel, Allan P., s.j., *The Jesuit Code of Liberal Education: Development and Scope of the* Ratio Studiorum. Milwaukee: The Bruce Publishing Company, 1938.

Furlong Cardiff, Guillermo, s.j., *Nacimiento y Desarrollo de la Filosofía en el Río de la Plata*. Buenos Aires: G. Kraft, 1952.

—— *Los Jesuitas y la Excisión del Reino de Indias*. Buenos Aires: Ediciones Theoria, 1960.

Henríquez Ureña, Pedro, *Literary Currents in Hispanic America*. Cambridge: Harvard University Press, 1945.

Jacobsen, J. V., *Educational Foundations of the Jesuits in Sixteenth Century New Spain*. Berkeley: University of California Press, 1938.

Kelemen, Pal, *Baroque and Rococo in Latin America*. New York: Macmillan, 1951.

Lanning, J. T., *Academic Culture in the Spanish Colonies*. New York: Oxford University Press, 1940.

Leonard, Irving A., *Books of the Brave; Being an Account of Books and of Men in the Spanish Conquest and Settlement of the Sixteenth-Century New World*. Cambridge: Harvard University Press, 1949.

Levillier, Roberto, *Don Francisco de Toledo, Supremo Organizador del Peru: Su Vida y Obra, 1515–1582*. 3 Vols., Madrid: Espasa y Calpe s.a., 1935.

Lohmann Villena, Guillermo, *El Arte Dramático en Lima durante el Virreinato*. Publicación de la Escuela de Estudios Hispano–Americanos de la Universidad de Sevilla. Madrid: Artes Gráficas, 1945.

Lopetegui, León, s.j., *El Padre José de Acosta s.j. y las Misiones*. Madrid: Consejo Superior de Investigaciones Científicas, 1942.

Mateos, Francisco, s.j., "Escuela Primaria en el Perú del XVI," *Missionalia Hispanica*, VIII (1951), 591–599.

—— "Una Carta Inédita de Alonso de Barzana," *Missionalia Hispanica*, VI (1949), 143–145.

Mörner, Magnus, *The Political and Economic Activities of the Jesuits in the La Plata Region. The Hapsburg Era*. Stockholm: Ibero–Amerikanska och Institutet, 1953.

Mörner, Magnus (ed.), *The Expulsion of the Jesuits from Latin America*. New York: Alfred A. Knopf, 1965.

Múzquiz de Miguel, José Luis, *El Conde de Chinchón Virrey del Perú*. Publicación de la Escuela de Estudios Hispano–Americanos de Sevilla. Madrid: Artes Gráficas, 1945.

Palma, Ricardo, *Tradiciones Peruanas*. Edición y Prólogo de Edith Palma. Madrid: Aguilar, 1957.

Picón–Salas, Mariano, *A Cultural History of Spanish America*. Translated by Irving A. Leonard, 2nd ed., Berkeley: University of California Press, 1963.

Sacchinus, Franciscus, s.j., *Historiae Societatis Jesu Pars Tertia sive Borgia*. Romae: Typis Manelfi Manelfii, 1649.

—— *Historiae Societatis Jesu Pars Quarta sive Everardus*. Romae: Typis Dominici Manelphi, 1652.

Sartolo, Bernardo, s.j., *El Eximio y Venerable Padre Francisco Suárez de la Compañía de Jesús en la Fiel Imagen de sus Heroicas Virtudes*. Salamanca: Andrés García de Castro, Impresor de la Universidad, 1639.

Sierra, Vicente D., *Los Jesuitas Germanos en la Conquista Espiritual de Hispano–América*. Buenos Aires: Talleres Gráficos de Padilla y Contreras s.r.l., 1944.

Tibesar, Antonine, o.f.m., *Franciscan Beginnings in Colonial Peru*. Washington, D.C.: Academy of American Franciscan History, 1953.

Valdizán, Hermilio, and Maldonado, Ángel. *La Medicina Popular Peruana: Contribución al "Folk–lore" Medico del Perú*. 3 Vols., Lima: Imprenta Torres Aguirre, 1922.

Vargas Ugarte, Rubén, s.j., *El Episcopologio del Antiguo Virreinato del Perú: 1513–1825*. Lima: 1940.

—— *Historia de la Compañía de Jesús en el Perú*. 3 Vols., Burgos: Imprenta de Aldecoa, 1963–65.

—— *Jesuitas Peruanos Desterrados a Italia*. Lima: 1934.

—— *Los Jesuitas del Perú*. Lima: 1941.

—— "1631–1931. Una Fecha Olvidada. El Tercer Centenario del Descubrimiento de la Quina," *Revista Histórica*, IX (1931), 291–301.

Varones Ilustres de la Compañía de Jesús, second ed., 9 Vols., Bilbao: Administración del Mensajero del Corazón de Jesús, 1887–1892. The first edition of this work appeared in Madrid between 1613 and 1736. The fourth volume of the second edition contains, based mainly on the

BIBLIOGRAPHY

Cartas Annuas and *Cartas Edificantes*, the biography of the Jesuits who worked in Peru, Nueva Granada, Quito, Paraguay and Chile.

Whitaker, A. P. (ed.), *Latin America and the Enlightenment*. New York and London: Appleton-Century, 1942.

Wethey, Harold E., *Colonial Architecture and Sculpture in Peru*. Cambridge: Harvard University Press, 1949.

INDEX

Academie des Sciences, 93–4
Acosta, José de, 22–7, 29, 30, 48, 49, 54;
on forced Indian labor, 55–6, 60, 72,
73, 78, 95; on Indian missions, 122,
124–6, 143, 147
Aguilera, Antonio, 108
Akademie der Wissenschaften, 94
Amat, Viceroy, 96, 117, 148, 149, 150,
151, 152
Andreu, Jacinto, 108
anesthesia, 107
Aranda, Count of, 148
arithmetic, 3, 4, 35
Arriaga, José de, 35, 41, 49, 78
Atienza, Juan de, 32–3
Augustinians, 4
auto de fe, 125–26
auto sacramental, 44
Avendaño, Diego de, 60; on forced-labor
draft, 61; on public administration,
65–6; on slavery, 68–9, 72, 83, 91, 147
Ávila, Esteban de, 27, 56, 60, 72, 78, 147

Balerini, Antonio, 81, 88
Banduri, Anselmo, 88
Barba, Alonso, 94
baroque, 46–7; way of life, 119 ff.
Barrasa, Jacinto, 43, 134, 139
Barzana, Alonso de, 49, 78, 121, 126
Berulle, 90
besoardicus lapis, 100, 101
bibliographies, 86
books, 9–10; written in San Pablo, 41, 51,
57, 60, 63, 72, 123; distributed by
San Pablo, 78–81; budget for, 77;
owned by San Pablo's faculty, 81–5;
medical, 106–08; *see also* library
Borgia, Francis, 7, 8, 9, 10, 11, 12, 16, 17,
18, 19, 20, 36
Bossuet, 87
Botero, John, 87, 90
Bourdaloue, 87
Bracamonte, Diego de, 12, 13, 15, 19, 131
Burg, Joannes, 100

Cabredo, Rodríguez, 98
Cabrera, Luis, 87
Calepino, Ambrosio, 86
Calvo, Juan, 107
caña fistula, 100, 112
Carbonell, Miguel, 88
Cardano, Girolamo, 107
Cárdenas, Fray Bernardino, 62, 63
Cartesianism, 96
Castillo, Juan del, 100, 106
Cavero, Hernando, 84
chaplains, 143–45
Charles III, 147, 152
Charlevoix, 89
Ciruelo, Pedro, 94
civil administration, 90–1
Cobo, Bernabé, 35, 47; on San Pablo's
library, 78, 85, 101, 133
Coello, Francisco de, 78
Contreras, Francisco de, 63
Contreras, Luis J. de, 83, 129
Copernicus, Nicolas, 93
Córdoba y Salinas, Diego de, 127
Corneille, 87
Cortesi, Giovanni B., 107
culteranismo, 43

Dante, 87
degrees, 21, 26, 30–1
Descartes, Rene, 94, 95
doctrinas, 17, 20, 23–4, 49, 120
Dominicans, 4–5, 14, 17, 28–9
Durán, Nicolás, 81–2, 119, 125, 129

economics, 91–2
Enlightenment, 93–6
Enríquez, Martín, 32, 132
Esteyneffer, Juan de, 109, 147
Euclid, 94

Falopio, Gabrielle, 107
Feijoo, Benito Gerónimo, 96
Fernández, Juan, 108
Ferrera, Juan de, 88

fireworks, 137–38
Fornés, José, 108
Franciscans, 4, 13, 14, 16

Galen, 107
Galilei, Galileo, 93
Garibay, Esteban de, 88
Garriga, Antonio, 38–40, 84
geography, 91–2
Goltzi, Hubert, 82
Gómez, Alonso, 101
González, Thyrsus, 38, 50; on the use of books, 84
Gracián, Baltasar, 87, 90
grammar, 4; textbooks, 40–1
Guicciardini, Francesco, 88
Gumilla, José, 92

Harvey, William, 107
Hawkins, Richard, 143
Hernández, Bartolomé, 121–22, 123, 125, 126
Herrera, Antonio de, 87, 88
Hidalgo, Bartolomé, 107
Hippocrates, 107
history, 87–9
Homer, 25, 34
Horace, 40, 43
Huancavelica, 55, 58–61
humanities, 13; school of, 22, 25, 26, 32–47, 97

Indians, 5, 21, 23; school for, 17, 24, 36; justice for the, 55–62; conversion of, 120–28; sodality for, 134
infirmary, 99, 101, 105–06; for the slaves, 70–1

Jauregui, Martín, 72

Kepler, Johannes, 93

laboratory: scientific, 95; pharmaceutical, 99–100, 106–07, 113, 115
Laínez, Diego, 97
languages, 5, 24, 42, 48–52, 86
La Palata, Duke of, 136, 140, 145
Larramendi, Manuel, 86

Lebrun, R. P., 89
Lechner, Andreas, 111
Leibniz, G. W. von, 94, 96
León Pinelo, Antonio, 91
library, 75, 76–7; budget for, 77; students', 81; private, 81–5; common, 85–96; medical, 106–08
Liñan, Melchor de, 136
Lipsius, Justus, 90
Loaiza, Fray Jerónimo, 1, 4, 5, 17, 49
Locke, 96
López, Juan de Dios, 108
López, Luis, 15, 132
Loyola, Ignatius, 46, 73; on libraries and books, 74–5, 83; on medicine, 97–8
Lyro, Ignacio, 111

Mabillon, 87
Mariana, Juan de, 88, 90
Martínez, Alonso, 5
Martinier, 93
mathematics, 4, 94
Mayer, Joseph, 109
medicine, 97–118; chairs of, 98
medicines, 98, 99; distributed by San Pablo, 100–02, 111–13; retail and wholesale of, 102–04
Mendo, Andrés, 90
Mendoza, Garcia Hurtado de, 98, 132
Mendoza, Hernando de, 98, 132
Mercati, Michele, 107
Mercuriale, Girolamo, 106, 107
Mercurian, Everard, 19–20, 22; on buying books for Peru, 76
Messia Venegas, Alonso, 101
Mestizos, 36, 49, 52
Miraval, Nicolás, 101, 102
missions, 120–31; against idolatries, 125–28; financing, 128–30
mita, 55–62
Molière, 87
Moncada, Baltasar de, 109–10
Moreri, Louis, 87
mulattos, 36–7; 52, sodality for, 133–34
Muratori, Ludovico Antonio, 88
music, 4, 16, 20, 47, 137

natural sciences, 91–5
Nazianzen, Gregory, 40

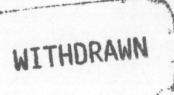
LE 68 .L5 M37 1968

Mart'in, Luis.

The intellectual conquest of
Peru

LE 68 .L5 M37 1968

Mart'in, Luis.

The intellectual conquest of
 Peru

DEMCO